LEXICOGRAPHICA Series Maior

LEXICOGRAPHICA

Series Maior

Supplementary Volumes to the International Annual for Lexicography
Suppléments à la Revue Internationale de Lexicographie
Supplementbände zum Internationalen Jahrbuch für Lexikographie

Edited by
Pierre Corbin, Reinhard R. K. Hartmann, Franz Josef Hausmann,
Ulrich Heid, Sven-Göran Malmgren, Oskar Reichmann,
Ladislav Zgusta

131

Published in cooperation with the Dictionary Society of North America
(DSNA) and the European Association for Lexicography (EURALEX)

Renata Szczepaniak

The Role of Dictionary Use
in the Comprehension
of Idiom Variants

Max Niemeyer Verlag
Tübingen 2006

Bibliografische Information der Deutschen Bibliothek

Die Deutsche Bibliothek verzeichnet diese Publikation in der Deutschen Nationalbibliografie; detaillierte bibliografische Daten sind im Internet über *http://dnb.ddb.de* abrufbar.

ISBN-13: 978-3-484-39131-4   ISSN 0175-9264
ISBN-10: 3-484-39131-6

Table of Contents

Acknowledgements

I wish to acknowledge the help I have received while working on this book, which is a revised version of my 2004 PhD dissertation.

My first thanks go to the Head of the School of English, Adam Mickiewicz University in Poznań, Professor Jacek Fisiak for the privilege to undertake my research in this particular institute.

It is hard to express adequately my gratitude to the Head of the Department of Lexicology and Lexicography, Professor Arleta Adamska-Sałaciak, my adviser. The time she generously devoted to reading the subsequent versions of my dissertation, constructive criticism, suggestions and continuous support for this undertaking are deeply appreciated.

I would like also to convey special thanks to the reviewers, Professors Jacek Fisiak and Tadeusz Piotrowski for insightful comments and positive assessment of my PhD thesis.

I also acknowledge the enormous help from friends and colleagues. I am extremely grateful to Professor Robert Lew for the invaluable information on statistical analysis and his assistance in the statistical processing of the data. Dr Ewelina Jagła deserves my special gratitude for volunteering as a co-rater of the linguistic material collected, and Dr Przemysław Kaszubski – for guidance on how to effectively exploit the British National Corpus for the purposes of this study. I am also indebted to Professor Joseph Kuhn and Professor Stephen Wright, as well as Mr Dwight Holbrook for kindly providing their interpretation of text samples used in the empirical part. Thanks are also due to the following staff of the School of English, Adam Mickiewicz University for help with administering the task booklets: Professor Roman Kopytko, Professor Joseph Kuhn, Professor Alicja Pisarska, Professor Przemysław Tajsner, Professor Jacek Witkoś, Professor Stephen Wright, Dr Elżbieta Adamczyk, Dr Aleksandra Jankowska and Dr Janusz Kaźmierczak.

Last but not least, I would like to thank all the anonymous students who took part in my experiment.

Poznań, October 2005

Renata Szczepaniak

Introduction

Due to lexicographers' unremitting interest in the opinions and expectations concerning their dictionaries one can already talk of a "user-perspective" (Hartmann 2001) well-established in lexicography. Not only the needs of dictionary owners, but also the way they approach the task of consultation and the influence of dictionary use on performance are thoroughly explored with a view to improving on new editions. The scale of over thirty-year research is marked by an increasing number of versatile, more and more specialised empirical studies, as well as by the need for a general overview and professional assessment of the quickly accumulating results (see, e.g., Diab 1990, Hulstijn and Atkins 1998, Nesi 2000, Tono 2001).

Despite rapid advances in the field, the not-so-uncharted waters of dictionary consultation leave much to explore. As noted by Hartmann (2001: 81),

> [t]he conditions of dictionary use can only be determined by accurate empirical observation. Among the parameters to be investigated are (various types of) dictionaries consulted by (various types of) users during (various types of) activities requiring (various types of) strategies.

In particular, the intuitively appealing image of the pedagogical dictionary as a tool for boosting comprehension of a written text has not yet been confirmed beyond doubt, and requires fresh research perspectives.

This study, by no means aspiring to become a final word on the subject, is an attempt to contribute to the steadily increasing body of "more dynamic observations of what real users do with real dictionaries in real situations of communicative deficit" (Tono 2001: 83). The situation of highly advanced students performing the complex comprehension task of decoding contextually modified idioms, viewed as a source of disruption to the fluent reading process, has been selected as a relatively unexplored niche, and, at the same time, a convenient springboard for investigating the situation of dictionary use in its entirety. It is hoped that this project, by setting out to disclose the roots of success or failure in the aforementioned task, will shed some light on the central dilemma of the usefulness of the monolingual dictionary for advanced reading.

Chapter 1 introduces the subject of receptive dictionary use as one of utmost concern to pedagogical lexicography. By emphasising the complexity of the reference act, it points to the need for a holistic treatment of the consultation process, without dismissing its final stages as falling outside lexicographic interest. A selective overview of relevant empirical findings is followed by some methodological considerations. Finally, the rationale for further research in the field is spelled out, and the scope of the present study delineated.

Since instruction in dictionary use is indirectly affected by views on the reading process, Chapter 2 summarises the tenets of three main reading theories, with special emphasis on the top-down model and its long-lasting influence on L2 reading, reflected in the "inference versus look-up" controversy.

Chapter 3 foregrounds the case of occasional transformations of idioms as a serious obstacle to the reception of the language of the press and fiction by non-native readers. Starting with some general remarks on the phenomenon of linguistic creativity, it specifies the meaning of the term *idiom* in the present study, and dwells on creative – as distinct from systemic – idiom variation. An attempt is made to explain the sources of difficulties in processing the former.

Chapter 4 highlights certain problems involved in using the monolingual learner's dictionary to tackle the comprehension deficit in question as a function of the treatment of idioms in the entry.

Chapter 5 discusses the procedure and results of the experiment designed to embrace the consecutive steps undertaken in the task of decoding idioms (process-oriented perspective) as well as their effectiveness (product-oriented perspective). The data is analysed in order to isolate patterns of consultation behaviour responsible for advanced learners' performance.

The study ends with conclusions and comments on the role of the monolingual learner's dictionary in the comprehension of contextually modified idioms. An attempt is made to extrapolate from the described case to the general picture of monolingual dictionary use in reading, as well as to point out possible lexicographical and pedagogical implications, and offer suggestions for further research.

1. Receptive Dictionary Use: Research Background

1.1. Primacy of receptive dictionary use

Much to the disappointment of lexicographers, most of the richness squeezed into a modern EFL dictionary, i.e., encoding information on syntax, frequency, usage, and the paradigmatic and syntagmatic relations that a lexical unit enters into, remains unused – a fact attesting to the conservatism of dictionary users, who traditionally treat a dictionary as an instrument primarily for decoding (Béjoint 1994: 152). Béjoint's (1981) 21-question survey investigating the use of monolingual English dictionaries by French students at the University of Lyon revealed that monolingual learner's dictionaries (MLDs) were more often used for decoding than for encoding activities regardless of the medium:

1. L2 > L1 translation: 86%
2. Written Comprehension: 60%
3. Written Composition, including L1 > L2 translation: 58%
4. Oral Comprehension: 14%
5. Oral Composition: 9% (Béjoint 1981: 216)

In Tomaszczyk's (1979) comprehensive study, the frequency of the use of a monolingual and bilingual dictionary for encoding (writing) (67.3%) slightly surpassed that for decoding (reading) (61.6%) in a heterogeneous group of foreign language learners. Also, 60.7% of Nuccorini's (1992: 92) Italian subjects reported receptive activities as the primary reason for consultation.

Theoretically, receptive dictionary use may occur in all tasks involving the comprehension of an L2 text, be it written or spoken, that is, in what are traditionally called "decoding", as opposed to "encoding", activities.[1] In practice, however, it is normally restricted to reading and L2 > L1 translation, although, as Scholfield (1999: 13) notices, some needs questionnaires (e.g., Béjoint 1981, Tomaszczyk 1979) reported isolated cases of dictionary use during listening. The scope of this study is limited to the use of the monolingual L2 dictionary; hence in further discussion a receptive situation will be synonymous with reading.

For readers, the most vital piece of information within the entry is meaning. Unsurprisingly, it ranks high in lists of information categories regarded as the most frequently sought after:

1. Meaning: 87%
2. Syntactic information: 53%
3. Synonyms: 52%
4. Spelling and pronunciation: 25%
5. Language variety: 19%
6. Etymology: 5% (Béjoint 1981: 215)

---

[1] The former include reading, listening, and translation from L2 into L1, whereas the latter are: writing, speaking, and translation from L1 into L2 (Béjoint 1981: 209).

The fact that 87% of Béjoint's subjects placed meaning among the three most often looked up pieces of information finds confirmation in the comparable data from Tomaszczyk (1979: 111), where 85% of subjects turned to the monolingual dictionary for meaning (definitions or equivalents). The Needs Research project into the use of LDOCE1 by intermediate students in six countries, carried out in 1980 by the Longman ELT Dictionaries Department, revealed that checking the meaning of words accounted for 60% of all look-ups (Summers 1988: 114). In Nuccorini (1992: 92) meaning was the reason for consultation in 75% of cases, with pronunciation coming next (14.2%). 99% of Wingate's (2002: 100) intermediate subjects consult the dictionary for meaning often or very often.

Given that the MLD emerges as a tool, above all, for solving comprehension problems arising in the process of reading, it is the interpretation and application of the meaning information in the entry that will be explored in the empirical part of this study.

1.2. Complexity of the reference act: Potential pitfalls

Even though checking a word in a dictionary is usually performed in a routine, largely mechanical manner, to think of research into the steps of dictionary use as dwelling on the obvious is to give the lie to the complexity of the strategies involved. Recurrent trends in dictionary-using habits have been incorporated in models of the consultation process, whose elements remain basically the same across several publications, the modifications depending mainly on whether they apply to the use of a dictionary for all language tasks (encoding and decoding), or only to reception.[2] The most recent model neatly summarises the results of prior research into the steps that readers follow in their consultations (Figure 1).

Steps one, two and three involve the recognition of the problem and the decision as to the need for consultation, both of which, if absent, automatically cancel further stages. Points four and five concern the reference skills: the search[3] for the appropriate entry and locating the desired information within the entry. Equally important, though frequently marginalised by students and teachers alike, is retrieval and comprehension of the relevant data, as well as integrating it back into context – a process undoubtedly requiring more than a cursory reading of the definition. The whole dictionary reference act is inextricably linked with inference, which not only frames it, as it were, but "is relevant as a *part* of dictionary use itself" (Scholfield 1999: 28). Firstly, the choice of the right sense requires that the user have some idea of the meaning inferred from context; secondly, the use of examples also requires some inferencing skills. Ideally, context and dictionary are used in a back-and-forth way to achieve the ultimate goal of the look-up process, that is "to understand the

---

[2] Cf. Béjoint (1994: 155–156). The models directly applicable to dictionary use in reading are to be found in Scholfield (1982, 1999) and Hartmann (2001).

[3] A terminological distinction should be made between a look-up and a search, which are often used interchangeably. As Atkins and Varantola (1998b: 87) point out, a look-up refers to a single look-up of one headword in one dictionary, whereas the group of look-ups or one look-up in one or more dictionaries relating to one problem constitutes a search. Therefore, only if a lexical problem is solved after one trial, is a look-up synonymous with a search.

meaning information given in the chosen subentry, and somehow to combine this with the meaning of the text where the unknown was met" (Scholfield 1999: 28). The evaluation of the outcome of one's efforts should crown the consultation.

Figure 1. Components of the consultation process (Hartmann 2001: 91)

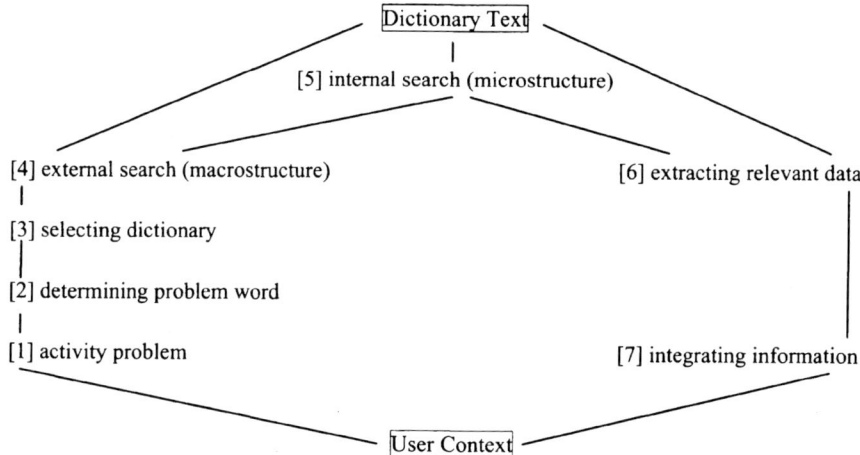

Receptive dictionary use, less complex perhaps than dictionary use for encoding purposes (see, e.g., Humblé 2001: 16, 101), is certainly not problem-free. Although the whole consultation process requires considerable effort, it is the user's macro- and microstructure skills that have received the most attention so far (e.g., Béjoint 1981; Atkins and Varantola 1998a, 1998b; Tono 2001: 116–142); stages six and seven, where errors are harder to detect, have been treated less extensively. However, unless allowance is made for these steps, the picture of dictionary use cannot be comprehensive. Only when dictionary users' behaviour has been dissected, can receptive errors be spotted, analysed and prevented in future. What follows is a recapitulation of the findings from previous research that account for the negative and, to a lesser extent, positive effect of the presence of a dictionary in situations of comprehension deficit.

1.3. Previous research

1.3.1. No effect of dictionary use on performance

One of the first studies on the role of a dictionary in the context of reading – Hosenfeld (1977, cited in Tono 2001: 30) – registered the adverse effect of looking-up words in a glossary on the reading process: the fluency suffered and students tended to decode word by word. Therefore, it was postulated that using a reference work should be treated as a last-resort strategy. Bensoussan, Sim and Weiss (1984),[4] who conducted four large-scale studies on the influence of the use of mono- and bilingual dictionaries on advanced students' success in L2 reading tests, obtained the most surprising results: "[e]xcept in the case of one text, no significant relation was found between students' test scores and dictionary use. It did not seem to make any difference on the test whether a student used a bilingual dictionary, a monolingual dictionary, or no dictionary at all" (Bensoussan, Sim and Weiss 1984: 268). Padron and Waxman (1988) managed to isolate fourteen strategies related to reading achievement on the basis of a reading comprehension test and a questionnaire on which students indicated how often they used each one. "Looking up words in the dictionary" was singled out as a negative strategy. Similarly, Neubach and Cohen (1988, cited in Nesi 2000: 37–39), who observed six students during a reading comprehension task in which the use of a dictionary was optional, report disappointing results.

Negative effect (or lack of positive effect) of the dictionary condition on reading performance, however discouraging, in itself does not prove the uselessness of a dictionary as a tool for assisting comprehension. Closer analysis of numerous factors interfering with efficient exploitation of the dictionary potential reveals the difficulty of creating conditions that would optimise dictionary-aided reading. Above all, the use of a dictionary in the experimental group and the subjects' reference skills cannot be taken for granted.

1.3.1.1. Ignoring the dictionary

It needs to be stressed that the mere availability of a dictionary in the experimental group rarely leads automatically to a multitude of reference acts. For a receptive situation of dictionary use to take place, the reader must experience a problem – a lexical gap that disrupts the reading process. Since "everyone has different degrees of word knowledge for different words, and, for many words, we simply do not need to have elaborated knowledge" (Stoller and Grabe 1993: 38), the lexical item may be either totally unfamiliar or, more likely in the case of advanced students, vaguely familiar. It is the latter, "incomplete" meanings that are probably the most frequent targets of good readers (Scholfield 1997: 285). Obviously, a reference act will take place on condition that the lexical gap is irreparable by means other than a dictionary (e.g., a native speaker's opinion, marginal gloss or highly informative context), and the item is truly important for comprehension. This relevance, as Scholfield (1999: 17–18) points out, might stem from the task type or from the unfamiliar item's role in activating appropriate schemata.[5] Difficult vocabulary items tend to negatively affect comprehension only when they appear in strategically important parts of the text; otherwise, they are simply skipped (Freebody and Anderson 1983, cited in Nation and Coady 1988: 99).

One of the frequently cited studies whose results gave lexicographers food for thought by reporting no influence of dictionary use on reading comprehension scores was Bensoussan, Sim and Weiss (1984). The replication of the experiment revealed that reading com

---

[4] The research in this case was motivated by the controversy between Israeli EFL teachers and administrators of examinations over the issue of dictionary use during examinations.

[5] The term, introduced by Bartlett (1932; 1995), refers to knowledge of the world that readers store in memory and may activate when processing new information; see section 2.1.

prehension tests may not be affected by a dictionary when: 1) the test checks comprehension of text and not of individual vocabulary items; 2) the dictionary does not provide the necessary information; 3) the user fails to identify keywords to be looked up (Nesi and Meara 1991: 639–643).

The more recent research by Hulstijn (1993) confirmed the positive relationship between word relevance and the reading goal on look-up.[6] Furthermore, it showed that easily inferable words were looked up less frequently than words whose meaning could not be easily guessed from context, although inferring ability turned out to be a factor of minor significance compared to vocabulary knowledge. Students with limited vocabulary knowledge tended to look up more words than advanced students,[7] but, surprisingly, greater inferring ability did not result in fewer consultations. Apparently, students were eager to check their inferences, which tallies with the results of Knight's (1994) investigation into the effect of bilingual dictionary use on incidental learning and reading comprehension in high- and low-ability students. Although fewer words per text-set were actually looked up by the low verbal ability group than the high-ability group, the correlation between the number of targets looked up and comprehension scores was high only in the former. Whereas there was a significant difference between the dictionary and no-dictionary condition for the low-ability group, the high-ability group seemed to be less dependent on vocabulary for comprehension. In the dictionary condition there was little difference between both ability groups (Knight 1994: 293). "[I]t appears that many high verbal ability students refer to the dictionary when they have already correctly guessed the meaning", Knight (1994: 295) concludes, thereby partly corroborating the opinion of Bensoussan, Sim and Weiss (1984: 271) that the more proficient students know enough to manage without a dictionary.

Predictably, intermediate and advanced L2 learners are more likely to look up words when reading a shorter text rather than a text of more than one page. Finally, the accessibility of dictionary information influences the frequency of look-ups, with an electronic dictionary having an advantage over a paper one (Hulstijn, Hollander and Greidanus 1996: 336).

All things considered, the effort of consulting a dictionary must be seen as worthwhile before the learner decides to interrupt the reading, especially since "[t]he dictionary continues to be seen as an instrument designed to provide quick and superficial support in case of emergency" (Béjoint 1994: 152).

1.3.1.2. Misusing the dictionary

Of all potential sources of failure in comprehension tasks despite the presence of a dictionary, inadequate reference skills figure as a major culprit. Regrettably, "[v]ery little attention

---

[6] Irrelevance of some target words to the completion of the task was also pointed out by Tono (2001: 75) as a factor responsible for the difference between his results and those of Bensoussan, Sim and Weiss (1984).

[7] That higher proficiency students tend to search the dictionary less than lower proficiency learners is also stated in Atkins and Varantola (1998a: 34) and Tono (2001: 112). On the other hand, Hatherall's (1984) advanced subjects used the dictionary more often than the less advanced ones. This surprising fact is explained tentatively: "[p]erhaps less advanced students are less confident of retrieving the necessary information and thus more reluctant to try" (Hatherall 1984: 187).

has been paid to how the learners' particular use of dictionaries affects results" (Tono 2001: 56). Bensoussan, Sim and Weiss (1984: 268) reject inadequate reference skills as an explanation for their puzzling results as "both too simplistic and too pessimistic to be useful", instead pointing to students' insufficient knowledge of syntax, or the so-called "threshold effect", according to which more than five per cent of unknown words in a text makes it unclear and prevents guessing.

Tono's (2001: 75–83) investigation into the effects of long-term dictionary use on reading comprehension proved the existence of a positive correlation between the overall results of the Dictionary Reference Skills Test Battery (DRSTB) and comprehension scores. Still, no straightforward relationship between DRSTB subscores and reading comprehension scores could be discovered. Apart from control over the reference skills, intensive training in dictionary use that the subjects had received was pointed out by Tono (2001: 75) as responsible for the difference between his results and those of Bensoussan, Sim and Weiss (1984).

Tight control over subjects' reference skills being an exception rather than a rule, insights into reference problems can be gained from error analysis and observational studies, such as Neubach and Cohen (1988, cited in Nesi 2000: 37–39). The major difficulties with the macrostructure search experienced by the subjects during the consultation were: alphabetic ordering, inability to identify the right headword, abandoning the search, experiencing frustration during the search, and continuing the search when the target item had been found. Similarly, McCreary and Dolezal (1999) report their subjects' difficulties in following the guidewords in alphabetical order (put down to the Asian background of many of the subjects) and unwillingness to follow the cross-references, perceived by many students as "too much work, too time-consuming, and... dependent on a fine and accurate knowledge of alphabetical order applied not just to the first letter of the word, but also to the second and third letters" (McCreary and Dolezal 1999: 132). However, it needs to be noted that the students had an American college desk dictionary, and not a learner's monolingual dictionary at their disposal, which might have affected the accessibility of information.

After the entry has been found, the user might run into difficulties with retrieving the information and understanding the definition. When searching the microstructure, some of Neubach and Cohen's (1988, cited in Nesi 2000: 37–39) students tended to read only the first definition and were uncertain about the word meaning they managed to arrive at. Similarly, Wingate (2002: 115) singled out reading only the beginning of the entry among the factors responsible for the lack of statistically significant difference in a comprehension task for intermediate learners of German in Hong Kong. In her study, moreover, the defining vocabulary was the most serious obstacle (41.7% of errors resulted from encountering unknown words in definitions), to be followed by derivational definitions (12.5%) and definition structure (4.2%).

What sort of consultation problems are advanced students likely to grapple with? Nesi and Haill's (2002) naturalistic and holistic research into receptive dictionary use provides particularly interesting findings. Although, as the authors admit, the portrait of "international students' normal receptive use of dictionaries" is imperfect due to a large number of variables left uncontrolled (e.g., mother tongues, language ability, dictionary-using skill, choice of dictionary, choice of look-up word, choice of text), the study offers an in-depth analysis of the problems that learners at university level might encounter in a natural situation of dictionary consultation. The data (77 reports on the way international under graduate students at a British University looked up five selected words from a text of their choice), collected over a period of three years, enabled the identification of five categories of look-up problems:

1. The subject chose the wrong dictionary entry or sub-entry (34 cases).
2. The subject chose the correct dictionary entry or sub-entry but misinterpreted the information it contained (11 cases).
3. The subject chose the correct dictionary entry or sub-entry, but did not realise that the word had a slightly different (often figurative) meaning in context (7 cases).
4. The subject found the correct dictionary entry or sub-entry, but rejected it as inappropriate in context (5 cases).
5. The word or appropriate word meaning was not in any of the dictionaries the subject consulted (8 cases) (Nesi and Haill 2002: 282).

Only the first type of error involves macrostructure skills; inadequate microstructure skills or lack of information induced the remaining error categories. Among the explanations for the misinterpretation of the entry is the "kidrule strategy"[8] (Miller and Gildea 1987, cited in McCreary and Dolezal 1999: 123), in which the familiar part of the dictionary definition is taken for the equivalent of the headword. To use an example, a child who looked up *erode* found a familiar-looking *eat out, eat away*, composed a sentence using *eat out* and finally replaced it with the new word *erode*, to obtain the curious construct *Our family erodes a lot* (Miller and Gildea 1987: 97–98, cited in McCreary and Dolezal 1999: 123). Wingate (2002: 165–167, 181) regards kidrule as a direct consequence of students' difficulty in comprehending and assembling meaning components into an equivalent of the target word:

> If a suitable equivalent is available in the definition and the learners manage to identify it, the look-up action will be successful. If a definition does not contain an equivalent, especially weaker subjects still search for one and accept unsuitable words instead, just because they are familiar (Wingate 2002: 181).

Another reason for misinterpretation was the "sham use" of dictionaries, i.e., disregarding or distorting the dictionary information so as to be able to retain one's preconceived notions:

> Students believed they had found their solution in the dictionary, but in reality, they had only read enough of the entry to confirm a preconceived idea, or simply deviated from the dictionary information on the grounds of interpretation and (personal) association (Müllich 1990: 487, quoted in Nesi and Haill 2002: 288).

Errors of the third type occurred because the subjects either had not recognised the discrepancy between definition and contextual meaning, or "no effort was made on the part of the subject to use the more generally applicable dictionary information to create context-specific 'value glosses'" (Nesi and Haill 2002: 289). Some of the subjects who committed errors of type four had problems with understanding the language of the definition, others did not recognise the possibility of a figurative interpretation or were influenced by precon

---

[8] Also observed with ESL students at an American university (McCreary and Dolezal 1999) and intermediate learners of German (Wingate 2002).

ceived notions. The dictionary evidently failed the students when the vocabulary item looked for was absent, or the explanation was formulated in a misleading or difficult way.

Types three and four of receptive errors bring to the fore the recurrent issue of context processing, already highlighted in McCreary and Dolezal (1999), where the dictionary, alone no better than guessing the meaning from context, turned out to be beneficial when combined with contextual information, thereby adding credibility to the practice of treating the use of contextual clues as an inseparable component of successful dictionary-aided reading rather than an alternative strategy. The context factor is germane to the discussion for yet another reason. The more difficult the text, the less successful the dictionary consultation is likely to be; in particular, the use of irony, colloquialism, slang, and metaphor is "liable to impair the use of monolingual dictionaries by clouding the meaning of lexical units in context", and "the less the user understands a text, the less reliable is the information obtained from the dictionary" (Müllich 1990: 486, 487; quoted in Nesi 2000: 39, 40).

All things considered, in a reading situation one would expect university students to be already equipped with sufficient searching strategies indicative of basic metalinguistic skills (e.g., knowledge of the alphabetical order, parts of speech), and the knowledge of lexicographical conventions (e.g., phonetic alphabet, grammar codes, lemmatisation) that every skilful dictionary user must possess. On the other hand, overt optimism about the later stages of the look-up might be unfounded: retrieval of the relevant information from the entry and its integration with the context requires considerable mental effort, a lot of which has already been invested in prior stages of the reference act.

1.3.2. Positive effect of dictionary use on performance

Several studies demonstrate a positive association between dictionary consultation and reading performance. Summers (1988) investigated the effects of dictionary use, or, to be precise, of different entry organisations, on production and comprehension, the latter being of immediate interest here. Special sample entries, prepared for eight previously selected unfamiliar words in three passages were followed by comprehension questions. It turned out that irrespective of entry design (whether it consisted of examples only, entirely of definitions, or of a definition plus examples), the use of the dictionary information always improved comprehension as compared with the control (no-entry) condition. In a similar study, Laufer (1993: 139) discovered that the traditional entry was the most effective: "[t]he learners will change their initial hypotheses about meaning when provided with additional information in the form of definition or example". Knight (1994) investigated the effect of bilingual dictionary use on incidental learning and reading comprehension in high- and low-ability students (105 learners of Spanish). Although the dictionary exerted positive influence on reading comprehension, the difference between the dictionary and no-dictionary condition was significant only for the low verbal ability group. Lew (2002b: 763) speaks of the relative advantage of the monolingual dictionary over other dictionaries in a decoding task: "[d]isappointingly for the monolingual dictionary enthusiast, it is in a rather perverse sense that the monolingual dictionary is *relatively more suitable*: its disadvantage is the least for the most advanced learners, but it is never really better than any other dictionary".

Regrettably, few studies reporting a favourable influence of the presence of a dictionary on reading comprehension performance analyse the causes of success, which, by default, must be attributed to the subjects' excellent reference skills and the reliability of dictionary information.

One of the exceptional investigations into the strategies of a good dictionary user is Tono (2001: 97–115). Data from the user profile questionnaire, observation of the use of dictionary conventions and of the look-up process during L2 > L1 translation with a bilingual dictionary in three groups of advanced,[9] intermediate, and elementary subjects, helped to single out certain characteristics of a skilled dictionary user. Among others, advanced learners' decisions to consult the dictionary were not rushed, but preceded by careful analysis of context. Although there were no major differences between successful and less successful users' macrostructure skills, time spent by the former on pre-consultation deliberations was immediately offset by high retrieval speed of information under the given entry, attesting to successful users' superior knowledge of the microstructure. Also, higher language proficiency gave advanced students an advantage over the intermediate and elementary group in understanding the entry. In the translation task the high-ability group made better judgements as to the target words to be looked up, and generally spent more time on the actual translation than on processing dictionary information than the low-ability group.

Neubach and Cohen (1988, cited in Nesi 2000: 37–39) notice that careful analysis of contextual information enables advanced students to get the gist of the passage before dictionary consultation, so that they use the dictionary mainly to confirm their mostly correct expectations, a finding consonant with that of Hulstijn (1993) and Knight (1994). In a similar vein, Wingate (2002: 117–118) mentions extensive use of contextual clues and hypothesising about the meaning before look-up as characteristic of good users.

In general, what few clues can be gathered from previous research about the assets of successful dictionary users is that they utilise contextual information properly, know what and where to look for, and are more skilled at retrieving the information from the entry than lower ability learners.

In view of the above findings, it becomes clear that in assessing the impact of the dictionary on learners' reading performance, a variety of factors, in addition to the mere presence of the reference work, needs to be taken into account. Not least among them are the accessibility of information and the way of presenting the meaning (definition structure, comprehensibility of the explanation or usability of examples). However, learner-related aspects, such as control over the number of initiated and realised reference acts and the extent to which the located information has been utilised, are equally important. Discrepancies in results and researchers' opinions about the usefulness of the dictionary stem, among others, from varying amount of attention given to such details, as well as from the diversity of design and methods applied, of which the most typical ones are discussed in the following section.

---

[9] The advanced subjects were MA holders – part-time teachers of English as a Foreign Language.

1.4. Methodological considerations[10]

The "very private matter" (Nesi and Haill 2002: 277) of dictionary use does not lend itself easily to inspection. Awareness that no single method can yield an exhaustive and impartial picture of normal, everyday consultation motivates "methodological plurality" (Hartmann 2001). Those scholarly endeavours in which the data, collected by various means, can be cross-checked, or "triangulated" (Nesi 2000: 12), are likely to be the most credible. The ever-growing diversity in methodological approaches manifests itself in their current non-matching classifications, as Hartmann (2001: 115) notices. This section, in highlighting the merits and weaknesses of major methods applied in investigating the influence of diction-ary use on performance and the process of consultation, aims to provide background against which the design of the experiment discussed in Chapter 5 can be better explained. Nesi's (2000) division into questionnaire-, test- and observation-based research will be adopted.

1.4.1. Questionnaire-based research

Questionnaire-based research or survey, an example of which is Tomaszczyk (1979) or Béjoint (1981), is an indirect method of collecting data, usually through techniques such as interviews, self completion or postal questionnaires, or attitude scales. All of these rely on retrospection or introspection, which undermines the reliability of the obtained data. To quote Hatherall's (1984: 184) well known criticism: "[a]re subjects saying here what they do, or what they think they do, or what they think they ought to do, or indeed a mixture of all three?" Nuccorini (1992) admits that in her survey teachers were far more accurate in filling in their questionnaires than students. The latter provided inconsistent data which, to make sense, called for the researcher's educated guesses. As Humblé (2001: 44) rightly observes, "[if] researchers themselves have to pick out the 'right' answers, then what is the use of going through the trouble of devising a survey?". Questionnaire-based research has also been criticised on the grounds that it makes unfounded assumptions about subjects' linguistic and lexicographic knowledge (Humblé 2001: 43–44).[11] Allegedly, questionnaires have lost their potential as a methodological tool in dictionary-user research:

> Examined 20 years later, the results of these first questionnaires seem obvious, even if they were not so at the time. It would not be surprising if more recent questionnaires only confirmed the con-clusions of the first ones. One can safely assume that this research method has by now yielded all its possible results. Questionnaires only investigate what *is* and not what *should* be or *could* be. The only practical conclusions to be drawn from them are what dictionary features learners use (and should be maintained), and what features they do not use (and should be eliminated).
>
> Since questionnaires depend heavily on what subjects *consciously* know or think they know, it seems logical that controlled experiments, or tests, would at some point take over (Humblé 2001: 44–45).

---

[10] For a detailed review of methods employed in all branches of dictionary user studies, see Diab (1990: 58–63), Hartmann (2001: 110–120), Tono (2001: 59–72).

[11] For that reason, among Lew's (2002a: 270) recommendations for questionnaire writers there is the following one: "don't use technical language that subjects might not understand".

Despite the increasing unpopularity of questionnaire-based research, its value has been recently reassessed and defended by Lew (2002a). It is argued there that charges directed at questionnaires apply equally well to observation-based research, where the reliability of measurement is affected by the Labovian observer's paradox. Moreover, questionnaires seem indispensable in the case of certain (e.g., attitudinal) aspects of dictionary use. Finally, as Lew (2002a) points out, differences in the profiles of dictionary use obtained from various surveys do not diminish surveys' reliability, but are a natural consequence of variables involved in distinct situations of dictionary use.

Whereas no questionnaire proper has been utilised for the purposes of this study, certain elements based on retrospection and self-reflection (e.g., familiarity rating scale, self-reports of look-up motivation, statements of one's familiarity with the dictionary or the level of difficulty when using the unfamiliar dictionary) have been introduced so as to supply and cross-check the data collected by other methods.

1.4.2. Test-based research

Test-based research includes all studies carried out under controlled conditions and aimed at obtaining objective measurable data on performance in reading tests (of interest here), vocabulary learning, and assessment of dictionary using skills (Nesi 2000: 12). As Humblé (2001: 48) states, "[i]n the case of *tests*, unlike questionnaires, it is primarily the *dictionary* which is being evaluated... Tests tend to blame the dictionaries for the bad results of the learners and question the dictionaries' effectiveness". The most commonly employed techniques within this category are experiments (or experimental tests) and quasi-experiments.

An experiment involves the observation of the effect of a change in the value of one or more independent variables on the dependent variable(s). For instance, in Knight's (1994) experiment, there were three independent variables: 1) exposure or no exposure to words in context before testing (within-subject variable); 2) verbal ability (between-subject variable) and 3) dictionary access (between-subject variable). The dependent variables were incidental vocabulary learning and reading comprehension. Experiments may involve the use of nonce words or specially designed dictionaries (Tono 2001: 144). The quasi-experiment resembles a true experiment but for the lack of randomisation in the selection of subjects (Tono 2001: 72).

Provided that the experiment has been appropriately designed and administered, test-based research yields manageable, quantifiable, relatively precise and objective data. As Nesi (2000: 32) recommends, sufficient attention should be paid to factors such as: the allocation of the dictionary, the subjects' familiarity with the dictionary, quantity of dictionary use, test format (the task should be as close to natural dictionary use as possible), objective test marking and data analysis. It is advisable to use only one type of dictionary within a group, make sure that the subjects represent a homogenous performance level, and work under the same time constraints (Hatherall 1984: 186–187).

Certain scoring measures, such as the multiple-choice format or direct questions, are likely to bias the answers by providing additional context (Nesi 2000: 32, Wingate 2002: 19). The former are akin to True/False questions in that they can often "be answered correctly without reading the passage, by just applying common sense, by extracting only minimal and superficial information from the reading text, or by receiving clues from other questions" (Wingate 2002: 19). Indeed, evidence from another research area has shown that performance in forced-choice tasks exceeds performance in explanation tasks in school-age children and adolescents (Nippold and Taylor 1995). In other words, multiple choice turns out to be too crude a method to reveal differences in understanding. In this respect, "explanation tasks are more demanding because they require the individual to actively generate – rather than simply select – an appropriate interpretation of an idiom" (Nippold and Taylor 1995: 431). As was mentioned in section 1.3.1.1., reading comprehension may not be affected by a dictionary when the questions test general comprehension of the passage rather than the vocabulary. Although the immediate recall protocol (e.g., Knight 1994), in which learners recount what they remember after reading the text, is commonly held as the optimum comprehension measure (Wingate 2002: 19), it entails the risk of the meaning of the target items being deliberately or unintentionally omitted from the report. Additionally, scoring is far more complicated than in the case of other comprehension measures.

Strict control of all variables, though guaranteeing the reliability of data, occasionally makes the task too artificial to reflect real-life situations of dictionary use (Tono 2001: 36). Test-based research can be used to verify hypotheses concerning the results of the consultation process. However, it does not have much explanatory power – it gives no indication whatsoever as to the procedures and stages employed during the search (Nesi 2000: 32). These are usually explored through observation-based research.

1.4.3. Observation-based research

According to Hatherall (1984: 184), "whatever the difficulties, the only reliable method of collecting data on dictionary user behavior is by direct observation. Ideally, in other words, the research would actually watch users in action". The aim of observation-based research is to discover certain patterns in the dictionary user's behaviour, instead of testing linguistic performance or reference skills. It generates, rather than tests, hypotheses (Nesi 2000: 33). The data is collected during the task or immediately afterwards by means of techniques such as observation (participant and non-participant), a protocol (think-aloud and its paper equivalent), or post-task interview.

In participant observation the observer engages in the activity, whereas non-participant observers "stand aloof from the group activities they are investigating and eschew group membership" (Tono 2001: 67). "Unobtrusive" observation may highlight interesting habits of individual dictionary users that cannot be discovered in large-scale quantitative studies. However, the generalisability of such studies is often limited due to a small number of subjects.

Another direct record of "what happens when a particular user works with a particular dictionary during a particular activity" (Hartmann 2001: 118) is a think-aloud protocol, in which the dictionary user verbalises his/her thoughts during the activity of looking-up. Verbal protocols are usually audio and/or video-recorded. One of the few studies of dictionary-use strategies in a comprehension task by means of a verbal protocol is Neubach and Cohen (1988, cited in Nesi 2000: 37–39). As with observation, the number of subjects must be very limited, unless a written protocol is used, e.g., in the form of Diab's (1990)

"Dictionary Using Diaries"[12]. Though undoubtedly interfering with the natural process of looking up, written protocols are a rich source of information otherwise unobtainable in large groups.

Another direct technique is a post-task interview, which can be "open or structured, recorded or unrecorded, conducted with subjects individually or in small groups" (Diab 1990: 61). An interview allows the researcher to ask additional questions concerning the completed task. However, since it relies on subjects' retrospection, that is, on what they think they have done, it is liable to the sort of criticism questionnaires have come in for. An example of a post-task interview is Neubach and Cohen (1988, cited in Nesi 2000: 37–39).

All techniques employed in observation-based research are time-consuming, sometimes expensive, and involve lengthy data processing in search of emerging trends. Above all, attention to the behaviour of individual subjects makes qualitative research of this kind "easily reduced to the level of anecdote if the processes of data collection and analysis are not recorded in detail" (Nesi 2000: 53). The need to eliminate contradictory evidence through data triangulation and re-assessment of samples via checking intra- and inter-rater reliability becomes even more pressing than in quantitative research.

Evidently, no method, whether questionnaire-, test- or observation-based, is capable of perfectly recreating natural conditions of dictionary use while remaining totally controlled and absolutely objective. One can only attempt to "to devise the study in such a way that what the subjects say they do and what they actually do can be compared" (Béjoint 1994: 148). This approach will serve as a model in the empirical part of this monograph.

1.5. Rationale for further research

Despite the fact that reading invariably pops up in questionnaires of students' needs as one of the most frequent occasions of dictionary use, the role of dictionary in decoding remains an unsettled issue: there are nearly as many negative as positive reports as to the effects of the dictionary condition on reading performance. Regrettably, "most studies were concerned only with whether or not dictionaries were *used* and not how *effectively* they were used" (Tono 2001: 75). Clearly, there is space for pursuing the association between comprehension scores and the quality of the look-up process, retrievable via studies called by Tono (2001: 83) "more dynamic" – concentrating not only on the end-product of consultation but also on its process. In order to link achievement to regularities in the consultation habits, the experiment reported in Chapter 5 combines elements of test-, observation-, and questionnaire-based research.

Although reference skills are a popular area of study, the question of what happens once the dictionary information has been located seems to have been neglected in the literature. In fact, if reference skills are to be understood traditionally as "the abilities required on the

---

[12] Nuccorini (1992) also employed this kind of self-report in various situations of dictionary use. The subjects had to fill in the information concerning the item looked up, minimal context, reason for consultation, occasion of consultation, dictionary consulted, whether the answer was found, the part of the entry it was found in, and the level of their satisfaction.

part of the dictionary user to find the information being sought" (Hartmann and James 1998: 117), the problem of handling the microstructure data falls outside the purview of lexicography.[13] The opposite view will be advocated in this study, that is, exploitation of the information will be considered at least as valid a factor determining the ultimate usefulness of a dictionary as the skills of finding the item in the macro- and microstructure.

Why should the perspective of highly advanced learners be valuable for dictionary-user research? On the face of it, they make poor subjects, looking up few words (Hulstijn 1993: 144, Atkins and Varantola 1998a: 34, Tono 2001: 112) to confirm largely correct guesses (Hulstijn 1993: 144, Knight 1994: 295). The opportunities to observe their consultation process are likely to be scarce. If, in general, "dictionaries are used more competently by the more linguistically sophisticated users" (Béjoint 1994: 151), testing their dictionary skills seems a bit of a nit-picking. Indeed, the discussion of consultation pitfalls so far has often been limited to lower-level or intermediate subjects. Potential difficulties of highly proficient students majoring in English as a foreign language have hardly been considered at all. However, one might argue that research which juxtaposes advanced learners' achievement with that of their lower-ability peers, instead of evaluating it in its own right, will inevitably create a favourable, though supposedly incomplete, image of the proficient learner – dictionary user. Whereas reference skills and linguistic sophistication are undoubtedly concomitant, advanced students are only relatively better dictionary users. Given a sufficiently difficult task, they may need to resort to the dictionary as often as less proficient ones, and likewise experience consultation problems, though probably of a different nature. Implicit in this study is the belief that a suitably challenging task should make a more sensitive tool for detecting potential receptive errors of proficient subjects. Accordingly, the empirical part re-traces the path followed by learners in search of the original meaning of idioms camouflaged in text in the dictionary and control (no-dictionary) condition.

The other side of the dictionary-aided-comprehension coin are the determinants of success or failure related to the reference work itself. As Wingate (2002: 3) explains,

> [d]ictionary-related reasons [for (in)effective dictionary use – R. S.] concern strengths or deficiencies in the way information is presented to the learners. They are relative to the proficiency level of learners... If more is known about user needs at different proficiency levels, dictionary information can be adjusted. This can for instance result in the development of different monolingual dictionary types for different levels.

In view of the fact that the upper intermediate level has been proved to be the proficiency threshold that needs to be reached if the use of the monolingual dictionary is to be effective (Wingate 2002), in theory, advanced learners should be capable of handling the dictionary information without any serious obstacles. Still, it is possible to reverse the usual question of the minimum linguistic attainment necessary for adequate dictionary use, and ask about the upper proficiency level at which the usefulness of the monolingual learner's dictionary drops, as well as inquire about the features behind the potential decline. In probing this matter, it is convenient to examine the entries for items regarded as representative of the "hard" section of the lexicon, frequently sought after even by proficient students; hence the choice of idioms as targets in the present study.

---

[13] This approach is espoused, e.g., by Humblé (2001: 16).

Since reading is the activity during which the effectiveness of dictionary use is to be tested, some rudimentary knowledge of the evolution of views on the character of the reading process and reading instruction – indispensable to our discussion – will be presented in Chapter 2.

2. Influence of L1 Reading Research on Instruction in L2 Reading and Dictionary Use

2.0. Introduction

Whether a receptive situation actually leads to dictionary use depends, to a large extent, on the kind of instruction that learners have received. This chapter highlights the main aspects of reading research in so far as they carry pedagogical implications. Also, it presents the results of related research initiated in response to the most powerful and lasting influence of one of the theories on reading instruction.

2.1. L1 reading models

The first models embodying the theories of the reading process date back to the mid-1950s and early 1960s (Samuels and Kamil 1988: 22). Three broad types have been distinguished in the literature and labelled, respectively, "bottom-up", "top-down" and "interactive"[1].

According to the behaviourist underpinnings of the audio-lingual teaching method of the 1960s, reading is a matter of habitual, stimulus-response reaction to the written symbol – pure "verbal mechanics", as Swaffar (1988: 129) put it. Consistently with the then popular idea of language as a structure, reading involves the linear recognition of lower-level elements to make sense of higher-order elements (from graphemes through words, phrases, clauses, sentences, to the meaning of whole paragraphs), and only by such a left-to-right operation can one succeed in, first, decoding (i.e., mechanically matching meaning to the symbol), and then, deriving the meaning (Chodkiewicz 2000: 44). As Samuels and Kamil (1988: 31) explain, "[b]ecause the sequence of processing proceeds from the incoming data to higher-level encodings, these descriptions of the reading process are called bottom-up models". Thanks to its text-boundedness, bottom-up processing is said to be data-driven (Carrell and Eisterhold 1988: 77). Implicit in this view of reading is the idea of meaning as a property of the text,[2] totally independent of the reader – decoder. The major accusation levelled against bottom-up models in the literature is that they represent subsequent processing stages of reading as insular and self-contained, and fail to account for context-effects in comprehension.

---

[1] These are blanket terms for a number of specific models. For a comprehensive overview of reading models, see Samuels and Kamil (1988); see also Chodkiewicz (2000: 43–49).

[2] This traditional view is reinforced by natural language, full of expressions attesting to the existence of the objectivist "conduit metaphor" (Lakoff and Johnson 1980: 10–11), according to which every lexical unit is a container holding some well-defined, context-free meaning (e.g., *It's difficult to put my ideas into words; Try to pack more thought into fewer words; Your words seem hollow; The sentence is without meaning*).

In reaction to bottom-up models and with the advent of cognitivism, a more mentalist, psycholinguistic, or "whole-language" approach (Samuels and Kamil 1988: 23) to reading developed. The top-down model redefines the activity of reading in terms of the graphic – and from then on frequently cited – metaphor of reading as a "psycholinguistic guessing game" (Goodman 1970). In Goodman's own words, reading

> involves an interaction between thought and language. Efficient reading does not result from precise perception and identification of all elements, but from skill in selecting the fewest, most productive cues necessary to produce guesses which are right the first time (Goodman 1970: 108).

To paraphrase this definition, the reader engages in the construction of meaning by creating hypotheses to be confirmed or verified on the basis of selected contextual clues. Hence, in contrast to the bottom-up view, readers are upgraded from the position of mere decoders to that of "active samplers of text... using predictions to take short-cuts in bottom-up processing of letters and words" (Haynes 1993: 47). Top-down models account for the fact that the higher-order stages of information processing interact with the earlier stages, and that the former "seem to be driving and directing the process and are doing the lion's share of the work" (Samuels and Kamil 1988: 31). Reading, by the tenets of the top-down approach, is essentially conceptually driven, not data-driven as in bottom-up models. Accordingly, reading comprehension is no longer text-bound. Rather, as Omaggio (1986: 100) notes, the text "provides direction for listeners and readers, so that they can construct meaning from their own cognitive structure (previously acquired or background knowledge)". The knowledge on which one draws in comprehending the text has been formalised in the schema theory, first developed by Bartlett (1932; 1995). Schemata are said to be interrelated knowledge structures, constructed of previous experience of the world which, along with the context, allow the reader to make predictions and create hypotheses concerning the meaning. When reading, one engages in "fitting meaning to existing schemata" (Omaggio 1986: 101).

Despite its immense popularity, the top-down approach has not been without flaws. Haynes (1993: 48) reports L1 studies which prove mastery of bottom-up processing, disclaimed in the psycholinguistic model, to be indispensable for fluent reading. Samuels and Kamil (1988: 32) argue that top-down models apply only to beginners; for a reader skilled in recognising words, generating predictions will be too time-consuming and inefficient. Conversely, for Eskey (1988: 93, 94), top-down models adequately render advanced, but not beginning reading because "[i]t is precisely this 'automaticity' [of decoding – R. S.] that frees up the minds of fluent readers of a language to think about and interpret what they are reading – that is, to employ higher-level, top-down strategies like the use of schemata and other kinds of background knowledge". The two seemingly disparate views are compatible in the light of Eskey's (1988: 95) distinction between two modes of understanding the use of top-down processing: as a word-recognition strategy and text interpretation method, the former characteristic of poor readers (prioritised by Samuels and Kamil 1988), the latter – of skilled readers (foregrounded by Eskey 1988).

The late 1970s and early 1980s brought about another change of scene in reading research – a reaction against top-down models in the form of interactive models of reading.[3]

---

[3] The term *interactive* has acquired several senses in reading research (Grabe 1988). It is important to distinguish between that pertaining to the reading process (as the interaction between the reader

Being a compromise, they accommodate the role of higher-level processes that involve context-generated predictions and expectations without excluding the perceptual in-coming data from the text. In line with this approach, "readers do graphophonemic processing of word-form and retrieval of their meaning, as well as inferencing from global and local context" (Coady 1993: 18). The roles of top-down (conceptually driven) and bottom-up (data-driven) processing can be elucidated as follows:

> Bottom-up processing ensures that the listeners/readers will be sensitive to information that is novel or that does not fit ongoing hypotheses about the content or structure of the text; top-down processing helps the listeners/readers to resolve ambiguities or to select between alternative possible interpretations of the incoming data (Carrell and Eisterhold 1988: 77).

The interactive approach does not proclaim the supremacy of either mode of processing; instead, they are presented as parallel and intertwined. According to Stanovich's (1980, cited in Chodkiewicz 2000: 46) interactive-compensatory model, extensive context processing in less efficient readers compensates for their inadequate word recognition skills, but, at the same time, the overall comprehension of the text suffers due to excessive concentration on word-processing. On the other hand, in skilful readers, who are capable of context-free word recognition, more cognitive capacity can be directed at text comprehension. Interestingly enough, Carrell (1988) reveals that, though the weakness of one strategy indeed leads to overreliance on either text-based processing (text boundedness) or knowledge-based processing (schema interference), it need not necessarily result in immediate processing-switch. As Carrell (1988: 108) demonstrates, "[t]he same skill deficiency (effortful decoding) may lead to one of two totally different comprehension styles – text-biased or knowledge-biased – depending on what the reader does in either persevering in the problem area or trying to escape from it".

In summary, the interactive approach indicates two interrelated planes of processing information – data- and concept-driven – as prerequisites for successful reading comprehension. Under the circumstances, "the fluent reader is characterised by both skill at rapid, context-free word and phrase recognition and, at higher cognitive levels, the skillful use of appropriate comprehension strategies" (Eskey 1988: 98).

2.2. Pedagogical implications

2.2.1. L2 reading instruction as influenced by top-down and interactive models

Of the three reading models, only the top-down approach left a strong and lasting imprint on EFL reading pedagogy, which readily and rather uncritically embraced the use of

---

and the text) and the one referring to reading models, meaning the interaction between information obtained from various (bottom-up and top-down) levels of processing, e.g., graphic features, letters, words, phrases, sentences, local cohesion, paragraph structuring, topics of discourse, inferencing and world knowledge (Grabe 1988: 57–59). See also Eskey (1988: 95–96).

prediction and context-based inference[4] as a convenient solution to the problems of foreign reading comprehension and the related issue of vocabulary acquisition.[5] Whereas teachers and the then current textbooks applauded the practice of unrestricted guessing of the meaning of words from context,[6] the use of the dictionary was discredited, if not downright rejected. Although the heyday of the psycholinguistic approach to reading falls on the late 1970s and early 1980s, as late as the late 1980s there still appeared articles advocating the view that "[t]he dictionary means security for many, of course, so this cannot be a prohibition, only an encouragement; but we should advise that the dictionary be used only as a last resort" (Nattinger 1988: 63).

Under the influence of interactive models, educational trends in reading and vocabulary acquisition have shifted: "instructional activities in this framework tend to place emphasis on teaching students to take advantage of all of their prior knowledge. As a result, vocabulary instruction is viewed in terms of the students' background knowledge of concepts as well as of word-forms" (Coady 1993: 6). In practice, it is recommended that "natural" guessing from context, appropriate for the less frequent vocabulary, be supplemented with the more explicit training in the case of the basic (core or "sight") vocabulary (Coady 1993: 16–17). The rationale behind this method is to be found in the schema theory, reinterpreted in interactive terms:

> Word-forms which are automatically and instantaneously recognised by a reader can be thought of as access portals to schemata. In effect, word-forms trigger an already existing network of knowledge which will then interact with other words/schemata, enabling a reader to arrive at comprehension of the overall meaning of the given text (Coady 1993: 11).

The rehabilitation of the word-centred bottom-up approach entails the reintroduction of the dictionary – a tool of improving lower-level processing – into the classroom. Nonetheless, the dictionary is no longer perceived as the primary and exclusive source of meaning, but as one of the additional, alternative routes to it. At the same time, inference ceased to be treated as a strategy intended to oust dictionary use:

---

[4] Inferencing has been viewed in the literature from at least three perspectives, viz. a receptive procedure, a potential learning procedure, and a learning objective (Chodkiewicz 2000: 134). In the course of our discussion, we will concentrate on guessing as a receptive, and not learning, procedure, although it is sometimes very difficult to separate the two, since comprehension is a prerequisite for learning.

[5] For a discussion of studies on the relationship between vocabulary and text readability, the effects of low-frequency vocabulary and pre-teaching of vocabulary on comprehension, see Nation and Coady (1988: 97–101).

[6] Context is a broad category. Linguistic context (sometimes referred to as "co-text") can be defined as "morphological, syntactic and discourse information in a given text which can be classified and described" (Nation and Coady 1988: 102). Chodkiewicz (2000: 81–82) mentions the distinction between local context (limited to a phrase/sentence immediately surrounding a given word) and global context (the text in which the word/phrase is encountered), as well as that between internal or "within the word" context (the information inherent in the morphology of the word) versus external ("within the text") context (all the information present in the text). Finally, one can speak of general (extralinguistic) context – "background knowledge of the subject of a given text" (Nation and Coady 1988: 102). In this study, the sense of linguistic external (several-sentence) context is used.

[t]op-down practice should also be retained in ESL reading classes...The goal of top-down reading instruction should not be absolute independence from the dictionary, but rather an increase in students' flexibility, knowing where and how to look for meaning when the handiest sources of information fail to make sense (Haynes 1993: 59).

Despite the fact that contextual guessing ceased to be presented as a comprehension strategy alternative to dictionary use, it continues to be viewed as a major help in understanding unfamiliar (especially infrequent) words within the interactive theory of reading. Since the issue has a bearing upon the problem of dictionary use and instruction, the major arguments put forward in the "context vs. dictionary" controversy, as well as selected results of research investigating the effectiveness of inference for comprehension, will be reported in section 2.2.2.

2.2.2. Inference as an alternative to dictionary use: Revision of arguments

Let us examine the pivotal arguments of inference-enthusiasts, which, to a large extent, translate into those of dictionary-sceptics.

2.2.2.1. The "no disruption" and "deep processing" argument

The widespread belief in the "banishment" of dictionaries from the classroom stems from the conviction that "if a student stops to look up words in the dictionary, this will slow reading speed and thus weaken comprehension. If one learns to skip or guess from context, integrative reading can still take place" (Haynes 1993: 48). To rephrase this argument, the alleged superiority of inference lies in its non-intrusive character: unlike dictionary consultation, guessing is said not to interfere with the short-term memory and the smooth reading process. While determining the meaning of unfamiliar words from context may be one of the essential subskills of intensive and cursory (extensive) reading (Van Parreren and Schouten-van Parreren 1981), the line of reasoning stressing the positive effects of guessing on the speed of reading is particularly unconvincing. According to Nation and Coady (1988: 104–105), the strategy of guessing from context consists of five steps:

1. Finding the part of speech of the unknown word.
2. Looking at the immediate context of the unknown word and simplifying this context if necessary.
3. Looking at the wider context of the unknown word...
4. Guessing the meaning of the unknown word.
5. Checking that the guess is correct.

Inevitably, these must take time and effort so one would be hard-pressed not to agree with the statement that "[i]nitially the strategy is a *major* interruption to the reading process while learners develop familiarity with the range of clues available" (Nation and Coady 1988: 105, emphasis – R. S.).

Ironically, the claim of the non-disruptive nature of guessing is subverted through another argument frequently cited by advocates of inference:

[T]he attempt to infer brings the unknown word into contact with an active searching and thinking process, involving consideration of possible meaning dimensions of the word (its denotation, field of application, syntactic behaviour, connotations, etc.)... Trying to learn a new word by looking it up in a dictionary is akin to rote learning; on the other hand, attempting to infer the meaning of the word provides for meaningful learning... (Honeyfield 1977: 36).

By definition, extensive mental processing inherent in guessing words from context must interfere with the fluency of reading. Also, in line with the above quotation, the multi-step process of dictionary consultation (cf. section 1.2.) would have to be regarded as thoughtless rote learning – a preposterous supposition. Laufer (1993: 132) contends that looking up and the subsequent working out of the meaning in context requires equally deep processing and, in addition, guarantees the reliability of the assimilated information.

2.2.2.2. Analogy between L1 and L2 reading

More importantly, as Haynes (1993: 48) points out, the hasty transfer of the "reading as a psycholinguistic guessing game" theory from L1 to L2 environment must be questioned at its roots for at least two reasons. Firstly, some studies in L1 reading show that fluent reading cannot be effected unless bottom-up processing has been mastered. Secondly, the analogy drawn between L1 and L2 reading is fallacious: L2 reading is a source of considerable difficulties and takes more time. Therefore, Haynes (1993: 50) concludes, "it seems premature to claim that since L1 readers often skip or guess at new words in context we must teach ESL students to do the same when they encounter new words". When an analogy has to be made, L2 readers resemble L1 low-skill rather than fluent readers (Coady 1993: 10). Indeed, ample empirical evidence confirms the suspicion that L2 learners' reading behaviour is nowhere near that of native speakers.

Carrell (1983), while studying the effects of background knowledge on reading within the context of the schema theory, made the disturbing discovery that

[n]either advanced nor high-intermediate ESL readers appear to utilize context or textual clues. They are not efficient top-down processors, making appropriate predictions based on context, nor are they efficient bottom-up processors, building up a mental representation of the text based on the lexical information in the text (Carrell 1983: 199).

Bensoussan and Laufer (1984), whose study was meant to reveal to what extent, if at all, context helps in guessing, came to similarly pessimistic conclusions. Context did not significantly improve lexical guessing – it helped in only 13 per cent of the answers for only 24 per cent of the words. Furthermore, the higher scores of good students could be attributed to their overall superior vocabulary knowledge, but not to their guessing abilities. Like weak students, they ignored unknown words, applied preconceived notions, made wild guesses or, at best, contextually-inappropriate guesses, turning to context as a last resort.

Similarly, Laufer and Sim (1985: 10) observe that both poor and good learners (when faced with a difficult passage), unable to use textual and extratextual clues to good effect, take "the line of least resistance – that is, the easy way out". In deriving the meaning, they cling to certain (usually familiar or familiar-looking) lexical items or disregard unfamiliar words, add whatever textual or extratextual knowledge they have to the meaning thus created, and impose a sentence structure on their frequently false interpretation. Syntactic structure has been found to be exploited least, or even ignored in favour of lexical cues. In view of such disappointing results, one must agree with the suggestion that "[i]f the cause of the type of reading presented here is an insecure language base, then, to remedy the situation, work on the language would be more beneficial than practice in the use of contextual clues, since the former is apparently a prerequisite for the latter", and that "[t]he solid language base that is required to enable the reader to use contextual clues seems to be mainly of a lexical nature..." (Laufer and Sim 1985: 10). Laufer and Sim (1985) basically confirm Van Parreren and Schouten-van Parreren's (1981: 238–239) conclusions concerning the syntactic, semantic, and lexical level errors during the process of guessing the meaning of unknown foreign language words from context. In most general terms, learners form premature, strong hypotheses on the basis of lexical rather than syntactic information, and are prepared to distort or disregard contextual information in order to maintain their guess, which they often fail to check against the immediate or wider context.

Statman (1987) points to the affective factor as a serious barrier to fluent foreign language reading, perhaps more salient than linguistic shortcomings. In line with the previous research, the subjects exhibited "panicky" reading (Statman 1987: 295) – absurd hypotheses and wild guesses based on random vocabulary items with blatant disregard for syntax. This undesirable behaviour, it is argued, can be put down to a range of emotional responses that a foreign text might induce, such as anxiety, fear, frustration and excitement:

> When the reader is experienced and confident in reading, he or she takes short-cuts, "knows" where to look for main ideas, jumps over difficulties and maintains multiple readings of ambiguous words and different schemata until context has resolved the meaning. In contrast, when the reader is unsure of himself, he or she remains trapped by the many decisions and alternative meanings presented by the text (Statman 1987: 298).

Furthermore, the guessing process may end in failure due to factors beyond the reader's control. Unsurprisingly, cue-adequate sentences foster word inference (Li 1988: 409), and a "pregnant", i.e., suitably rich, context, certainly improves the guessability of the meaning (Mondria and Wit-de Boer 1991[7]). Nonetheless, one needs to acknowledge the fact that explicitness is an exception rather than a rule in natural, unedited texts. As Laufer (1997) rightly points out, there exist "words you can't guess" because context is not redundant enough (the case of nonexistent contextual clues) or the clues happen to be in unfamiliar words (unusable contextual clues); besides, the clues might be misleading or suppressed, for example, by background knowledge.[8] Whereas a sufficiently informative immediate context may somehow guide second language readers to the meaning of an unknown word,

---

[7] Additionally, their findings invalidate the popular assumption that retention is directly proportional to context informativeness. This argument, related to vocabulary acquisition and not comprehension, will not be pursued further.

[8] For a detailed discussion of the problem of not very perspicuous context clues, presented as a manifestation of the inherent inexplicitness of natural language, see Stein (1993).

their plight is only aggravated in the case of global clues hidden in longer stretches of text (Haynes 1993: 54).[9]

There is always a risk that an incorrect guess will be retained despite conflicting evidence, like in the experiment by Statman when "[h]aving once established a hypothesis, even those students who claimed to have read to the end stuck to it grimly in spite of later evidence against it" (Statman 1987: 296). Similarly inflexible behaviour was registered by Laufer and Sim (1985) and Van Parreren and Schouten-van Parreren (1981).

Finally, in order to attempt a guess, the reader must recognise an item as unfamiliar, and here L2 learners fail again in that, unlike native speakers, they "are often unsure whether a word is really new or not. Thus it is not surprising that any flash of familiarity in a word arrests their attention, making the context fade into the background" (Haynes 1993: 58). Common is misidentification resulting from an incorrect analysis of morphological or graphophonemic structure of a lexical item (Haynes 1993: 55–56). According to Bensoussan and Laufer (1984: 26), it is the somewhat familiar words, as opposed to totally unfamiliar ones, that stand the least chance of being guessed correctly – more often than not, they will be ignored as too familiar to be worthy of investing the effort. Under what Laufer (1997: 25) terms "words you think you know" or "deceptively transparent" (DT) words, five categories are subsumed: words with a deceptive morphological structure, idioms, false friends, words with multiple meanings, and synforms (similar lexical forms) (cf. Huckin and Bloch's (1993) "mistaken ID" words). On account of the covert nature of sense distortion caused by DT words, they easily lead to further misinterpretations of context and of the remaining unfamiliar words, in this way perpetuating the deleterious effect on text comprehension (Laufer 1997: 27).

2.2.2.3. Usefulness of inference for infrequent words

The misguided analogy between the L1-L2 reading manner notwithstanding, the value of guessing from context as an EFL comprehension strategy is dubious for another, perhaps even more compelling, reason. Paradoxically, research has shown inference to be least useful for infrequent vocabulary items – those singled out as primary candidates for guessing and incidental learning within the top-down and interactive reading theory (Na and Nation 1985: 39–40). A closer look at this seemingly counterintuitive argument is in order.

According to Schatz and Baldwin (1986), the use of high-frequency words and highly constrained, artificial contexts might have enhanced context effects in previous studies. To avoid bias, they designed three experiments testing the extent to which the meaning of low-frequency words is inferable in natural contexts. In the first experiment, the subjects assigned to the context and no-context condition were given a multiple-choice vocabulary test. In Experiment 2, another group of students were given words-in-isolation and words-in-context tests from four content areas ("newspapers", "magazines", "history textbooks", and "science textbooks") so as to eliminate content as a factor influencing the context-

---

[9] Interestingly, complaints about L2 readers' poor integrating skills are echoed in lexicographic research reporting learners' difficulty in assembling the meaning components of a dictionary definition into one equivalent (cf. section 1.3.1.2.).

effects. Experiment 3 was a replication of Experiment 1, but students were asked to write full definitions instead of answering multiple-choice questions and the raters did not know which condition they were scoring. The lack of statistically significant context effect in either of the three studies is explained against the background of Finn's (1977-1978, cited in Schatz and Baldwin 1986: 450) "transfer feature theory", which suggests an inverse relationship between the amount of information a word carries and its guessability. Put simply, the more predicable a word is in context, the lesser the amount of information it carries. Since "[o]ne assumes that authors use low-frequency words not for the purpose of teaching word meanings, but for the purpose of adding information or constraining the text" (Schatz and Baldwin 1986: 451), it follows that the strategy of guessing from context is unlikely to work for high information, rare words that are often unfamiliar. The study offers cogent reasons for the reexamination of the practice of overemphasising guessing from context and for the reinstatement of the dictionary as a far more reliable source of meaning. As the authors argue,

> [t]raditionally, dictionary use is the *last* step taken to get the meaning of a low-frequency word. This look-it-up-as-a-last-resort strategy may be appropriate for word recognition, but not for the comprehension of high-information words that are not in the reader's lexicon (Schatz and Baldwin 1986: 451).

This opinion, consonant with Knight's (1994: 295) appeal for the re-examination of the practice of encouraging students to guess meaning from context, deserves special attention in view of studies hinting at word variable as more highly correlated with comprehension achievement than the ability to guess the meaning or get the gist of the text (Anderson and Freebody 1981, cited in Laufer 1997: 20).

2.3. Concluding remarks

However shaky the analogy between L1 and L2 reading, one of the L1 reading theories – the top-down model – has exerted a particularly profound influence upon EFL reading instruction by popularising the strategy of guessing the meaning from context as a viable alternative to dictionary use. The substantial literature expounding the advantages of context clues as a comprehension strategy (e.g., Honeyfield 1977, Li 1988, Na and Nation 1985, Van Parreren and Schouten-van Parreren 1981) or indicating their limitations (e.g., Bensoussan and Laufer 1984, Haynes 1993, Huckin and Bloch 1993, Laufer 1997, Laufer and Sim 1985, Mondria and Wit-de Boer 1991, Schatz and Baldwin 1986, Stein 1993) yields no unequivocal answer to the all-important question of the effectiveness of guessing (as opposed to dictionary definition) during the activity of reading.[10] Though artificial, constrained context will undoubtedly boost comprehension, it would be unrealistic to

---

[10] Disappointing as this may be, one needs to take heed of the fact that a fully objective assessment seems methodologically unfeasible due to the difficulty of telling the contextual information from that extracted from the dictionary (Scholfield 1997: 296). One cannot simply assume that the dictionary condition excludes the use of inference.

expect redundancy from the majority of authentic texts. It is even more far-fetched to take the reading and inferencing skills of foreign learners for granted or to equate them with those of native speakers. The process of guessing at the meaning of unknown words must be at least as much of an interference as the act of looking words up. Neither is it possible to state at present which involves more mental processing and is thus more conducive to learning. Last but not least, it is doubtful whether infrequent words indeed make ideal candidates for guessing.

The above evidence is by no means to be taken to imply that there is no place for inference in EFL reading. As Van Parreren and Schouten-van Parreren (1981: 237) remark, "[i]t is self-evident that a reader who is not able to use context adequately will have to refer to the dictionary continually and in many cases will not be able to choose the correct alternative". In fact, guessing from context becomes a valid strategy only if the guess can be verified, a practice particularly commendable in the case of key-words, the good grasp of which is essential for the activation of the appropriate schemata, and for further guessing from context (Scholfield 1997: 285). Consequently, dictionary use is to be viewed as a safeguard against the weaknesses of guessing, rather than as a last-resort strategy. Simultaneous use of dictionary and inference seems best suited to the needs and habits of readers, who often feel insecure when unable to verify their guesses. Significantly, the use of the dictionary (or glosses) and contextual information yields better results than either strategy in isolation (Davis 1989; Hulstijn, Hollander and Greidanus 1996; McCreary and Dolezal 1999). As Chapter 3 demonstrates, in the case of idiomatic modifications, the combined use of dictionary and contextual information becomes an absolute necessity.

3. Creative Use of Idioms – a Stumbling Block to L2 Reading

3.0. Introduction

In view of the negative effect of difficult vocabulary items on text readability, knowledge of such semantically complex items as idiomatic expressions constitutes one of the prerequisites for fluent L2 reading. Mastery of English idioms is certainly to be expected of teachers as one token of their near-native command of a language. Disappointingly, no matter how excellent their lower-level reading skills and how massive their receptive vocabulary, rapid idiomatic phrase recognition in the case of learners remains an unattainable goal. According to Arnaud and Savignon (1997), native-like proficiency with respect to complex lexical items is beyond the reach of even highly advanced students (in that case, French teacher trainees of English). Idioms, likened by Johnson-Laird (1993: ix) to riddles, are notoriously "'hard words': that proportion of the headword list of a dictionary which consists of specialist, varietal and rare items that are barely attested in general corpora of English" (Moon 1992: 499). Unsurprisingly, they enter L2 learners' sight vocabulary late (or never). The scale of the problem is widely acknowledged, as reflected in numerous publications tackling the issue from the pedagogical point of view:[1]

> [W]e can imagine how difficult it is for learners to go from their native language (in which the definitions of the idioms are also often vague) to another language (in which the speakers again have only a vague idea of what the idioms mean) and to capture the meaning and patterns of use of the foreign language idiom while learning its idiomatic form (Lattey 1986: 228).

If decoding canonical forms of idioms (whether on their own or in context) is a tall order, learners' plight can only be aggravated when unfamiliar idiomatic expressions are used creatively and take on shapes distinct from their dictionary versions.

This chapter brings up the issue of creativity in the use of language, one manifestation of which is original idiom variation, as an impediment to EFL reading. It demonstrates that, thanks to their discourse distribution and functions, idiom modifications contribute substantially to the overall text meaning. Besides, it dwells on the nature of the difficulties which non-native readers experience upon encountering innovative forms of idioms. This is achieved by characterising creative (as opposed to systemic) variation, discussing selected aspects of psycholinguistic research into idiom comprehension, and, finally, pointing out the limited role of context clues in aiding the interpretation of transformed idioms.

---

[1] E.g., Alexander (1978: 24–30, 1992b); Irujo (1986a, 1986b); Lattey (1986).

3.1. Creativity in the use of language: Non-native speakers' dilemma

To a layperson, linguistic creativity in the Chomskyan sense (everyone's free gift to generate and understand an infinite number of sentences using the finite set of rules of the language) sounds not half as attractive as the notion of creativity from everyday usage, translating into independence from conventional thinking. Whereas the adjective *creative* brings to mind only positive synonyms (such as *inventive, imaginative, original* or *ingenious*), the adjective *conventional* connotes – next to *accepted, expected, standard – run-of-the-mill, common, prosaic, routine, stereotyped, pedestrian, clichéd, trite* or *platitudinous*. In British society, the contempt for anything that smacks of the commonplace in language dates back at least to the 18th century, when, as Alexander (1978: 21) claims, proverbs were rejected as vulgar sayings of the working class. Derogatory connotations of fixed phrases seem to be perpetuated:

> [t]he prejudices and social enmity implicit in negatively loaded words like 'cliché', 'stock phrase' or 'hackneyed phrase' are a widespread and potent feature of the class structure of British society... In order to cater for changing needs and fashions sayings are continually coined and integrated into the language. It so happens that some acquire a social stigma while others do not (Alexander 1978: 21).[2]

Undoubtedly, creativity, incessantly pursued by entrepreneurial speakers/writers, is one of the most coveted features of any linguistic production. It is attempted for multifarious reasons: "[s]peakers – some more than others – invent words and phrases to force us to pay attention, to amuse us, to astonish us, and to challenge us. And they create new ways to convey old meanings for the sheer joy of invention" (Johnson-Laird 1993: ix). All the same, as Lewandowska-Tomaszczyk (1983: 98) notes, linguistic creativity is not limitless – a balance must be struck between the two opposite forces of the conventional and the creative inherent in language. It is the inseparable link between the old and the new that allows "rearrangements and/or multiplication of the known stereotypical patterns, ...introducing new elements to the existing patterns by establishing new connections between them, by their reconfigurations etc., so that the result may be a creation, more or less distant to [sic] the old constructs" (Lewandowska-Tomaszczyk 1983: 98).

Contrary to common belief, creativity consisting in the choice of unconventional linguistic forms, though not an inborn quality, is not the prerogative of poetic or literary language. Still, original language use, characteristic of intelligent, educated native-speakers' speech (frequent in news reports or witty repartee) probably remains beyond L2 learners' reach, at least in terms of production. Götz (1986: 87) claims that "[i]diomatic jokes by foreigners are considered to be an encroachment on native speaker group territory, unless, of course, the foreigner's performance is (near-) perfect in all respects, and in that case he or she is regarded as being (almost) one of the natives". Howarth (1998: 30) suspects that literal uses of conventional phraseological expressions may be taken as a sign of non-nativeness. Since most learners' knowledge of L2 idioms is all but native-like, variation places a considerable burden on the comprehension of the sometimes hardly recognisable

---

[2] With the politically incorrect notion of class consciousness on the decline, it would be interesting to examine the more current associations the British have on this subject.

expressions, whose intended sense, far from the autonomous meaning of a dictionary lexeme, needs to be actively constructed. The discussion in the remaining part of the chapter is restricted to one vehicle of linguistic creativity that poses a serious threat to non-native reception of everyday texts, namely idiomatic expressions.

3.2. The scope of the term *idiom* in the present study

Linguistic terms that embrace the common understanding of *idiom* as "an expression whose meaning is different from the meaning of the individual words" (MEDAL), reflected in learner's dictionaries, are *pure idiom* and *figurative idiom*, being two initial points on the cline of idiomaticity, which stretches from the most syntactically and semantically "frozen" idioms proper, through figurative idioms, restricted collocations, to free combinations (Howarth 1998: 28).

Traditionally, a pure idiom is "a non-literal set expression whose meaning is not a compositional function of its syntactic constituents but which always has a homonymous literal counterpart" (Fernando 1978: 337). Noncompositionality, the most salient feature ascribed to idioms, can be exemplified by *kick the bucket*, which does not mean 'kick the pail', but 'die'. The semantic consequence of noncompositionality is opacity, which justifies the treatment of idioms as non-literal, metaphorical language. Commonly regarded as "dead metaphors", historically they are "the end point of a process by which word-combinations first establish themselves through constant re-use, then undergo figurative extension and finally petrify or congeal" (ODCIE: xii). Whereas a pure idiom (e.g., *shoot the breeze*) is perceived as opaque, that is, totally unmotivated, this is not the case with figurative idioms (e.g., *move the goalposts*), whose origin remains recognisable to the reader (Howarth 1996: 24).

The fact that idioms are said to possess a homonymous literal counterpart[3] makes them particularly suitable for creative exploitation, e.g., *blow away the cobwebs* can mean not only 'do something in order to help yourself to think more clearly and have more energy', but also 'remove the net of sticky threads made by a spider'. To be fully idiomatic, an expression cannot be an individual, single occurrence, but must transcend the boundaries of private idiom to become public idiom, to use Fernando's (1996: 66–67) terminology. Institutionalisation implies conventionality.

Apart from figurative and pure idioms[4] – the latter representing model examples of the category, also qualified in the literature as "proper", "classical" or "idioms par excellence" – *sentence idioms*, i.e., proverbs and sayings, will be included in the scope of the present discussion on the grounds that they also serve as a template for colourful allusions and modifications. Although they do not function as idioms in colloquial language, in the East

---

[3]   The argument for the existence of literal counterparts of pure idioms has been weakened by corpus research (Moon 1998b: 91). Normally, context resolves ambiguity potential in the canonical form, and the literal meaning is only occasionally restored in punning.

[4]   In the empirical part of this study only pure idioms will be used so as to forestall the effect of transparency on comprehension.

European lexicographic tradition the term *idiom* subsumes proverbs (Hudson 1998: 20–21). The difference between idioms proper and proverbs is that the latter are usually complete sentences, convey folk wisdom and occasionally have literal meaning (e.g., *an apple a day keeps the doctor away*) (Hudson 1998: 21).

3.3. Distribution and function of idioms in discourse

The majority of fixed expressions are poorly represented in the corpora. In the 18 million-word Oxford Hector Pilot Corpus (OHPC) 88% of idioms and all proverbs occurred with frequencies of less than one token per million words (Moon 2001: 230). Similarly, of the 248 proverbs that Cignoni and Coffey (2000) searched in the 16 million-word Italian Reference Corpus, 48.4% were not found at all, and for 52% the frequency was low.

Idioms (including proverbs) tend to appear in journalism, and, to a lesser extent, fiction (Moon 1998a: 68ff). For instance, Cignoni and Coffey (2000) observed over 80% of proverb tokens in journalism, and in the Bank of English Corpus (329 million words at the time), tabloid journalism had the highest incidence of idioms (nearly twice as much as the average) (Moon 2001: 233ff.). On the other hand, in the same corpus, the use of idioms in spoken English and formal information-oriented texts (e.g., expository non-fiction, academic and business writing) was limited.

Though searching for them in the corpora might resemble "looking for needles in a haystack" (Moon 1999), idioms fulfil too vital a role in discourse to be dismissed as superfluous adornments. First of all, idiom occurrences in journalism are associated with key positions, such as titles, headlines, internal section headings, introductory and concluding sentences (Cignoni and Coffey 2000: 552, Fernando 1996: 144, McCarthy 1992: 60). Hence, idioms will act like strategic signposts, substantially influencing predictions affecting the overall sense of the text and its structural units. Moreover, infrequent pure idioms (within the category "metaphors") and proverbs (within the category "formulae") are primarily evaluative, and only secondarily informative (Moon 1998a: 221). As much as 89% of all fixed expressions with metaphorical or simile content located in the corpus had an evaluative function, which implies that "the use of institutionalised metaphors is stylistic,[5] bound up with evaluation, and centred on the interaction" (Moon 1998a: 225). Rarely strictly referential, idioms represent "graphic ways of conveying an opinion" (Moon 1999: 272) or "impressionistic packages of information" (Fernando 1996: 188). The following two fragments exemplify, respectively, positive and negative evaluation implicit in idioms:[6]

---

[5] For an investigation of the stylistic properties of phraseological units in various text genres, see Gläser (1998).
[6] Interestingly, negative evaluation in idioms is twice as common as positive one (Moon 1998a: 247). This, Moon explains, might mean two things: either negative evaluations are simply more obtrusive, or the number of negatively evaluating fixed expressions indeed surpasses that of positively evaluating ones, which would be commensurate with the periphrastic nature of idiomatic expressions.

(1) I thought the way we were taking corners was getting stale, so we had decided to vary them from near to far post. It *did the trick*, as they looked dangerous. Paul Kee did well making some great saves to keep us in the game. (OHPC: journalism, Moon 1998a: 246)

(2) Stores remained *in the doldrums*, with the latest retail sales figures confirming the difficulties of the high street. (OHPC: journalism, Moon 1998a: 246)

Thanks to an indirect, vague way of expressing attitude and evaluation, idioms commonly function as politeness devices: they create solidarity, express sympathy and mitigate judgements (Moon 1998a: 260–269). In this, they resemble

> a kind of euphemism, the use of which makes it more socially acceptable to make a personal opinion-comment about an event or relationship than the use of a non-idiomatic expression of the same message would be. If I describe Alice as *laughing up her sleeve*... I most probably do not think that *laughing up one's sleeve* is a very laudable activity. Chances are that I will communicate this feeling of mine – but I haven't actually said that I don't think well of Alice's behaviour (Lattey 1986: 224).

What additionally facilitates the transmission of attitudes through fixed expressions is their being the embodiment of collective experience and shared values – the portion of the lexicon so culturally marked that it is referred to as "a language of culture" (Teliya et al. 1998). As Moon (1998a: 259) remarks, "[a]ppeals and challenges to FEIs [fixed expressions, including idioms – R. S.] therefore become appeals and challenges to the culture and its ideology".

On the whole, idioms tend to occupy strategic positions in discourse, where they carry a wealth of emotive, attitudinal and cultural overtones, essential to the full comprehension of the intended message. Though the pragmatic orientation governing the usage of idioms entails subtleties hardly ever captured in traditional definitions, it constitutes one aspect of near-native command of the language, and as such deserves special attention in an advanced EFL classroom.

3.4. Idiom variation: A marginal phenomenon?

The force of the claim that idioms are completely "frozen" is weakened, among other things, by the phenomenon of variation, reflected in the corpora, which "show up the woolliness, indeterminacy, and instability of idioms" (Moon 1996: 254). In the 18 million-word Oxford Hector Pilot Corpus, about 54% of fixed expressions has been found in a form other than canonical (including 14% with two or more variations) (Moon 1998a: 120).[7] According to data from the same corpus, idiom frequency correlates strongly with variability, which undermines the argument that common idioms are stable and therefore less likely to vary. Even constructions thought of as the most inflexible occasionally turn up in their non-canonical forms, e.g., *kick the pail* and *kick the can* have both been encountered in the 'die' sense in American English (Moon 1998a: 123). Certain idiom variants may become so

---

[7] In Cignoni and Coffey's (2000: 553) corpus-based study only 25% of occurrences of proverbs were cited in their basic form.

popular as to blur the identification of their citational form, thus questioning the legitimacy of the very notion (Moon 1998a: 121). The fact that the phenomenon is widespread in journalism, well known for its role in paving the way for institutionalisation and language change (Moon 1998a: 121), makes it the more valid for investigation. The increasing popularity of this research issue is marked by a growing number of publications and scholarly events, to mention just one – the Fourth International Symposium on Phraseology (ISP4), held in April 2001 – devoted entirely to the topic of idiom variation.

3.4.1. Systemic variation

Idiom variation can be broadly divided into two types: systemic and creative (Gläser 1998), the latter also referred to as "exploitation" (Moon 1996, 1998a). The terms *variability* versus *variation* are sometimes used to render the institutionalised/creative distinction (Nuccorini 2001: 194).

Systemic variation – "within the constraints of the lexicological/phraseological system" (Gläser 1998: 129–130) – is recorded in dictionaries and thus "prescribed" (Fernando 1996: 68). Systemic variation can be lexical or systematic (Moon 1996).

In lexical variation, variable items are often synonymous, e.g., *bang/beat the drum, sb's head on a plate/platter, give sb a dose/taste of their own medicine; push/drive sb over the edge; be walking/treading on eggshells* (Moon 1996: 247). Further, lexical variation may denote differences between varieties of English, e.g., *That's the way the cookie crumbles* (British, American and Australian) vs. *That's the way the ball bounces* (American, informal); *king of the castle* (British) vs. *king of the hill* (American); *have green fingers* (British and Australian) vs. *have a green thumb* (American).

Systematic variation, according to Moon (1998a: 139), "displays some sort of regularity", "reflects deeper grammatical systems and relationships or concepts". It involves both syntax and lexis, e.g., *let the cat out of the bag – the cat is out of the bag; turn the tables – the tables are turned; have one's knife out – the knives are out* (Moon 1998a: 142); *blow the whistle – whistle-blowing – a whistle-blower; break the ice – ice-breaking – an ice-breaker* (Moon 1996: 250) or *get/have a raw deal; get/keep/have one's eye in; give/get/receive a good hiding; have/get/develop cold feet* (Moon 1998a: 139).

Another type of systemic variation are antonymous idioms: *off the record/on the record; have all your marbles/lose your marbles; keep your cool/lose your cool* (Moon 1996: 250). Besides, certain idioms and proverbs can function in their truncated, shortened form, for instance, *it's the (last) straw that breaks the camel's back – the last/final straw; every cloud has a silver lining – a silver lining* (Moon 1996: 251). There are also clusters of idioms called idiom schemas that "have some reference in common, a metaphor in common, and cognate lexis, but without (necessarily) any fixed structure or fixed lexis" (Moon 1998a: 163), such as the cluster of idioms denoting 'crazy', 'stupid': *one sandwich short of a picnic, several cards short of a full deck, a few gallons shy of a full tank, two beanshoots short of a spring roll, a bishop short of a chess set, several hatstands short of a cloakroom, one number short of a logarithm* (Moon 1996: 252).

Institutionalised, systemic variation will not be further explored here (for a discussion, see Moon 1998a: 124–170).

3.4.2. Creative variation

3.4.2.1. Definition and characteristics

The phenomenon variously referred to in the literature as the "nonce use of idioms", "creative modifications", "contextual/occasional transformation" of idioms, "one-off variation", the "creative adaptation" of idioms, or – a particularly graphic one – "extracting the maximum juice from words" (Redfern 1997: 267), illustrates how language naturally shuns triteness and how, if the latter threatens certain expressions, they are quickly disposed of or "renewed" because it "it seems cleverer to allude to them than simply use them" (Moon 1988: 107). What distinguishes this type of variation from systemic variation is the intention of the writer:

> The first [category of change – R. S.] is that of slight adaptations of a syntactic, grammatical or semantic nature, where the writer has probably unconsciously adjusted the form of the proverb and the reader may remain unaware of this fact. The second is that of significant lexico-semantic changes in which it is clear that the writer has consciously changed the proverb to create a particular effect (Cignoni and Coffey 2000: 551).

Veisbergs (1997: 156) defines creative variation as "intentional, subjectively and stylistically motivated transformations of the meaning of the idiom in its contextual use". Similarly, Glucksberg (1993: 19) puts emphasis on the purposefulness of the alteration, as well as on the listener's/reader's ability to discover it. For example, *kick the pail* might be recognised as meaning 'die', but such a variation would be perceived as unmotivated, unacceptable, and, most likely, would be viewed as a mistake (Glucksberg 1993: 20).

In exploitation, carefully selected ingredients of the standard meaning are skilfully manipulated to achieve a desirable, usually humorous, effect. The new contextually-bound form is no longer an instantiation of the canonical form, but a loose reference to it. Being an example of semantic productivity, not just flexibility, exploitations prove that creativity in idioms – typically seen as trite and stereotypical – is not a contradiction in terms. At this point it is useful to invoke Hobbs's (1979, cited in Cacciari 1993: 32) "life cycle" of an idiom:

> creative and alive metaphor → familiar metaphor → "tired" metaphor → "dead" metaphor[8]

In the third stage a direct link between the two domains replaces the familiar, established interpretative path. Finally, the metaphorical origin of the expression (its "history"), is lost (Cacciari 1993: 32). For an idiom's life cycle to encompass idiom variation, another link is needed:

---

[8] It needs to be noted that the view of idioms as "dead metaphors" has been undermined by studies showing that native speakers have consistent intuitions about the analysability of idioms and use recurrent mental images in proverb interpretation, which implies the influence of conceptual metaphors providing a link between a proverb and its figurative meaning (e.g., Gibbs 1990, 1993, 1995; Gibbs and Beitel 1995).

creative and alive metaphor → familiar metaphor → "tired" metaphor → "dead" metaphor → "resurrected"[9] metaphor

Apparently, an idiom is creative twice in its long life. First, at its "birth", because "[e]very idiom is the result of a personal innovation at a particular point in time" (Fernando 1996: 18).[10] Second, at its "reactivation", when, as soon as the dormant or virtually "dead" metaphor is so well established that it runs the risk of becoming a platitude, the old sign is "remotivated" (Nerlich and Clarke 2001: 6) to look almost as attractive as the brand new expression it once used to be. The "rebirth" aspect of the phenomenon is reflected in various fancy epithets with which it has been showered in the literature, to mention just a few: the "unfreezing" of fixed expressions, "renewal" of idioms, "recycling" of set expressions, or lexical "revitalisation".

To round off this largely theoretical section, it seems useful to demonstrate how creative variation can stretch the original meaning to the limit. Consider the following:

(3) *Can't see the wood for the trees* (decontextualised canonical form)
(4) After you've spent years researching a single topic you get to a point where you *can't see the wood for the trees* (canonical form in context)
(5) After you've spent years researching a single topic you get to a point where you *can't see the forest for the trees* (systemic variant)
(6) *Seeing the Forest and the Trees:* The legacy of Nazism did not altogether disappear from Germany after World War II. In a pine forest northeast of Berlin a 60-m. swastika of larch trees planted by a Hitler supporter in the 1930s becomes visible every autumn. Not only the trees live on. So does the ideology... (creative variant; *Time*, December 4, 2000: 26)

3.4.2.2. Categorisation

Veisbergs (1997: 157) divides creative transformations into structural ones, affecting both the structure and the meaning of an idiom, and semantic ones, affecting only the meaning.[11] According to this categorisation, the structural transformations of an idiom may be the result of addition, insertion, allusion, ellipsis, or substitution (where the substitute word may be a synonym, antonym, or a paronym – a formally similar word), e.g.,

(7) *So priceless* a bird in the hand is worth two in the bush [addition]
(8) A bird in the hand is worth two in the *economic* bush [insertion]
(9) Why chase *the two birds* when *one* is *up for grabs*? [allusion]
(10) *A bird in the hand,* I thought, and accepted his offer [ellipsis]

---

[9] The term used in Swanepoel (1992: 304).
[10] As Johnson-Laird (1993: ix) put it, "the creation of idioms also reflects new conceptions of the world, new ways in which individuals construct mental models of the world, and new ways in which to convey their contents vividly. It is through idioms... that the truly creative nature of human expression reveals itself. Idioms are the poetry of daily discourse".
[11] Compare Coffey's (2001) *de-composition*, where "the MWU [multiword unit – R.S.] has not undergone significant formal changes, but rather the focus has been given to one or more of the MWU's single-word components", and *re-composition*, where "the MWU's form has very evidently been changed, one or more key words having been replaced by other words" (Coffey 2001: 217).

(11)   *A competent minister* in the hand is worth *many generals* in the bush [substitution] (Veis-
berds 1997: 158).

In semantic transformations, on the other hand, sustained or extended metaphor, zeugma,
and dual actualization (i.e., of both the idiomatic and the literal, compositional reading) are
said to be typical. Veisbergs exemplifies them with *pay a compliment,* which, strictly
speaking, in not an idiom, but rather a restricted collocation with the verb used in a figurative sense:

(12)   They're all so badly off these days that they can only pay compliments [dual actualization]
(13)   While she liked paying compliments, she also appreciated those who knew how to earn them
       [sustained metaphor]
(14)   He paid a compliment and my bill [zeugma] (Veisbergs 1997: 158).

Contrary to Veisbergs' claims, it seems that a structural change does not always affect the
meaning of an idiom. Even if meaning is altered in the case of addition, insertion, allusion
and substitution, it remains intact when ellipsis is used. Leaving out certain elements does
not have to destroy the semantics of the expression alluded to, so, e.g., *A bird in the hand...*
evokes *A bird in the hand is worth two in the bush.* Similarly, a truncated saying (e.g.,
Blood's thicker...) in a context supporting only the standard dictionary reading involves no
deviation from the conventional meaning whatsoever, as opposed to the complete standard
form of the same saying in a scientific text that activates the normally dormant literal reading.

Since the semantic distance between the canonical and contextual version is of immediate significance to comprehension, a scale of creative transformations congruent with the
gradual immersion of idioms in context will be proposed here (Table 1).

Table 1. One-off idiom variation: Degrees of semantic change

Transformation type	Example
I. Despite structural transformation (usually ellipsis or allusion) the original meaning re-mains intact.	She had gone over in her mind the other people she might talk to... Her other friends were elsewhere, in other towns, other cities, other countries, and writing it in a letter would make it too final. The lady down below... that was the bottom of the barrel; she would be like the relatives, she would be dismayed without understanding. (*scrape the bottom of the barrel,* Atwood 1969: 213)
II. The idiomatic mean-ing is reinforced, made more precisely applica-ble to a particular situa-tion (usually by addition, insertion, or substitu-tion); it is possible to replace the transforma-tion with the canonical form.	[the surgeon said:] 'It won't be noticeable... Your boyfriend may see a faint line when he kisses you, but if he's that close he probably won't be looking.' Sexist asshole, I said, but to myself. No point in biting the hand that sews you. (*bite the hand that feeds you,* Paretsky 1987: 85, quoted in Leppihalme 1997: 61–62)

Transformation type	Example
III. The idiomatic meaning is not reinforced. Instead, "the original metaphor is reversed or inverted" (Moon 1998a: 171); the canonical form and the transformation are not substitutable.	...Dolly's "mother" was six years old when she was cloned. That may explain why Dolly's cells show signs of being older than they actually are—scientists joked that she was really a sheep in lamb's clothing. This deviation raises the possibility that beings created by cloning adults will age abnormally fast. (*a wolf in sheep's clothing*, Time, February 19, 2001: 38)
IV. The idiomatic and the literal meanings are both activated ("dual actualisation", according to Veisbergs 1997: 159).	Cecily: This is no time for wearing the shallow mask of manner. When I see a spade I call it a spade. Gwendolen: I am glad to say that I have never seen a spade. It is obvious that our social spheres have been widely different. (*call a spade a spade*, Wilde ([1899] 1983: 46)
V. Only the literal meaning of the idiom (or its element) is activated ("demetaphorisation", according to Moon 1998a: 173).	Toot Your Own Horn (title) The railroading simulator may not be quite as thrilling as a flight simulator, but getting freight from the depot to the delivery site on time can be remarkably satisfying... Best of all, you can blow the whistle whenever you want. Purists will miss the paper-mâché mountains..., but their loved ones will appreciate the extra space in the rec room. This could change Christmas morning forever. (*toot one's own horn*, Newsweek, October 5, 1998: 10)
VI. Neither the idiomatic nor the literal meaning of the canonical form are activated.	Plastic makes perfick (title of an article about plastic surgery; play on *practice makes perfect*, The Sunday Express , May 12, 1991, quoted in Veisbergs 1997: 160)

This categorisation displays a gradual increase in literal bias, and the resultant growing distance between the usual, conventional and context-modulated meaning. Type I displays absolutely no deviation from the original meaning. The opposite extreme is when context does not activate idiomatic meaning at all, and it seems that non-native readers stand no chance of successful comprehension of a passage with transformations of type V and VI. Therefore, for the purposes of the present study, only modifications of type II, III and IV will be used, i.e., those in which the semantics has been affected by context, but the idiomatic meaning has been retained to some extent. In other words, the semantic criterion will be given priority over the formal one: a given variation will be treated as truly creative if it involves some alteration, however slight, in the conventional meaning, whereas the structure of an expression might or might not be modified.

What is the exact nature of the difficulties that L2 readers face on encountering creatively modified idioms? The following section attempts to address the question by reporting relevant results of psycholinguistic research. Unfortunately, for the most part, the research conducted so far concerns native speakers' comprehension of familiar idioms in canonical form.

3.5. Interpreting idiom variants

How non-native speakers are to acquire the ability to interpret unfamiliar transformed idioms remains a bit of a mystery. However,

> it seems that there are indeed rules or perhaps conventions: the metaphor and meaning must be maintained and the variant lexis must be recognised as belonging to a particular lexical set. Successful decoding requires recognition of the lexical pattern, the metaphoricality, and the meaning appropriate to the context (Moon 1998a: 168).

Let us now scrutinise the nature of recognition and comprehension problems in turn.

3.5.1. Identification

How is it possible that familiar idioms and proverbs, even considerably distorted, can be instantly recognised by native speakers and foreigners alike? According to Norrick (1985: 45), the "kernel", i.e., the minimal recognisable unit, calls forth the whole proverb. For instance, *Remember the early bird* suffices as a warning against late arrival (Norrick 1985: 46). In a similar vein, Cacciari and Tabossi (1988, cited in Titone and Connine 1999: 1665–1666) claim that the complete meaning can be accessed through a sufficient portion of an idiomatic string, called the "idiomatic key" (the so called "configuration hypothesis"). Flores d'Arcais (1993: 81) distinguishes between the point of idiom uniqueness (usually the last word of an idiom), at which the phrase can be interpreted only as an idiom, and the point of idiom recognition, which may precede the point of idiom uniqueness and depends on context and idiom familiarity. For instance, *spill* is likely to be the recognition point of *spill the beans* although its point of uniqueness is *beans* (Flores d'Arcais 1993: 81).

It needs to be noticed that the above theories, in stressing the accessibility of an idiom as dependent on conventionality and familiarity – a function of users' experience – mean little to non-native speakers. Unfamiliar idioms, if modified, cannot be accessed via key words at all, because of the total ignorance of the idiomatic pattern. Another obstacle to recognition is that they often look deceptively familiar or are "deceptively transparent", to use Laufer's (1997) wording, and therefore unlikely to attract readers' attention.

3.5.2. Comprehension

The major difficulty in interpreting idioms seems to be the fact that their meaning cannot be derived from the meanings of their constituent words. As noncompositional models of comprehension explain, the stipulated meaning of familiar idioms is retrieved via "direct look-up"[12]. Higher speed of understanding idioms in their idiomatic senses than in their literal senses (Gibbs 1985), or than their literal paraphrases and variants (McGlone, Glucksberg and Cacciari 1994), as well as the facilitating effect of familiarity on reading

---

[12] For a review of noncompositional models of idiom comprehension, see e.g., Cacciari and Glucksberg (1991: 218–219), Glucksberg (1993: 4–5), Titone and Connine (1999: 1656–1661).

speed (Cronk, Lima and Schweigert 1993, Cronk and Schweigert 1992, Forrester 1995, Schweigert 1991), attest to the validity of the noncompositional approach. However, the view of idioms as "long words" has been undermined by psycholinguistic evidence demonstrating that idioms, like all linguistic expressions, are not devoid of internal structure, in which constituent word meanings contribute to the meaning of the whole idiom. Let us recount the major arguments for the compositionality of idioms as a convenient background for the discussion of learners' comprehension of variant idioms.

As Stroop (1935, cited in Cacciari and Glucksberg 1991: 219) demonstrated, language comprehension is nonoptional and automatic: subjects could not help noticing word meanings even when they were explicitly told to ignore them and concentrate on the colour of the ink instead. Furthermore, according to Glucksberg (1991: 150), word meanings contribute to idiom comprehension and use in at least three ways. Firstly, they constrain the use of an expression, even in opaque idioms (e.g., since kicking is a discrete act, one may say *He lay dying all week*, but not *He lay kicking the bucket all week*). Secondly, idioms retain their meaning after some of the words have been replaced, which is a manifestation of lexical flexibility (e.g., it is possible to say *crack/break the ice,* but not *crush the ice*). Finally, old idioms become vehicles for new meanings, semantic productivity rather than mere flexibility coming into play here. The last point, of direct relevance to the present study, deserves more attention.

Cacciari and Glucksberg's (1991: 225) subjects, when faced with a variant idiom *Roger always bit off much less than he could chew*, provided sensible interpretations, such as *He did less than he could; Roger never pushed himself; He did not challenge himself,* etc. Since production of such interpretations involved more than a simple retrieval of the stipulated meaning, this suggests that "idioms are recognised and identified as having their own meanings, but are also treated as linguistic entities and analysed as such" (Cacciari and Glucksberg 1991: 238). Apparently, as Howarth (1998: 29) argues, unconventional use of a familiar expression results in readers' "unnatural" awareness of its compositionality and the consequent need to refer to the context. Similarly, McGlone, Glucksberg and Cacciari (1994) conclude that idioms display compositional qualities and require linguistic processing like literal strings on the grounds that idioms in their variant forms were read as quickly as their literal paraphrases. This finding, incompatible with the standard view of idioms as long words, according to which comprehension of variant idioms should take considerably longer than that of literal paraphrases, can be accommodated by the "phrase-induced polysemy model" (Glucksberg 1993: 11). In line with this theory, as a result of frequent use, a popular idiom's constituent words acquire the idiom-specific meaning, in addition to their context-free meaning, e.g., *spill*, apart from 'be lost from a container', denotes also 'reveal (a secret)', in consequence of its frequent usage in *spill the beans*. When direct access fails, as is the case with variant idioms that don't match the canonical form of the original idiom, the contextually appropriate (i.e., phrase-induced) meaning of a word is accessed and normal linguistic processing ensues (Glucksberg 1993: 11). Like the configuration hypothesis, this model relies on previous linguistic experience for an idiom's reconstruction, and so it hardly applies to the situation of learners encountering unfamiliar idioms, when no awareness of the phrase-induced meaning of an idiom's constituents can be taken for granted.

"What kind of interpretation can people provide when they meet an unknown idiom, or one that is very unfamiliar or difficult to remember?", one might ask after Flores d'Arcais (1993: 94). In one of his experiments, native speakers employed four categories of princi ples in order to provide paraphrases for unfamiliar decontextualised idioms: 1. Analogy to a known idiom; 2. Use of semantic properties of one of the words of the idiom; 3. Metaphoric extension of the action or state described in the phrase; 4. Literal meaning. Extensive use of such strategies in the comprehension of unfamiliar idioms proves that semantic information in idioms' constituents is utilised; thus, idioms are analysable units, with semantic and syntactic structure available and activated when necessary (Flores d'Arcais 1993: 96–97).[13]

The computation of the meaning of novel or infrequent idioms resembles the processing of metaphors (Flores d'Arcais 1993: 86), and is explicable in terms of Giora's (1999) "graded salience hypothesis", which states that it is the idiomatic meaning of familiar idioms, more salient[14] than the literal one, that should be activated in both idiomatically and literally biased contexts;[15] on the other hand, "[p]rocessing less familiar idioms should be similar to processing less familiar metaphors. It should activate their salient literal meaning in both types of contexts. However, in the literally biasing context, the literal meaning should be the only one activated" (Giora 1999: 923). The findings of one of Giora and Fein's (1999) experiments bear out the assumptions of the graded salience hypothesis:

> comprehension of less-familiar idioms, in which the idiomatic meaning is no more salient than its literal interpretation, activated both the literal and the idiomatic meanings in the idiomatically bi-ased context. However, in the literally biasing context, it was the more salient literal meaning that was highly activated, whereas the less salient idiomatic meaning was only marginally evoked (Giora and Fein 1999: 1614).

Analogous results were obtained for processing less-familiar metaphors.

In like manner, Katz et al. (1998) argue that unfamiliar idioms and proverbs are neither idiomatic nor proverbial and would be read literally out of context. In context, however, "literal meaning is aroused for unfamiliar proverbs even when the context in which it is used supports the proverbial nonliteral sense, and the nonliteral sense is generated only when there is sufficient contextual support for that sense" (Katz et al. 1998: 166). To give an example, if *Wake up and smell the coffee!* were a novel saying, it would be read literally, at least initially, even when the person addressed had clearly been wide awake. On the other hand, its figurative sense 'recognise the truth or reality of something' would be evoked exclusively in a nonliteral, idiomatic context.

The situation of non-native speakers' comprehension of idioms is less clear due to the scarcity of research. According to Schraw et al. (1988), foreign learners, who lack lexicalised representations of idioms in their memory, tackle unfamiliar idioms as if they were novel metaphors, using a word-by-word analysis of the statement. For example, one subject in his paraphrase of *chew the fat* suggested that lifting weights helped *chew fat off the body*

---

[13] Cacciari (1993: 40–41) singled out five types of similar interpretative strategies on the basis of 32 self-reports, in which the subjects explained how they arrived at paraphrases of unfamiliar idioms.

[14] "A meaning of a word is salient, if it is coded in the mental lexicon. The degree of salience of a meaning of a word, or an expression, is a function of its conventionality, familiarity, or frequency" (Giora 1999: 921).

[15] Confirmation of greater salience of the idiomatic meaning comes from studies reporting informants' subjective assessment of the frequency of the literal and idiomatic sense (e.g., Popiel and McRae 1988, Cronk, Lima and Schweigert 1993). Compare Schweigert (1991), who claims that less familiar idioms foster a literal reading, the finding, however, not to be borne out in Forrester (1995).

(Schraw et al. 1988: 421). Moreover, in generating the meaning of unfamiliar idioms, they tend to rely on contextual information. Similarly, Liontas (2002) demonstrates that literal interpretation of idiom elements is obligatory regardless of the presence of context and type of an idiom. For idioms with small conceptual-semantic image (CSI) distance (degree of opacity), immediate transfer from L1 will facilitate comprehension.[16] On the other hand, the interpretation of idioms that are non-matching, the most difficult for learners, will require, apart from simple translation, additional mental effort and context-based inferencing procedures. In general, non-native speakers' comprehension of idioms seems to entail bottom-up processing, which must be supplemented with top-down processing in the case of non-transparent idioms.

Presumably, creative modifications of unfamiliar idioms – the case under discussion – will be read compositionally at first because of both the unfamiliarity of their canonical form and its unconventional use. Whereas the deviation from the canonical form may be overlooked because the meaning has been accessed right away from a partial lexical cue in the case of modifications of familiar idioms,[17] with modifications of unfamiliar idioms it is likely to remain unnoticed because the original idiomatic meaning has not been retrieved at all. Beside the structure of the lexical phrase, non-native speakers' interpretation of unfamiliar idioms is guided by attention toward context. The use of context as a reading comprehension strategy, hardly a straightforward issue on its own, is beset with additional difficulties in the case of idiomatic expressions.

3.5.3. Limited usability of context

Normally, context should influence the reception of an idiom by signalling idiomaticity (recognition stage) and offering clues as to its possible meaning (inferential stage). Unfortunately, in the case of non-native speakers reading variant idioms, these comprehension-facilitating functions of context may be inaccessible.

First of all, context that fosters complete or partial demetaphorisation or dual actualisation – a common feature in creatively transformed idioms – substantially reduces non-native readers' chances of perceiving the idiomaticity of the encountered syntagm. This pertains particularly to idioms with homonymous literal counterparts. As was said, processing less familiar idioms (let alone completely new ones) requires the activation of the literal meaning regardless of context bias, while the idiomatic meaning surfaces only if the context supports that meaning. It follows that a literal or ambiguous context surrounding an unfamiliar idiom will fail to induce awareness of idiomaticity in a reader. Additionally, transformations, often disrupting the continuity of the idiomatic form, act as a further factor inclining the learner to consider an idiomatic phrase to be a regular compositional string.

Guessing the meaning of idiom variants from context seems to be likewise constrained. As Moon (1998a: 185) remarks, "[i]n the case of an unfamiliar FEI which involves an opaque metaphor, the hearer/reader may be unable to deploy either analogy or real-world

---

[16] Compare Irujo (1986a), where learners relied on their L1 knowledge to understand identical idioms, similar idioms also invited interference from L1, and different idioms were the hardest to interpret.

[17] To use Howarth's (1998: 30) example, *he seems to be carrying the rap* will be taken for the intended meaning: *he seems to be carrying the can.*

knowledge. The context or co-text will typically shed light on the intended meaning, but not always". Authentic texts are only occasionally as redundant as those employed in linguistic experiments such as Forrester (1995).[18] What is more, "deceptive transparency" (mentioned in 2.2.2.2. and 3.5.1.) often pre-empts any guessing from context as there is no awareness of unfamiliarity.

Inferring the meaning of idioms is bound to be impeded not merely due to scarcity of relevant contextual clues, but also as a result of the peculiar status idioms enjoy in the lexicon. Being rare and of high information value, idioms enrich the text and raise its attractiveness. However, in the light of Finn's (1977-1978) transfer feature theory (see 2.2.2.3.), the more an item contributes to the contents of the message, the harder it is to infer. In other words, the most semantically loaded expressions become the pivots of the whole text, the remainder of which is usually "rarefied", and, consequently, offers no or sparse usable clues. The strongest version of this position appears to be the argument that, unlike metaphors, citational forms of idioms – the base for the distorted form – do not need disambiguating context; they are "unambiguous, meaningful units on their own, meaning the same thing in all contexts", as Nuccorini (1988: 153) put it. Looking up idioms only occasionally involves having to choose the right meaning because they are rarely polysemous in the usual sense of the word.[19] Idioms might be viewed as self-contained stories in their own right, unaffected by the topicality of a specific co-text, and explicable in terms of Lakoff's (1993) notion of the specific and generic-level schema. For instance, the proverb *Blind blames the ditch* involves the following specific-level schema:

There is a person with an incapacity, namely, blindness.
He encounters a situation, namely a ditch, in which his incapacity, namely his inability to see the ditch, results in a negative consequence, namely, his falling into the ditch.
He blames the situation, rather than his own incapacity.
He should have held himself responsible, not the situation. (Lakoff 1993: 233)

According to Lakoff (1993: 233), this is an instance of a generic-level schema, stripped of details such as a blind man falling into a ditch, and therefore applicable to a wide range of situations, all of which must share the following elements:

There is a person with an incapacity.
He encounters a situation in which his incapacity results in a negative consequence.
He blames the situation rather than his own incapacity.

---

[18] In this investigation of the influence of familiarity and context literalness on idiom comprehension, familiar and made-up idioms with their semantic equivalents were used (e.g., *fly in the ointment/smudge on the sheepskin; swallow a camel and strain at a gnat/drink a reservoir and splutter on a capful*), with reading time as a dependent variable. A significant familiarity effect, though no context effect, was observed for idiomatic phrases and their equivalents (i.e., familiar idioms had a shorter reading time than unfamiliar ones, and semantic equivalents were read faster if they were associated with familiar idioms, in both figurative and literal contexts).

[19] Around five per cent of expressions in the 18 million-word Oxford Hector Pilot Corpus are polysemous (Moon 1998a: 188). One of the rare examples of a fixed expression that is polysemous and possibly ambiguous in context is *A rolling stone gathers no moss*, meaning (1) 'people who move around a lot will never acquire wealth, position, stability, and so on' (negative evaluation); (2) 'people who move around a lot will never grow stale and dull' (positive evaluation) (Moon 1998a: 249).

He should have held himself responsible, not the situation.

The abstract generic-level schema limits the occurrence of this particular proverb to certain contexts conforming to that schema, which, notwithstanding, retains its integrity throughout and remains a complete story even when stripped of specific contextual elements. In this sense, idioms are independent, and "[it] is the context-independence of idioms that contributes to the fluency of communication" (Howarth 1996: 55). To give two more examples, *put your money where your mouth is* and *the grass is always greener on the other side of the fence* evoke the following generic-level schemata:

> *put your money where your mouth is:*
> There is a person who supports something.
> This support is expressed verbally.
> Someone else thinks that this person should express his/her support with actions.

> *the grass is always greener on the other side of the fence:*
> A person finds himself/herself in a certain situation.
> He/she thinks that his/her situation is not as good as the situation of people somewhere else.
> Someone else thinks there is no objective reason for this person to be continually dissatisfied with his/her situation.

Thus, contextual independence of idioms manifests itself in the fact that they are interpretable and unequivocal in minimal context, and, as in the case of proverbs, may function as complete utterances. To use Halevy's (1996: 225) metaphor drawn from the field of biology, idioms seem to resemble words with an "impermeable membrane":

> Words with pre-established meaning have a pattern which determines the same content for each context, or they are operative also in minimal or neutral contexts. With these words the context acts merely as a kind of filter while, on the other hand, when the selected meaning is unestablished or indeterminate the context acts rather as a stimulus for a productive process which "generates" the sense in question (Halevy 1996: 225).

When the "impermeable membrane" of the stable canonical meaning starts "leaking", and lets in the contextual meaning through the "gaps" in the citational form, an idiom loses much of its independence. As a variant, it is bound by context, which "injects the available old signs and their meanings with new life" (Nerlich and Clarke 2001: 6), sometimes leading to "ambiguation in context", i.e., multiplication of senses of the normally stable meaning. Under the circumstances, even a heavily redundant context must leave the reader at a loss as to the meaning of the canonical form, and without the knowledge of the source of the transformation, comprehension cannot be complete. When original elements of an idiom have been replaced, the inferred meaning will be neither the stipulated dictionary meaning nor the writer-intended meaning, but rather that of a supposedly new idiom, worked out solely on the basis of the form encountered in the text, incidental contextual information, and analogy with L1 or L2 idioms.

The final problem, indirectly pertinent here, relates to the issue of idiom learning. Should lengthy processing and initial difficulty in interpretation improve retention (Craik and Lockhart 1972, cited in Tono 2001: 26), idiom modifications stand a better chance of being acquired than their citational versions, especially when the dictionary explanation has been read only cursorily, as is often the case.[20]

All things considered, the role of context in helping learners to understand novel uses of idioms is severely limited. It may (but need not) foster the recognition of idiomaticity, and is of little use in detecting the source of the transformation, which is a necessary condition for successful comprehension.

3.6. Concluding remarks

Idioms, appearing, more often than not, in their non-standard forms, and at strategic points of discourse, impose a serious burden upon non-native reception of authentic texts of the press and fiction. Apart from performing informative functions, they normally carry evasive attitudinal and evaluative connotations, recognition of which is crucial to the complete comprehension of the message. Unpredictable one-off variation, not registered in dictionaries, poses special difficulties, which seem to be directly proportional to the degree of formal and, more importantly, semantic distance from the canonical version. In other words, readers' chances of decoding variation depend on the contextual entanglement of an idiom and the extent to which its idiomaticity becomes activated. As psycholinguistic findings indicate, L2 readers will utilise the knowledge of individual lexical items – components of an idiom – and context clues to arrive at an interpretation of unfamiliar opaque idioms. However, when context "ambiguates" the canonical meaning, it cannot facilitate appropriate guesses at the origin of the transformation. Therefore, the constructed meaning will be that of an allegedly new idiom combining elements of the canonical form interspersed with fragments of context, but not the author-intended sense involving an allusion to the standard expression. Altogether, success in grasping the sense of innovative uses of idioms with no external reference looks precarious, unless of course they are highly transparent or have a close match in L1.

---

[20] For example, Howarth (1996: 55) makes reference to paradoxical results when the subjects could recall the unconventional (literal) uses of idiomatic sentences better than standard idiomatic meanings.

4. The Monolingual Learner's Dictionary as an Aid to Coping with Idiom Variation

4.0. Introduction

The dictionary potentially aids the comprehension of variant idioms by supplying the thing alluded to, i.e., by substituting for native speakers' previous linguistic experience of the stipulated meaning. The effectiveness of the allegedly straightforward solution of dictionary consultation will depend on whether the explanation can be easily located, understood and properly applied in a given context. The ignorance of either the dictionary or context meaning unavoidably results in misinterpretations and the allusion falling flat. Is the information on idioms in an MLD entry always accessible? How does it convey the semantic and pragmatic complexity of idioms? Ultimately, the answer bears upon the issue of the usefulness of the monolingual learner's dictionary for advanced students, for whom rare and complex lexical items such as idiomatic expressions constitute a large proportion of targets. In an attempt to address these questions, this chapter examines the presentation of idiomatic meaning in learner's dictionaries. It does not, however, include a contrastive analysis of coverage, placement policy or prominence given to idioms in the entries, which have already been discussed in, e.g., Alexander (1992a, 1998), Bogaards (1996: 285–287) or Herbst (1996: 335–336).

4.1. Findability: Cross-referencing

Table 2 presents a sample of 30 idioms consisting of at least two lexical words, together with cross references and the headword under which they can be found in four MLDs.

Table 2. Cross-references to idioms in four learner's dictionaries

	LDOCE3	OALD5	COBUILD2	MEDAL
1) at the drop of a hat	@drop hat → drop	@drop hat → drop	@hat drop → hat	@drop hat → drop
2) blow hot and cold	@blow hot → blow cold → blow	@blow hot → blow cold → blow	@hot blow → hot cold → hot	@blow @hot cold ----------

	LDOCE3	OALD5	COBUILD2	MEDAL
3) carry the can	@carry can → carry	@carry can → carry	@can carry → can	@carry can → carry
4) twist/turn the knife	@knife twist → knife turn -----------	@knife twist → knife turn [1]	@knife twist → knife turn[2]	@knife twist-------- turn--------
5) find your feet	@find foot → find	@find foot → find	@foot find → foot	@find @foot
6) fly by the seat of your pants	@fly @seat pants → seat	@seat fly -------- pants → seat	@pants fly ----------- seat → pants	@seat fly ----------- pants --------
7) lead sb a (merry) dance	@lead merry ---------- dance → lead	@lead merry -------- dance → lead	@dance lead ----------- merry → dance	@merry @dance lead ----------
8) kick over the traces	@kick @trace	@kick trace → kick	------------------	------------------
9) go against the grain	@go against @grain	@grain go[3]	@grain go -------------	@grain go -------------
10) cramp sb's style	@cramp style → cramp	@cramp style → cramp	@cramp style → cramp	@cramp style→ cramp
11) cut your teeth on	@cut tooth → cut	@tooth cut[4]	@tooth cut → tooth	@cut tooth → cut
12) drive a wedge between sb and sb	@drive @wedge	@drive wedge → drive	@wedge drive ----------	@wedge drive----------
13) drop a clanger/brick	@drop @clanger brick → drop	@drop clanger →drop brick → drop	@clanger drop ------------ brick ------------	@clanger drop ----------- brick----------
14) not see sb for dust	@dust see → dust	------------------	------------------	@dust see--------------
15) sit on the fence	@fence sit---------------	@sit fence → sit	@fence sit → fence	@fence sit → fence
16) send sb off with a flea in their ear	@flea send ------------ ear → flea	@flea send ----------- ear → flea		@flea send------------- ear--------------
17) flog sth to death	@flog death------------	@flog death → flog	------------------	@flog death ------------
18)move the goalposts	@goalposts move→goalpost	@move goalpost→move	@goalpost move→goalpost	@goalpost move→goalpost
19) kick sb upstairs	@kick upstairs→kick	@kick upstairs→kick	------------------	@kick upstairs----------
20) not cut the mustard	@cut @mustard	----------------	@mustard cut→mustard	@cut @mustard

---

[1] Instead of a providing a cross-reference, the dictionary informs the reader that "[m]ost idioms containing *turn* are at the entries for the noun or adjective in the idiom".

[2] "*Turn* is used in a large number of other expressions under other words in the dictionary. For example, the expression 'turn over a new leaf' is explained at *leaf*" (COBUILD2: 944).

[3] "Most idioms containing *go* are at the entries for the nouns or adjectives in the idioms" (OALD5: 506).

[4] "Most idioms containing *cut* are at the entries for the nouns or adjectives in the idioms" (OALD5: 289).

	LDOCE3	OALD5	COBUILD2	MEDAL
21) the thin end of the wedge	@thin end -------------- wedge→thin	@thin end→thin wedge→thin	@wedge thin-------------- end---------------	@wedge thin-------------- end--------------
22) born on the wrong side of the blanket	@born wrong ----------- side ------------- blanket ---------	@born wrong→born side→born blanket→born	------------------	------------------
23) keep the wolf from the door	@wolf door --------------	@wolf door→wolf	@wolf door ------------	@wolf door -----------
24) keep one's eyes peeled/skinned /open	@eye peel→eye open→eye	@eye skin→eye peel→eye	@eye peel→eye	@eye @peel skin--------- open--------
25) butter would not melt in one's mouth	@butter melt→butter mouth ------------	@butter melt→butter mouth→butter	------------------	@butter melt→butter mouth -----------
26) make hay while the sun shines	@hay sun→hay shine --------------	@hay sun→hay shine→hay	@hay sun -------------- shine -----------	@hay sun ---------------- shine -------------
27) bark up the wrong tree	@bark wrong ------------ tree --------------	@bark wrong→bark tree→bark	@tree bark→tree wrong→tree	@bark wrong ------------ tree→bark
28) live by one's wits	@live wit→live	@live wit→live	------------------	@live @wit
29) laugh on the other side of one's face	------------------	@laugh side→laugh face→laugh	------------------	@laugh side --------------- face→laugh
30) not have a leg to stand on	@leg stand→leg	@leg[5]	@leg stand--------------	@leg stand→leg

@ = at
→ = cross-reference
--------- = the lexical item/the cross-reference is absent

The dictionaries are rarely unanimous in their choice of the headword under which to treat a given idiom. This, however, is a minor problem, as "[d]ictionary users do seem to expect all multi-word units to have one element that is more important than the others, and they seem to prefer to look them up within the entry for this element" (Béjoint 1994: 161), be it the rarest or the first lexical word. Advanced users are experienced enough not to give up the search upon failure to hit the right headword at first attempt. Unfortunately, any alteration of the canonical form (e.g., through substitution, addition or truncation) reduces the accessibility of the dictionary information. The only viable solution is careful cross-referencing from each lexical word component of the idiom. However, several departures from this procedure can be observed in the above small sample: 14 cross-references are lacking in 29 definitions in LDOCE3, 3 – in 28 definitions in OALD5, 12 – in 21 definitions in COBUILD2, 25 – in 28 definitions in MEDAL. The policy of failing to provide cross-references seems idiosyncratic. Equally obscure are the reasons for certain idioms being "privileged" and explained twice, e.g., idioms 6, 8, 9, 12, 13, 20 in LDOCE3, and 2, 5, 7,

---

[5] "Idioms containing *stand* are at the entries for the nouns or adjectives in the idioms" (OALD5: 1161).

20, 28 in MEDAL. CIDE dispenses with cross references altogether and instead guides the user by listing idioms, together with their "address" (i.e., page number, column and line) under each main word entered in the phrase index at the back of the dictionary. Bogaards (1996: 287) is critical of this policy on the grounds that "[s]ince most fixed expressions contain only two content words, looking up the one or the other gives a fifty percent chance of finding the solution. Going first to the 'Phrase Index' always necessitates a double search procedure". Nonetheless, considering that a headword in CIDE corresponds to a separate sense, and the layout of the entry is not very transparent, finding the desired idiom would, in all probability, be even more puzzling if it were not for the specification in the index.

4.2. Semantics

4.2.1. Defining style

Like other lexical items in the macrostructure, idioms are explained either by means of conversational COBUILD-type sentences or by traditional substitutable definitions. The former incorporate a typical context of usage and address the user directly (e.g., "If you have to carry the can...", "If someone has you over a barrel...", "If you say that some-one..."). Apart from COBUILD2, the remaining dictionaries make occasional use of the "If-definition" format: CIDE most frequently (15 COBUILD-like definitions in 39 entries out of a sample of 40 searched items), LDOCE and MEDAL – only sporadically (2/39 and 1/38 respectively) (see Appendix 1); no such definitions have been observed in the 38 idiom entries located in OALD5. Given that idioms tend to function as situational comments, the COBUILD defining style, which embeds the expression in its typical surrounding, seems to serve the purpose better. For instance, the substitutable definitions of *go against the grain* (the expression pertaining exclusively to 3rd person inanimate subjects) in OALD5: "(to be) contrary to one's nature or instinct" or in MEDAL: "to be completely different from what you feel is right, natural, or normal for you" are wanting in naturalness. These are to be contrasted with the more successful approximation of the meaning of the idiom in COBUILD2 and LDOCE3 respectively:

If you say that an idea or action goes against the grain, you mean that it is very difficult for you to accept it or do it, because it conflicts with your previous ideas, beliefs, or principles.
If something that you have to do goes against the grain, you do not like doing it, because it is not what you would naturally do.

4.2.2. Metalanguage

Idiom explanations, like all definitions in MLDs, are written with the help of defining vo-cabulary,[6] which consists of about 2000 words in LDOCE3, under 2000 in CIDE, 3500 in

---

[6] The idea of defining vocabulary originates in the "vocabulary control movement" of the 1930s, which aimed at identifying the minimal section of vocabulary that would facilitate language access

OALD5, and under 2500 in MEDAL. COBUILD2's editors speak of 2500 commonest words of English having been used in most of their definitions. Though defining vocabulary – the innovation implemented by LDOCE1 in 1978 – has been embraced by modern pedagogical lexicography as a welcome solution to the problem of circularity, and has since become one of the tokens of user-friendliness, its effectiveness for learners of various competence levels has, to my knowledge, never been put to test. While the pedagogical value of simple definitions may be high, the risk of achieving simplicity at the expense of accuracy, pointed out, e.g., by Carter (1998: 153), is never far away and seriously undermines the merits of defining vocabulary.

Limitations imposed upon the metalanguage are likely to blur finer distinctions of meaning, the direct consequence being an occasional lack of discreteness of the meaning of distinct idioms as presented in the dictionary. Thus we have, e.g., "to be blamed or punished for something that is someone else's fault as well as your own" as a definition of *carry the can* and "to be blamed for someone else's faults or crimes" as an explanation of *be/get tarred with the same brush* (LDOCE3).

The opposite situation arises when several dictionaries display discrepancies in the treatment of the same item. By way of exemplification, let us compare the definition of *lead sb a (merry) dance* in five dictionaries (Appendix 1, definition 9). Even though the first part of the definition is more or less uniform across the dictionaries and expresses, roughly, the idea 'cause someone to feel bad', the ensuing specifications vary, depending on which way of making someone feel bad is stressed as typical: keeping somebody in the dark about your further move, making them do unnecessary things (such as following from place to place), or telling them lies... One risk of including such concrete examples in the definition is that the qualifier "esp" or "for example" may be easily overlooked, and, if the specification captures the user's attention, it may lead to an overextension, so that e.g., OALD5's definition can be retained as "make someone follow from place to place", whereas the last part of MEDAL's definition might inspire a user to interpret the idiom as "lying to someone". Inevitably, lexicographers, working with various corpora and guided by personal judgement, arrive at solutions that emphasise different aspects of meaning. However, if defining vocabulary were regarded as an implementation (however imperfect) of the ideal of the Natural Semantic Metalanguage (Wierzbicka 1972, cited in Wierzbicka 1999), it should foster the identification of the lowest common denominator for different situational contexts of usage, and thus render the definitional content quite uniform across dictionaries.

Moreover, striving after brevity and maximal simplicity may result in too general or too narrow definitions. Restricted metalanguage by no means forestalls imprecision and misguided formulation of a definition, which then becomes as useless as (or has an even more detrimental effect than) one that is incomprehensible on account of complex vocabulary. Examples of inadequately presented idiomatic meaning are not hard to spot. CIDE's explanation: "If someone *kicks over the traces* they behave badly and show no respect for authority" fails to account for the fact that "disrespect for the authority" is not a permanent,

---

by foreign learners and help lexicographers define words (Carter and McCarthy 1988: 1–11). A particularly influential development turned out to be Michael West's General Service List, published in 1953, consisting of 2000 words selected on the basis of objective and subjective criteria (such as frequency, universality, or utility), and supposedly giving access to about 80% of words in any English text (Carter and McCarthy 1988: 6–8).

but an acquired characteristics of an agent (not a perpetual anarchist). Yet another idiom, *go against the grain,* is explained in MEDAL as: "to be completely different from what you feel is right, natural, or normal for you". What seems to be misleading here is the far too neutral word *different,* which implies a cool, matter-of-fact evaluation rather than personal involvement of the subject, far better expressed with *be contrary to* or *conflict with, clash.* Similarly imprecise is the statement that *make no bones about doing something* is "not to try to hide your feelings" (CIDE). One makes no bones about something that others may not like, or may disapprove of, rather than about one's love or sympathy. The explanation of *move the goalposts* in OALD5: "to change the accepted conditions within which a particular matter is being discussed or a particular action taken" does not indicate explicitly that the purpose of moving the goalposts is to make life difficult for others. The definition of *the thin end of the wedge* in LDOCE3 – "an expression meaning something that you think is the beginning of a harmful development" – fails to add that this "something" seems unimportant at first. On the other hand, CIDE's explanation of the same idiom – "[i]t's *the thin end of the wedge* means that something bad can be started by something quite small" – sounds crude. The definition of *carry the can:* "to be the person considered responsible for something" (MEDAL) does not make clear that the sense of *responsible* is not simply 'in charge/in control', but 'answerable', 'to blame', and that the person carrying the can usually shuns this responsibility. Similarly, MEDAL's laconic definition of *twist/turn the knife:* "to make a bad situation even worse" misses the interactive aspect altogether: twisting the knife normally involves making the situation worse for another, not for oneself. Also, the explication "If you *give* someone *the slip* you escape from them" (CIDE), even if followed by an example (*If you're not interested in a bloke you can always give him the slip in a bar as crowded as that*), seems too broad in that it does not give any hint as to the purposefulness of the action – one is unlikely to say (unless jokingly) that, e.g., a toddler gave her mother a slip in a crowded supermarket. Finally, the sense of *give sb the elbow* is not restricted to ending a relationship with someone, as shown in CIDE or MEDAL, but can also mean 'dismiss sb from a job'.

Apart from inaccuracy, the dictionarese using defining vocabulary is frequently accused of being "clumsy and unnaturally circumlocutory" (Carter 1998: 153), the fault of long-windedness pertaining especially to COBUILD2's definitions, e.g.,

If you say that someone cut their teeth doing a particular thing, at a particular time, or in a particular place, you mean they began their career and learned some of their skills doing that thing, at that time, or in that place.[7]
If you say that you are playing devil's advocate in a discussion or debate, you mean that you are expressing an opinion which you do not agree with in order to make the argument more interesting. If you say that someone else is playing devil's advocate, you mean that you disapprove of them because they are pretending to hold an unpopular opinion in order to make an argument more interesting.

---

[7] Compare this with the short definition in OALD5 – "to gain experience from something". This explanation, on the other hand, oversimplifies the matters by failing to mention that it is the first experience that is at stake.

4.2.3. Presentation of meaning

The analytical definition mediates the meaning by breaking it down into smaller blocks or semantic descriptors, at the same time leaving their re-assemblage to the reader. Knowledge thus obtained is, as Piotrowski (1994: 154) calls it, "cold, intellectual", as opposed to the synthetically presented knowledge encapsulated in equivalents:

> Niewiele wysiłku wymaga się od użytkownika, a wiedza, jaką otrzymuje, jest „gorąca", ponieważ tylko dobry odpowiednik potrafi mu dać przynajmniej przybliżone czucie językowe.
> [Little effort is required of the user, and knowledge thus received is "hot", because only a good equivalent can convey at least an approximate language feeling to the user] (Piotrowski 1994: 154, translation – R. S.).

This inherent property of the analytical definition makes it a less than efficient tool for explicating idioms. As Lattey (1986: 228) notes, "in using idioms we make a comment on the situational context, above and beyond what can be captured in a paraphrase", and even native speakers experience difficulties in putting their finger on the hardly reducible idiomatic meaning. A paraphrase, however elaborate, rarely entails "the language feeling". The meaning in dictionaries being an abstraction, a result of individual judgement, it is subject to further abstraction when users attempt to synthesise the analytically presented information according to their own criteria, abilities, linguistic experience, intelligence, etc. It follows that what the dictionary user accepts as the true meaning of an expression is in fact twice removed from the original meaning by dint of this "user's abstraction of lexicographers' abstraction". It is thus of utmost importance for lexicographers' idealisation to be possibly true to life. Even minute inconsistencies and imprecision in the formulation of definitions, over- or underspecification will be magnified and perpetuated in the process of the "user-meaning" construction.

In brief, in defining idioms, lexicographers face an unenviable task. A neat, brief and simple description may overshadow the complexity of idiomatic meaning. A long-winded one sometimes leaves the user none the wiser – the more components there are to be synthesised, the more probable it is that some of them will be lost "along the way", thereby further diluting the already insipid meaning of the dictionary explanation.

4.2.4. Examples[8]

Not all idiom entries are equipped with examples. Table 3 presents the average number of examples in a sample of 40 idiom entries (see Appendix 1) in five learner's dictionaries.

---

[8]   For an extensive discussion of examples for receptive purposes, see Bogaards (1996: 298–300).

Table 3. Number of examples in a sample of 40 idiom entries

Dictionary	LDOCE3	OALD5	COBUILD2	CIDE	MEDAL
No. of idiom entries located (out of 40 initiated searches)	38	38	28	39	37
Total no. of examples	24	18	25	39	8
Average no. of examples per entry	0.63	0.47	0.89	1.00	0.22

In this small sample, CIDE's idiom entries are the richest in examples, to be closely followed by COBUILD2.[9] LDOCE3 and OALD5 provide about half the number of illustrative sentences given in CIDE and COBUILD2, and in MEDAL they are a rarity. CIDE is exceptional in occasionally limiting the information on idioms to an example of usage, with an explanation in brackets (13 cases in 39 entries). This technique, while convenient when the bracketed information is short (e.g., *These actions* go against *the grain* (= principles) of *the party*), produces a slightly cumbersome effect in the case of more elaborate interpolations (e.g., *Did it take you long to* find *your* feet (= become familiar with your new surroundings and be able to do things on your own with confidence) *when you started your new job?*).

As to the contents of examples, some add little above what has been stated in the definition, and few are self-explanatory, e.g.,

(1) *I'd go to the Far East at the drop of a hat* (LDOCE3)
(2) *He blows hot and cold about getting married* (OALD5)
(3) *Why am I always left to carry the can?* (LDOCE3)
(4) *As usual, I was left to carry the can* (CIDE)
(5) *The all-party meeting was a damp squib* (COBUILD2)
(6) *It is the turn of Latvia to twist the knife* (COBUILD2)
(7) *Bates gave the police the slip* (LDOCE3)
(8) *I think the researchers are barking up the wrong tree* (CIDE).

The idioms in the above sentences could as well be replaced by other, even non-synonymous items. This considerably diminishes the helpfulness of an idiom entry for decoding – users do expect examples to clarify the meaning and often prefer them to definitions (Humblé 2001: 61).

The use of examples is not without problems. Just as the use of context, and, to some extent, definitions, it involves inference and the inevitable risk of erroneous guesses. Bearing in mind the difficulties in transmitting the meaning of the word unequivocally through

---

[9] Cf. Herbst's (1996) results of the investigation into the number of examples in all entries (including idioms) between *need* and *nervy*: COBUILD2 had the greatest absolute number (221), and was followed closely by CIDE (208). The fewest examples were discovered in LDOCE3 (143); OALD5 had 194.

examples, Humblé (2001: 64) recommends: "[t]he best one can do is attempt not to suggest a false meaning". The danger of misleading illustrative sentences might be avoided through greater redundancy in the entry, which, as Wingate (2002: 161, 218, 224) observes, substantially increases comprehension. Therefore, perhaps it would be advantageous to enrich and adapt authentic examples so that they become a recapitulation and reinforcement of the meaning from the definiens rather than a mere presentation of a random collocate.

4.3. Pragmatics

Even though all learner's dictionaries employ usage labels (such as *approving, derogatory, euphemistic, figurative, formal, informal, jocular, ironic, offensive, impolite, humorous, old-fashioned*), pragmatic information is included in idiom entries on a rather irregular basis. Table 4 shows its occurrence in the entries of 10 idioms with evaluative overtones, selected from Moon (1998a: 244–277) (see Appendix 2).

Table 4: Pragmatic information in 10 idiom entries

	Information in	LDOCE3	OALD5	COBUILD2	CIDE	MEDAL
1) drag one's feet	Definition	+	--	--	--	--
	Example	±	+	+	--	--
	Metalinguistic comment	+	--	--	--	--
2) you can't have your cake and eat it	Definition	--	--	+	--	--
	Example	--	±	±	±	±
	Metalinguistic comment	+	+	+	--	--
3) make a mountain out of a molehill	Definition	--	--	+	--	--
	Example	--	--	+	--	--
	Metalinguistic comment	--	+	+	--	--
4) wash one's hands of sth	Definition	--	--	--	--	--
	Example	--	--	--	--	--
	Metalinguistic comment	--	--	--	--	--
5) put the cart before the horse	Definition	--	--	+	--	+
	Example	--	--	+	±	--
	Metalinguistic comment	--	--	+	--	--

	Information in	LDOCE3	OALD5	COBUILD2	CIDE	MEDAL
6) scrape the bottom of the barrel	Definition	--	--	+	--	--
	Example	--	±	--	±	--
	Metalinguistic comment	+	--	+	--	+
7) wash dirty linen in public	Definition	--	--	+	+	--
	Example	--	--	+	--	--
	Metalinguistic comment	--	+	+	+	--
8) put all one's eggs in one basket	Definition	--	--	--	--	--
	Example	--	--	±	±	--
	Metalinguistic comment	--	--	--	+	--
9) fan the flames of sth	Definition	--	--	--	--	--
	Example	--	--	+	--	--
	Metalinguistic comment	--	--	--	--	+
10) rock the boat	Definition	--	--	+	--	±
	Example	±	±	±	±	±
	Metalinguistic comment	+	+	--	+	+
Summary	Definition	+	--	+ + + ++ +	+	+ ±
	Example	± ±	+ ± ± ±	+ +++ + ± ± ±	± ± ± ± ±	± ±
	Metalinguistic comment	+ +++	+ +	+ + ++ +	+ + +	+ + +

+ information present
± information implied
-- information absent

Judging by the number of pluses or "half-pluses", COBUILD2 seems to be the most generous in supplying pragmatic information on idioms. What is more, it is the most explicit in that it sensitises the user to the discourse function of an expression by placing the capitalised and framed term PRAGMATICS in the extra column. An entry marked in this way normally contains clues as to the attitude the item is intended to express, e.g.,

If you say that someone is making a mountain out of a molehill, you are critical of them for making an unimportant fact or difficulty seem like a serious one. *The British press, making a mountain out of a molehill, precipitated an unnecessary economic crisis.*
If you say that someone is scraping the barrel, or scraping the bottom of the barrel, you disapprove of the fact that they are using or doing something of extremely poor quality.

The information about the pragmatic value of an expression is often smuggled in examples, e.g.,

(9) *This puts the cart before the horse; elections should follow, not precede, agreement on a constitution* (COBUILD2)
(10) *I want to sell the house, but my husband is dragging his feet* (OALD5)
(11) *I can't tell what he wants – he keeps blowing hot and cold* (LDOCE3)
(12) *The government has blown hot and cold on this bill, and we just don't know where they stand now* (MEDAL).

Only in COBUILD2 is pragmatic information incorporated into definitions quite regularly.

Some idiom entries fail users by dismissing the attitudinal or evaluative associations, of which LDOCE3, OALD5 and MEDAL happen to be particularly frugal. To quote two examples of matter-of-fact, connotation-free statements,

wash one's dirty linen in public: to discuss private subjects or problems in public: *Washing football's dirty linen in public does nothing for the game* (MEDAL)
put all one's eggs in one basket: to depend completely on one thing or one course of action in order to get success (LDOCE3)

Scarcity of connotations in dictionaries comes as no surprise in light of the strong lexicographic tradition of the Aristotelian, analytical definition, which dwelled on differential (essential, "necessary and sufficient") properties (i.e., core meaning, identified with sense), and relegated connotations to the status of residual, or peripheral, meaning (Kövecses 1989: 2). Although cognitive semantics neutralises the core versus connotation distinction, lexicography follows suit only reluctantly, for obvious reasons of space limitations and difficulties in separating the linguistically relevant from the individual or the encyclopaedic associations. Nonetheless, the case of idioms, especially those fulfilling evaluative, beside informational, functions, calls for re-examination of this approach. If paraphrase strips stylistically marked words of what constitutes their essential part, the missing emotional load can be recovered by learners only with the help of explicitly stated information. Otherwise, the rich overtones of the message encoded as, for instance, *He dropped a clanger; That really got my goat* or *She'll hit the roof!* will remain obscure to the foreign learner.

4.4. Applying dictionary information in context

It goes without saying that effort invested in the location and comprehension of the idiom entry is likely to be wasted if it is not accompanied by extra processing, directed at adjusting the dictionary and the contextual meaning. This can become quite intricate when the transformed form considerably diverges from the canonical version. The prospect of protracted deliberations aimed at figuring out the sense of the dictionary meaning as applied in the specific context might appear too daunting – the definition can be taken at face value without further adjustments. Alternatively, as was mentioned in section 1.3.1.2., the use of stylistically marked language (to which variant idioms obviously belong) blurs the lexical meaning in context, and, as a result, the dictionary definition is likely to be easily rejected as inappropriate.

Successful exploitation of the entry is uncertain for yet another reason: variation in the use of idioms is virtually a non-issue in dictionaries. Only in COBUILD2's additional column can there be found information on regular, systemic variation in the form of a comment: "Verb/Noun inflects". Examples, in general, do not demonstrate one-off modifications at all, barring cases that border on institutionalised variation, such as *have a political axe to grind.* One of the rare example sentences in which a non-standard form of an idiom has been used is *The Prime Minister* cut *her political* teeth on (= got her first political experience from) *student debates* (CIDE). Whereas it takes a lot more than a dictionary entry to account for all existing (not to mention possible) modifications of an idiom, incorporation of one or two examples of variants on a regular basis might suffice to imbue learners with the idea of the potential of idioms for exploitation. As Humblé (2001: 105) rightly observes, electronic dictionaries, where space is no longer an issue, can accommodate long corpus-generated lists of sentences with idioms in their non-canonical versions.

4.5. Concluding remarks

In the case of decoding idiom variants, dictionary consultation – regarded sometimes as choosing the line of least resistance – seems to be the solution nearly as heavily beset with obstacles as contextual inference. Only precise cross-referencing guarantees the accessibility of information when part of an expression has been deleted or replaced. Moreover, there is a risk that the full import of an idiomatic expression will not be available to the user due to the methods of meaning presentation typical of monolingual learner's dictionaries. Among others, the analytical definition phrased in the restricted defining vocabulary, and merely broaching the pragmatic aspect, is not ideally suited to the task of expounding the hard-to-paraphrase, intricate and connotation-loaded items in question. Little clarification is offered in examples, which are, in general, few and far between, and seldom extremely informative. Last but not least, the learner might have serious problems with consolidating the definition with the context-specific meaning. In this respect, the dictionary, with its avoidance of anything atypical, is not very helpful.

5. The experiment

5.0. Introduction

Although the following study is certainly not free from the fault of artificiality induced by the methods of data collecting, care has been taken, in the choice of the task, materials and the dictionary, to minimise the risk involved in any partly observational quasi-experimental research, namely that it may "require users to look up words they would not necessarily wish to look up, in dictionaries that they would not normally consult, for purposes that they may not understand or subscribe to" (Nesi and Haill 2002: 277).

5.1. Aims

The present empirical study attempts to explore the effect of dictionary use on reading comprehension performance of highly advanced EFL learners. Given that prior research has proved that finding an item is rarely a problem for advanced students, and exploitation of the entry presupposes mastery of searching procedures, in-depth investigation of the latter has been abandoned. Instead, special emphasis has been laid upon the retrieval of the information on meaning from the dictionary and integrating it with the context to understand the passage.[1] The generally formulated research issue: "Does dictionary use significantly improve comprehension scores in the target situation? How can the results be explained in view of learner- and dictionary-related factors?" will be considered against the background of several more specific questions:

1. Is context alone a reliable predictor of meaning?
   a. How accurate is the interpretation of the new semantic product, i.e., context-specific idiomatic meaning?
   b. How accurate are the inferences concerning the canonical meaning of idioms?
2. What kind of look-up behaviour can be observed
   a. Have all target items been looked up and found?
   b. Have all target items recognised as unfamiliar been looked up?
   c. Have familiar target items been looked up for confirmation?[2]
3. What were the trouble spots in the case of failed consultation acts: poor findability or misinterpretation of the entry?
4. Does a successful consultation act guarantee success in the comprehension task? (To what extent do learners apply the newly acquired information to verify their initial hypotheses about the meaning of the passage?)

---

[1] The strategy of extracting relevant information from the dictionary and utilising it in text comprehension is called "search-do reading" by Mitchell (1983, cited in Hartmann 2001: 90).

[2] For the answer to research question 2, see 5.7.4, 5.7.5 and 5.7.6. The remaining issues are dealt with in 5.8.

5. What are the results of processing contextual and dictionary information during reading as reflected in the definitions of standard idiomatic meaning?

5.2. Design

Certain assumptions based on prior research results govern the design of this experiment:

1. The presence of the dictionary does not guarantee its use: resting one's judgement on the bare figures of final comprehension scores in the dictionary group may yield a false picture of the (in)effectiveness of the dictionary.
2. Nothing about dictionary use can be taken for granted, even with proficient subjects; only by comparing what they say they are doing with their actual behaviour and quantitative data can one hope for a realistic and explanatory account.
3. The task should be suited to the level of students' linguistic competence in order to increase the likelihood of consultations for unfamiliar items.

The experiment has been designed with a view to recreating the natural situation of dictionary use when readers mark the vocabulary items they wish to look up, and access the dictionary information only after the completion of the comprehension task so as to verify their inferences. Accordingly, one of the groups (henceforth Group B) performed the reading comprehension task (paraphrasing the underlined fragment), availed themselves of the dictionary, and then entered corrections to paraphrases in the space provided. In this way, the impact of inference and the dictionary information could be separated and the possible disruptive influence of the search on the fluency of the reading process – prevented. In view of the fact that the mere availability of a reference work does not automatically lead to every student looking up every target item and every search ending in success, all instances of consultation were registered in written protocols, even though the author's true focus were only the target items. The latter, unlikely to be skipped because of the task's demands, were at the same time not so conspicuous to the readers as to reveal the purpose of the experiment or discourage close scrutiny of the surrounding text. Comprehension was measured via two tasks, that is, the paraphrase mentioned above (a device more sensitive than multiple-choice questions or a summary) and, in the final stage of the experiment, the definition, so as to highlight different aspects of comprehension: of the contextualised expression and its dictionary version, elicited by means of word cues. Whereas the evaluation of the difference between the "dictionary and "no dictionary" condition for the paraphrase task was feasible within one group (i.e., Group B before and after consultation), the results of the post-consultation definition task had to be compared with those in the control group (hereafter Group A), which replicated the experiment except the opportunity to use the dictionary.[3] Pre-knowledge of the lexical unit was controlled explicitly through self-reports: familiarity rating and a table of look-up behaviour relying on retrospection (in Group B),

---

[3] In the absence of the dictionary, Group A did not correct their original paraphrases (in practice that would have meant poring over the same task just after completing it). Therefore, Group A functioned as the control group only for the definition task. Its additional role was to verify the pre-consultation results obtained in Group B.

and familiarity rating, to be compared with the actual quality of idiomatic forms and definitions (in Group A).

5.3. Target items

The decision to use idioms as lexical targets was dictated by several factors. Firstly, notoriously difficult idioms are one of the primary reasons for consultation, which means that they are perceived by foreign learners as a source of major disruption to the reading process. In Béjoint's (1981: 217) questionnaire idioms top the list: 68% of the subjects look for idioms very often; in Tomaszczyk (1979: 111) the percentage is even higher: 72%. If the occurrence of a single unknown vocabulary item could make a sentence, or even an entire text, incomprehensible in certain contexts (Wittrock, Marks and Doctorow 1975, cited in Tono 2001: 15), it is even more likely for an unknown idiom, let alone an unrecognised allusion to an unfamiliar idiom, to be comprehension-wrecking. Thus idioms, usually unfamiliar or only vaguely familiar to the majority of subjects, seem to make optimal targets in a situation when pre-testing the knowledge of lexical items would defeat the project.

Another thing is the deficiency of lexicographic studies in the field. Despite evidence from needs questionnaires, research on idioms in the context of dictionary user-oriented studies is still underdeveloped. So far, it is the skills in finding idioms in the macro- and microstructure that have received the most attention;[4] the skills of utilising the dictionary explanations of idioms while reading have been explored to a lesser extent. The need for research directed specifically at dictionary use in interpreting unfamiliar idioms in texts has been voiced, e.g., by Bogaards (1996: 285), who observes that "nothing is known about the sensibility of foreign learners to the fixed or idiomatic status of word combinations they come across without knowing their meaning". According to Tono (2001: 142), closer investigation of idiom look-up strategies at sentence and paragraph level might shed some light on the overall picture of cognitive strategies of dictionary use. Finally, the issue of idioms deserves attention especially in view of research findings that show an adverse effect of stylistically marked language on the difficulty of the text, and consequently, on dictionary use (Müllich 1990: 486, cited in Nesi 2000: 39).

The rationale behind using occasionally modified, and not canonical, forms of idioms is twofold. Although idiomaticity has been thoroughly explored, it is usually the "fixedness" aspect that has been emphasised. Regrettably, "[c]omparatively little attention has been paid to the dynamics of fixed expressions in real-time discourse, and the extent to which this is relevant to practical lexicography" (Moon 1992: 493). Systemic variation fares better; however, the more creative modifications are usually treated marginally. Another advantage of using one-off forms is that, being highly original, they resemble nonce-words in that they help to control the previous knowledge of idioms. Furthermore, since occasional modifications are not simple applications of dictionary meaning, it is easier to separate the two factors of context and dictionary information than in the case of standard, canonical forms, and thus possible to detect departures from what should be the standard procedure of

---

[4]   See, e.g., Béjoint (1981), Atkins and Varantola (1998a, 1998b) or Tono (2001: 116–142).

matching the dictionary entry against the contextual information. In other words, occasionally transformed idioms, non-existent outside a given text, necessitate considering context as inextricably linked, and not alternative, to dictionary use.

5.4. Materials

One of the criticisms levelled at linguistic experiments is that they are often, as Moon (1998a: 32) put it, "suspect" from a corpus linguistic perspective: "explorations and discussions of variation and transformation are typically intuition-based rather than data-driven: they depend on invented examples and so may not reflect real usage" (Moon 1998a: 32). Apparently, only the use of authentic texts can test the hypotheses that claim to reflect the actual processes of interpretation (Moon 1998a: 36). In order to address this recommendation, contexts from the British National Corpus were used as material for the task booklet (see Appendix 3 and 4). The original body of 50 texts was reduced to five on the basis of the author's subjective judgement of familiarity, transparency, and the degree of transformation of the target items (idioms likely to be unfamiliar and rather opaque, with both the form and the meaning changed, were included). The fragments were eventually tailored to a manageable size of 7–9 lines or 134–165 words. One paragraph – number four – had to be disregarded in the final analysis of the data; otherwise, it would have been responsible for distorting the picture of dictionary use by inducing the floor effect.[5] The texts were not graded or controlled for difficulty, which on the one hand might be perceived as one of the flaws of the present study, but on the other contributes to the naturalness of this written language sample.

5.5. The dictionary

The choice of one monolingual dictionary was imposed upon the subjects so as to control the contents of the information in the entry. In the second stage of the experiment all subjects from Group B had *Longman Dictionary of Contemporary English*, 3rd edition

---

[5] It turned out that, far from being merely a matter of greater user-friendliness, precise cross-references become indispensable in the case of transformed idiomatic expressions that have been truncated or have had one of their key components replaced. Even though many students were so set on finding *put your commitment where your mouth is* that they turned to the unlikely headword *put* as a last resort, no one managed to locate it due to the idiom *put your money where your mouth is* lacking a cross-reference from *mouth* to *money*. As this prevented even the most persevering users from arriving at the desired entry and became a source of considerable frustration, the original numbers assigned to each idiom and the surrounding paragraphs have been retained, so we have Idiom1, Idiom2, Idiom3, and Idiom5. The absence of Idiom4 is telling in that it points up insufficient cross-referencing as one of the factors reducing the usefulness of a dictionary in reading comprehension.

(LDOCE3) at their disposal. This particular dictionary was selected for purely practical reasons: its popularity and availability. As there are a large number of copies of this edition in the Poznań School of English library, even those students who did not use LDOCE3 on a daily basis were likely to be familiar with its layout and conventions.

5.6. Experiment

5.6.1. Subjects

Group A comprised 75 fourth-year students at the School of English, Adam Mickiewicz University in Poznań, Poland.[6] All students were native speakers of Polish representing a high level of proficiency in English – as English teacher trainees they had passed a proficiency-level examination in English the previous term.

Group B was composed of 68 (53 fifth- and 15 fourth-year) students at the School of English, Adam Mickiewicz University in Poznań, Poland, from eight seminar groups (5–15 people each). All students were native speakers of Polish representing a high level of proficiency in English comparable with that of the subjects from Group A. More or less homogenous dictionary reference skills could be expected of the students, who need to use the monolingual English dictionary efficiently for numerous assignments on a daily basis.

Group B were informed that the purpose of the experiment was to measure dictionary-aided reading comprehension of authentic texts. They worked at their own speed in 1–1.5-hour sessions at the times of their regular seminar classes. The experiment consisted of four sections, each beginning with a briefing in Polish. The first two parts had to be handed in together before section three could begin, which in turn had to be completed before the subjects went on to section four. After the first task (identical with section one in Group A), the subjects were allowed to use the dictionary if they wished. They were asked to record every step of their consultation acts in the table provided, and to utilise the space underneath for any corrections to the answers from section one. Having finished, they reported on whether they used the same dictionary at home, and if not, whether they found searching LDOCE3 troublesome. After sections one and two had been handed in, the students were explicitly told to extract the idioms from the underlined fragments and to reflect upon their motivation for the use of the dictionary (or its lack) in a table. In section four the subjects were instructed to form idioms using word-cues, rate idiom familiarity on a scale of 1 to 5, and to write short definitions.

---

[6] At the time, i.e., in October 2002, the "3+2" system od studies (a three-year BA programme plus a two-year MA programme) had already been implemented at the School of English of Adam Mickiewicz University in Poznań, Poland. The subjects were the last group of students to participate in the old five-year MA programme.

5.6.2. Procedure

Group A were informed that the purpose of the experiment was to measure reading comprehension of authentic texts. They worked during their regular lecture time in one 60–80-minute-session. Since the consecutive sections of the test had to be handed out successively, only after the previous task had been completed, the session had to be divided into three parts, lasting, roughly, 30–10–20 minutes each,[7] so as to enable efficient and quick distribution and collection of the booklets in a group of 75 subjects. A briefing in Polish preceded each section. Task one was to read five paragraphs and provide English or Polish paraphrases of the underlined fragments. The subjects were advised to disregard the formal accuracy (i.e., spelling, grammar) of their paraphrases. In the next section they were explicitly told to extract the idioms from the underlined fragments and to rate their familiarity on a scale of 1 (very well known) to 5 (completely unfamiliar).[8] The last part instructed the subjects to form idioms using word-cues (those parts of the idioms that remained unaltered in context, i.e., the parts common to the canonical and the modified form),[9] and to write short definitions.

5.6.3. Scoring procedures

Paraphrases
To score the paraphrases of the sentences containing modified idioms and the corrections to paraphrases (in Group B), Nippold and Martin's classification system (1989: 61) for the conventional idiom explanation task was adapted (see Table 5). Two raters scored the answers independently, checking them against the established interpretation (provided beforehand by three native speakers) and the classification system. Correct responses scored 1, partly correct ones were credited with a half point, incorrect ones – 0. Interscorer agreement was 0.93 (Group A), 0.91 (Group B), and 0.92 (Group B – corrections to paraphrases). The contentious cases were later discussed and agreed upon.

---

[7] The estimates of the time devoted to each section were possible after earlier observations of students from Group B, and proved largely correct as almost everyone managed to complete the task before the assigned time.

[8] The familiarity rating scale, based on Nippold and Rudzinski (1993: 730) and Nippold and Taylor (1995: 428), appears somewhat counterintuitive (the highest numerical value corresponds to the lowest familiarity value). Therefore, the students were instructed to pay special attention to its meaning.

[9] As it was impossible for Group A to recall the canonical forms of the idioms unless they had known them before, responses to cued recall, apart form eliciting definitions that would show the influence of processing the paragraph content on the generic idiomatic meaning extracted from the context, helped to verify the validity of familiarity rating.

Table 5. Scoring system used for the paraphrase task

Example sentence: "Tarring the whole of the Austrian public with the Haider brush is unfair."	
Correct (1)	The response captures the idiomatic/ambiguous meaning of the fragment, e.g., "To think of the Austrian public as having the same faults as Haider is unfair."
Partly correct (0.5):	
Related	The response is vague or reflects only a partial understanding of the idiomatic/ambiguous meaning of the fragment, e.g., "Treating the Austrian public like Haider is unfair."
Incorrect (0)	
Literal	The response reflects the concrete meaning of the fragment, e.g., "Covering the Austrian public with tar using the brush of the Haider type is unfair."
Unrelated	The response has nothing to do with the accurate idiomatic/ambiguous meaning of the fragment, e.g., "Urging the Austrian public to do sth is unfair."
Restatement	Part of the expression or paragraph was repeated or reworded without adding any new information, e.g., "The fact that we tar the whole Austria with the Haider brush is not fair."
No Response	The answer space was left blank or the student answered: "I don't know".

Cued recall and definition task

The standard of correctness for the cued recall task was the canonical form of idioms. The following scoring system was used:

1. Correct (score: 1): the idiom was recalled in its canonical (dictionary) form.
2. Partly correct (score: 0.5): the form departs slightly from the canonical one (e.g., lack of articles, incorrect article, wrong preposition).
3. Incorrect (score: 0): the idiom was recalled in a form other than the canonical one.

The standard of correctness for the definition task was the conventional (dictionary) meaning. The scoring system for definitions again draws on the criteria in Table 5.

1. Correct (score: 1): the definition captures the conventional meaning of the idiom (as explained in reference works), e.g., "be considered to have the same faults as sb else".

2. Partly correct (score: 0.5): related, i.e., the response is vague or reflects only a partial under-
    standing of the conventional meaning of the idiom, e.g., "treat sb like sb else".
3. Incorrect (score: 0):
    a. Unrelated: the definition has nothing to do with the accurate conventional meaning of the id-
        iom, e.g., "urge sb to do sth".
    b. No Response: the answer space is left blank or the student answered: "I don't know".

Advanced students of English are unlikely to produce literal answers or restatements when
explicitly asked to form and explain idioms; therefore, the categories "literal" and
"restatement" from Table 5 were dropped as superfluous.

Statistical measurement
T-tests for correlated samples were run so as to check the difference between the "no dictionary" condition (Group B before dictionary consultation; henceforth B/1) and the
"dictionary" condition (Group B after consultation, hereafter B/2) for the paraphrase task.
The same type of test was carried out to check the difference between the two conditions
for each of the four texts. Also, t-tests for independent samples were performed for the
definition task.

5.7. Results

5.7.1. Paraphrase task

The results of the paraphrase task are presented in Table 6 and Figure 2.

Table 6. Mean score and standard deviation in the paraphrase task

	A		B/1		B/2		Difference (B/1 vs. B/2)
	Mean	SD	Mean	SD	Mean	SD	
Paraphrase 1	0.36	0.44	0.35	0.44	0.38	0.43	0.03 (8.6%)
Paraphrase 2	0.05	0.18	0.03	0.12	0.04	0.17	0.01 (33%)
Paraphrase 3	0.27	0.38	0.25	0.33	0.31	0.33	0.06 (24%)
Paraphrase 5	0.13	0.29	0.10	0.25	0.34	0.42	0.24 (240%)
Average	0.20	0.18	0.18	0.17	0.27	0.22	0.09 (50%)

Sample size A = 75; Sample size B/1=B/2 = 68

Figure 2. Paraphrase quality

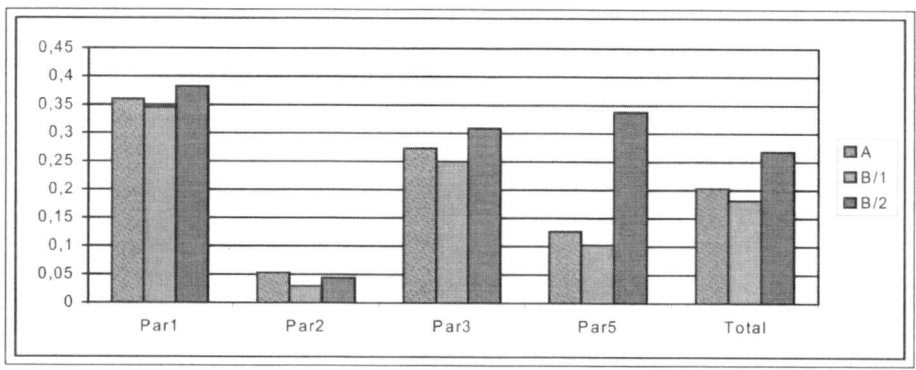

The mean quality of paraphrases in Group A and Group B before look-up turned out to be similar: 0.20 and 0.18 respectively. If we were to line the paraphrases in the order of deteriorating quality, for both groups Paraphrase1 was the easiest; the next best in quality were Paraphrases 3 and 5; Paraphrase2 fared badly. Considering the fact that the groups were not randomised, they show a remarkable uniformity of performance, with Group A scoring somewhat higher. After look-up, performance in Group B picked up by 50%.[10] The greatest improvement can be observed in the case of Idiom5, whereas only a minimal change – with Idiom1. The 27% result of the dictionary group after consultation is comparable with those for high verbal ability groups reported in Knight (1994) – 27% and Wingate (2002) – 32.3%.

In addition to the mean quality of paraphrases, another confirmation of the comparable language aptitude of the groups comes as a by-product of scoring, in the form of the distribution of correct, partly correct and incorrect paraphrases in Group A and B before look-up, to be compared with that in Group B after look-up (Table 7).

Table 7. Proportion of correct, partly correct and incorrect answers

	Correct			Partly correct			Incorrect		
	A	B/1	B/2	A	B/1	B/2	A	B/1	B/2
Par1	28%	28%	28%	16%	13%	21%	56%	59%	51%
Par2	1%	0%	1%	8%	6%	6%	91%	94%	93%
Par3	16%	9%	10%	23%	32%	41%	61%	59%	49%
Par5	7%	4%	24%	12%	12%	21%	81%	84%	56%
Total	13%	10%	16%	15%	16%	22%	72%	74%	62%

Group A and Group B before consultation have an almost identical proportion of partly correct answers, with a two-percent difference between incorrect answers, and a three-percent difference in correct answers. Altogether, correct and partly correct answers con

---

[10] Cf. Knight (1994) – 18% rise in the high ability group using a bilingual dictionary; Summers (1988) – 36% and 33% improvement in the "definition + example" condition.

stitute 28% in Group A and 26% in Group B, against 72% and 74% of incorrect answers in the respective groups. Among incorrect answers, only 13 paraphrases in Group A (4% of all answers) and 15 in Group B (6%) belonged to the category "literal". In 11 cases (4%) in Group A and nine cases (3%) in Group B there was no answer, i.e., the space was left blank or the student answered "I don't know", "No idea", etc.

5.7.2. T-test results for the paraphrase task

Table 8 presents the results of the t-tests for paired samples, which checked the differences between mean scores in Group B before and after dictionary consultation a) for the whole paraphrase task; b) for each of the four paraphrases.

Table 8. Paired samples t-test results for the paraphrase task (B/1 vs. B/2)

	Df	t-score	p-level
Paraphrase 1	134	0.81	42.06%
Paraphrase 2	134	0.71	47.71%
Paraphrase 3	134	2.06	4.16%
Paraphrase 5	134	4.36	0.003%
All paraphrases	134	3.82	0.02%

The difference of scores in the "no dictionary" and "dictionary" condition is significant at the 0.02% level. The difference between the scores for individual paraphrases in both conditions turned out to be statistically significant in the case of Paraphrase5 at the 0.003% level, and only just significant for Paraphrase3 (at the 4.16% level).

5.7.3. Familiarity rating

Mean values of familiarity rating[11] are presented in Figure 3.

Figure 3. Familiarity rating

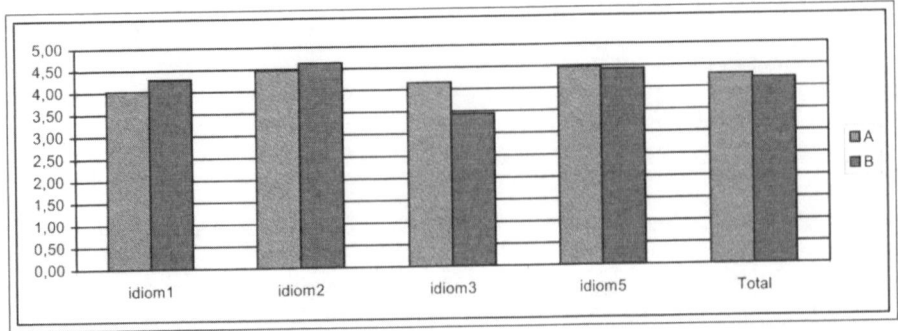

Ranges of familiarity:
1–1.66 = high familiarity
1.67–3.32 = moderate familiarity
3.33–5.0 = low familiarity

Whatever the individual differences, all idioms were rated as belonging to the "low familiarity" range, with Idiom3 (3.44) only approaching "moderate familiarity" in Group B, thus confirming the adequacy of the selected target items. The total means are similar, with Group A's familiarity (4.29) somewhat lower than that of Group B (4.20).

In order to test the reliability of the students' estimates, Group B's rating was compared with their self reports of look-up behaviour (section 5.7.5). The subjects were inconsistent in six cases (2%), when they contradicted themselves by rating the idiom as "(very) well known" and then claiming that they had not known the item and therefore checked it/but did not check it. Any further verification of the reported knowledge was not feasible: this group were to write forms and definitions of idioms only after dictionary consultation, and the quality of paraphrases before look-up could hardly be used as indicative of the awareness of the canonical form.[12] For that reason, Group A's data was used so as to discover any bias that the subjects may have displayed in reporting their familiarity with the idioms, namely, the quality of forms and definitions was checked against the rating. The instances when the students were positive about their (very) good acquaintance with the idiom, but scored 0–0, 0–0.5, or 0.5–0 in the cued recall and definition task, or when they admitted that they had not known the idioms at all, but provided correct forms and definitions, were taken as possible causes of distortion. The results are presented in Table 9:

Table 9. Reported vs. actual idiom knowledge in Group A

	Overestimates	Underestimates
Idiom1	9	2
Idiom2	6	0
Idiom3	7	1
Idiom5	4	3
Total	26 (9%)	6 (2%)

per cent relative to the total number of reports, i.e., 300

Apparently, the actual familiarity of idioms is likely to be about 7% lower than the rating shows. Given the analogous structure of both groups, this finding might be extended to Group B as well. On the whole, the comparison of self-reports with actual data proves a high degree of the subjects' language awareness, their ability to assess their knowledge quite precisely and responsibility for the adequate completion of the task.

Although familiarity influenced the quality of responses to a certain degree (the first two most familiar idioms scored the highest in Group A and the two least familiar idioms scored

---

[11] Considering the scale adopted, a more adequate, albeit awkward, term would seem to be the "(un)familiarity rating".

[12] Actually, neither the knowledge of the canonical form guaranteed success in paraphrasing, nor was the appropriate paraphrase necessarily a conclusive proof that the idiom was indeed familiar.

the lowest in Group B), the role of this intervening variable was limited. For one thing, the difference in average familiarity between both groups was not reflected in the difference in average paraphrase quality: Group A, for whom the idioms were less familiar, were able to outstrip Group B in the paraphrase task. As to individual cases, Idiom3, rated as the best known by Group B, scored worse than the less familiar Idiom1, and worse still than Idiom3 in Group A, whose reported knowledge was considerably lower. Moreover, the same rating values did not coincide with equal quality of the respective paraphrases (cf. Idioms 2 and 5 in Group A) and vice versa (Idiom1 scored almost identically in both groups despite a 0.26 difference in familiarity).

The meagre impact of familiarity on scores might be explained in two ways. Firstly, differences within the low familiarity range do not visibly affect comprehension. Secondly, contextual information, as a true levelling factor, overrides the effect of (un)familiarity discrepancies.

5.7.4. Idioms searched and found

Table 10 provides the proportion of searches and successful searches per idiom (out of 68 possible consultations) and the total proportion of searches and successful searches (out of 272, i.e., the number of all possible searches).

Table 10. Proportion of idioms searched and found

	Idioms searched	Idioms found	Success rate
Idiom1	72%	72%	100%
Idiom2	93%	90%	97%
Idiom3	62%	62%	100%
Idiom5	84%	78%	93%
Total	78%	75%	97%

In view of the fact that numerous other words were searched, a 78%-look-up confirms high relevance of the idioms to the task[13] and corroborates the expectation voiced earlier that advanced students will need to use the dictionary as much as the lower-proficiency learners provided that the text is suitably difficult. Almost all initiated searches ended in finding the idiom. Idiom2 was not located twice, and Idiom5 – four times, which accounts for a three-percent failure. Apparently, the subjective impression of (un)familiarity influenced consultation decisions, as illustrated in Figure 4 and Table 11.

---

[13] Cf. 85% look-up of relevant words in Hulstijn (1993: 144).

Figure 4. Searches per idiom (%)

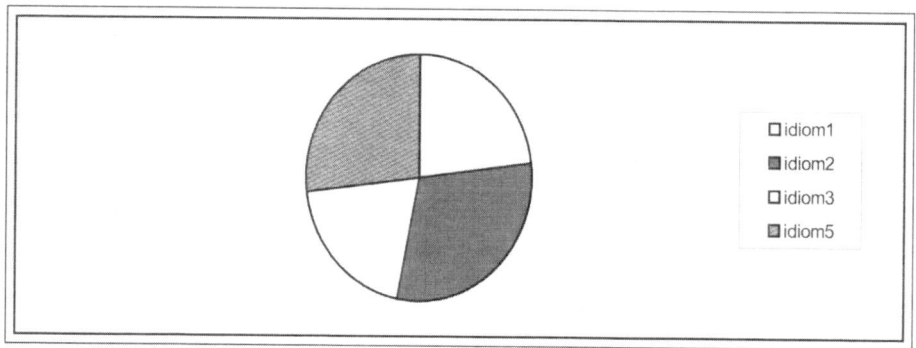

Idioms 2 and 5 were the most popular targets (accounting for 30% and 27% of all searches, respectively), whereas Idiom 1 constituted 23% of all searches, and Idiom 3, the most familiar one, was responsible for only 20% of searches. Paradoxically, the number of consultations was not proportional to improvement rate (Table 11).

Table 11. Familiarity/Look-up/Improvement

	Familiarity	Look-up	Improvement
Idiom3	3.44	62%	24%
Idiom1	4.29	72%	8.6%
Idiom5	4.43	84%	240%
Idiom2	4.63	93%	33%

5.7.5. Reported look-up behaviour

Figure 5 and Table 12 account for the students' motivation behind their consultation decisions. Self-reports reveal a similar pattern for Idioms 1, 2 and 5, looked up primarily because they were recognised as unfamiliar. Surprisingly, the second most common practice was to ignore unfamiliar target expressions (21% with Idiom1, 7% with Idiom2), or to search for familiar ones (12% with Idiom1, 6% with Idiom2 and 12% with Idiom5). The least often reported behaviour was that of not bothering to find familiar idioms. Idiom3 was approached in a different manner. As it was the most familiar one, 35% of searches were initiated in order to confirm the students' knowledge, and only 31% – because the item was unfamiliar. On 21% of occasions the decision was not to track down Idiom3 even though the learners admitted that they did not know it.

72

Figure 5. Reported look-up behaviour

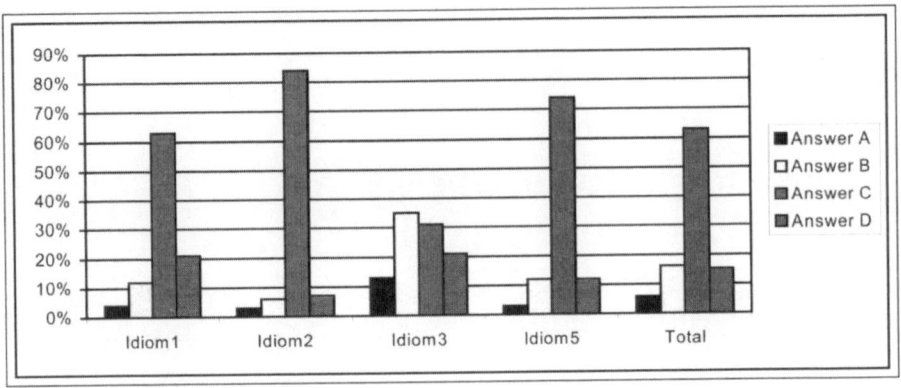

percentage relative to the number of answers per idiom (68) and to the total number of answers (272)

Answer A – "I knew the idiom so I didn't look it up"
Answer B – "I knew the idiom but I looked it up"
Answer C – "I didn't know the idiom so I looked it up"
Answer D – "I didn't know the idiom but I didn't look it up"

Table 12. Self-reported look-up behaviour

	Searched	Ignored
Unfamiliar	63%	15%
Familiar	16%	6%
Total	79%	21%

percentage relative to the number of answers per idiom (68) and to the total number of answers (272)

In general, it was the furtherance of knowledge rather than its corroboration that motivated the overwhelming majority of the reference acts: 63% of answers reported having looked up unfamiliar idioms (hardly surprising in view of familiarity rating values), whereas only 16% mentioned checking the meaning of familiar items.[14] Not all expressions recognised as unfamiliar were looked up: in 15% of self-reports the subjects admitted to having ignored unfamiliar expressions. Finally, 6% of decisions was not to look up idioms because one already knew them. The total number of items looked up corresponds almost exactly to the actual proportion of initiated searches (78%), confirming the reliability of self-reports.

5.7.6. "Paths"

In their search for meaning, the subjects who decided to look up the target words followed one of the "routes" or "paths" below:

---

[14] In the light of the actual proportion of the "confirmation paths" and Group A's slight tendency to overestimate their knowledge, even 16% looks like an inflated figure.

A: "Improvement"	incorrect/partly correct paraphrase – look-up – correct paraphrase
B: "No improvement"[15]	incorrect paraphrase – look-up – incorrect paraphrase
	partly correct paraphrase – look-up – partly correct paraphrase
C: "Confirmation"[16]	correct paraphrase – look-up – correct paraphrase
D: "Deterioration"	partly correct paraphrase – look-up – incorrect paraphrase
	correct paraphrase – look-up – incorrect/partly correct paraphrase

Although neither path B nor C leads to any real positive change in the answers, lack of the "dictionary effect" in path C is only natural as there is no space for improvement, unlike in path B. Table 13 shows the total number and proportion of paths undertaken.

Table 13. Path types: total number and percentage

Paths	Total Number	Proportion of path type out of all		
		Successful searches (205)	Initiated searches (211)	Possible searches (272)
Improvement	46	22%	22%	17%
No improvement	132	64%	63%	49%
Confirmation	12	6%	6%	4%
Deterioration	15	7%	7%	6%

Figures in the last column represent the proportion of paths out of all opportunities for consultation, of which, as was seen, not all were taken. The "successful searches" column attests to the influence of the actual use of the dictionary (rather than merely its presence) on performance, and therefore will be the subject of further discussion.

Closer analysis of the paraphrases shows that 35% (46) of the stunning proportion of 132 "no improvement" paths involved no change, repetition or restatement. The remaining 65% corresponds to incorrectly altered answers. By combining this information with the data in the "successful searches" column, one obtains a more precise picture of the effect of dictionary use on performance in the situation under discussion:

---

[15] The "no improvement" path covers both the prevailing instances of failed attempts to correct the initial answers and the cases of the paraphrases being left unchanged despite dictionary consultation.

[16] The term does not refer to the students' subjective impression of having upheld their intuitions, but to confirmation resulting from the scoring procedure. It needs to be noted that accurate paraphrases following look-up were rarely verbatim repetitions of the initial correct versions.

74

Figure 6. The effectiveness of dictionary use

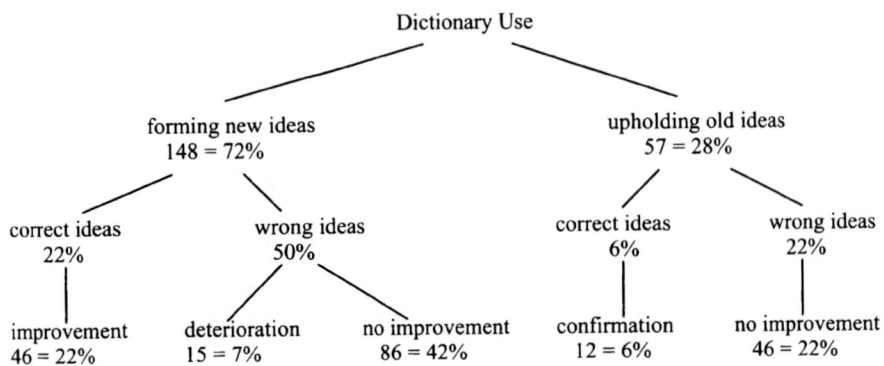

Disappointingly, dictionary use yielded negative results in 72% (50% + 22%) of cases by fostering or corroborating erroneous ideas, and generated or supported positive ideas in merely 28% (22% + 6%). Out of 46 "improvement" paths only 19 involved a full-point increase, and 15 "deterioration" paths reduced the scores by one or by half a point. Consequently, the final score after consultation turned out to be as low as 0.27.

5.7.7. Cued recall and definition task

The experimental group were able to recall the form of idioms significantly better than the control group. The dictionary helped most with the form of Idiom2, and the recall of the remaining three idioms increased incredibly symmetrically (Table 14, Figure 7).

Table 14. Recall task

	Group A		Group B		Difference
	Mean	SD	Mean	SD	
Idiom1	0.17	0.32	0.47	0.39	0.30
Idiom2	0.00	0.00	0.35	0.47	0.35
Idiom3	0.13	0.25	0.43	0.38	0.30
Idiom5	0.33	0.47	0.63	0.49	0.30
Average	0.16	0.17	0.47	0.25	0.31

Figure 7. Recall task

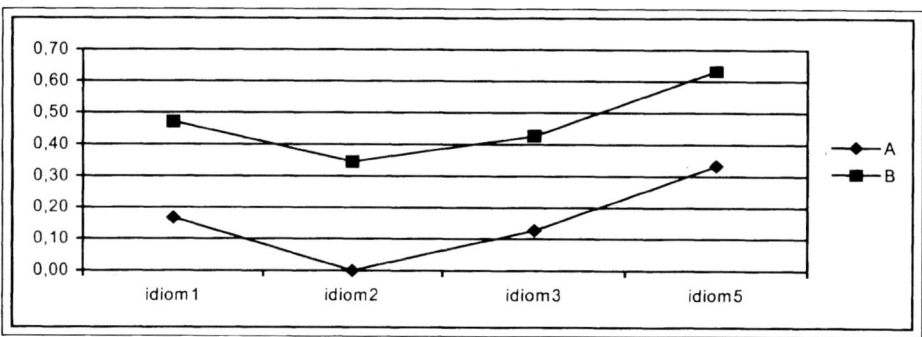

The dictionary affected the comprehension of idioms in their canonical forms even more favourably (Table 15, Figure 8): the mean score in the definition task increased from 0.11 in Group A to 0.51 in Group B. The most spectacular growth occurred with definitions of Idiom1. The remaining means rose almost as remarkably. Unfortunately, it was impossible to establish whether correct explanations reflected genuine comprehension in the case of direct quotations from the dictionary.

Table 15. Definition task

	Group A		Group B		Difference
	Mean	**SD**	**Mean**	**SD**	
Idiom1	0.11	0.27	0.60	0.40	0.49
Idiom2	0.07	0.18	0.53	0.43	0.46
Idiom3	0.04	0.18	0.40	0.39	0.36
Idiom5	0.19	0.39	0.52	0.49	0.33
Average	0.11	0.12	0.51	0.24	0.40

Figure 8. Definition task

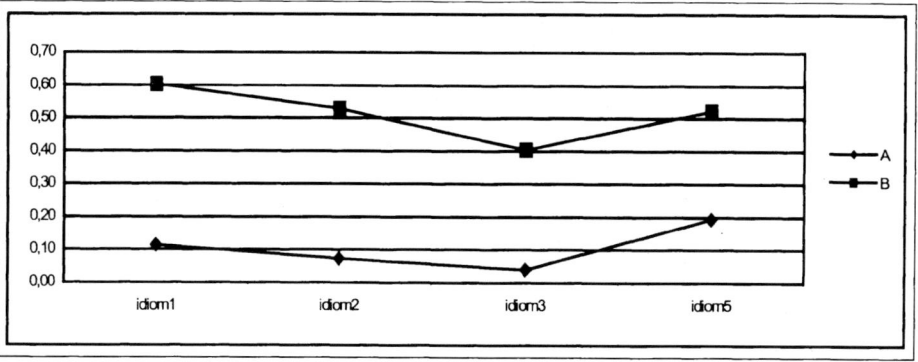

5.7.8. T-test results for the definition task

Table 16 presents the results of the t-tests for independent samples, which checked the difference between mean scores in the definition task in Group A and Group B a. for the summary data; b. for each of the four idioms. The difference is statistically significant at p<.0001.

Table 16. Independent samples t-test results for the definition task (A vs. B)

	Df	t-value
Definition1	141	8.66
Definition2	141	8.41
Definition3	141	7.31
Definition5	141	4.43
All definitions	141	13.35

p<.0001

5.7.9. The dictionary variable

34 subjects (50%) used LDOCE3 at home. 35% of the remaining 34 students (18% of the total number of 68) experienced some problems while using a dictionary other than their own: 2 people found it "quite difficult", and 10 – "slightly difficult". On the other hand, 22 students (65% of those who were not accustomed to using LDOCE3; 32% of the total) found it easy to consult. Altogether, 82% of the subjects (with those who used it on a daily basis accounting for 50%) experienced no serious consultation problems, whereas 18% complained about the inconvenience of having to search the unfamiliar-looking macro-structure. However, in view of the almost complete success in finding the item in the mac-rostructure, the "dissatisfaction factor" can be safely dismissed as not affecting advanced learners' ability to find idioms.

5.8. Discussion

Research question 1a: *Is context alone a reliable predictor of meaning: How accurate is the interpretation of the new semantic product, i.e., context-specific idiomatic meaning?*

The scores for paraphrases in the "no dictionary" condition demonstrate the limitations of contextual clues as comprehension facilitators. While the difficulty of the paragraphs has not been graded or controlled, they do not all represent the same level of complexity, which seemed to play a more significant role in boosting or hampering comprehension than idiom familiarity itself. One could even know the target item, but be bewildered by the intricacies of the contextually transformed meaning. One student's words succinctly summarise this paradox: "Kieruję się tu znajomością idiomu *throw books at sb* [sic], jednak nie wiem, co zrobić z resztą" ["I am guided by the knowledge of the idiom *throw books at sb* (sic) but I don't know what to do with the rest."]. Let us look at each of the four contexts in turn, starting with the paraphrases that presented the greatest difficulties for the subjects.

Paraphrase2 (of the fragment containing the idiom *be/get tarred with the same brush*) involves encyclopaedic knowledge on the Anglo-American policy towards Iran after WWII and refers to American history as a British colony. In addition, the context is not very informative as far as the meaning of the target item is concerned. The scarcity of useful contextual clues, coupled with low familiarity of the idiom and its considerably changed form (substitution), resulted in nearly total failure in the comprehension of the underlined fragment, with some subjects attempting random guesses, such as: *The United States shouldn't be bothered with the problems of other countries; The United States should not be bothered by the colonial battles; The United States should not be despised by the British colonies; The USA should not be affected by the British-Arab antagonism; The United States should stay away from the colonies.*[17]

The next poorly scoring paraphrase involves Idiom5, modified by means of insertion/addition to become *have a technological axe to grind*. In this case, context provides more clues to the meaning of the idiom and does not require any special world knowledge of the readers. However, interference from the Polish saying *twardy/ciężki orzech do zgryzienia* 'a hard/tough nut to crack' influenced many interpretations, which refer to it either directly or implicitly, e.g., *Each vendor has to struggle with technological problems himself; Każdy kontrahent ma własny orzech do zgryzienia* 'Each contracting party has his/her own nut to crack'. Another frequent misinterpretation stresses the particular method, way, approach, etc. that each vendor has, for instance: *Each vendor has his own way of doing things (technologically); Each vendor has his/her own technological methods or tools to make the material get the satisfying shape (to achieve his/her goal); Każdy ma swój własny sposób* 'Everyone has their own way (of doing things)'.

The third context is also informative (without being overinformative), but tricky in that it supports the literal as well as the idiomatic reading (dual actualisation, coupled with insertion). Unsurprisingly, the fragment containing the idiom *throw the book at sb* invited the largest number of literal or partly literal interpretations (10 out of 13 in Group A and 12 out of 15 in Group B), e.g., *Mr Simpson would throw every accessible book in his huge library at him; Pan Simpson byłby nawet w stanie poświęcić książki swojej imponującej biblioteczki by rzucić nimi w niego* 'Mr Simpson would even be capable of sacrificing books from his impressive bookcase so as to throw them at him'; *Oskarżałby go w swojej bibliotece* 'He would accuse him in his library'; *Mr Simpson would give vent to his anger with the help of a book from his library*. Other common interpretations stressed Mr Simpson's anger, obviously as a result of clinging to the comprehensible *would go purple in the face* preceding the idiom and bottom-up decoding of the phrase; for instance, *Mr Simpson would react violently; Mr Simpson would be extremely angry with him; Obrzuciłby go wyzwiskami/zrobiłby awanturę* '(Mr Simpson) would hurl abuse at him/give him a row'; *Pan Simpson byłby oburzony* 'Mr Simpson would be indignant'.

---

[17] All linguistic examples are presented in their original version (as they appeared in the students' booklets).

Despite the rich and even redundant context surrounding Idiom1 (*a feather in one's cap*), the scores, though the highest, were not very impressive. The students, on seeing the familiar word *success*, which indeed captured the sense of the idiom, apparently read the rest of the text only perfunctorily. The deceptive simplicity of this particular fragment, as it were, lulled their attentiveness and induced the "looking (or, rather, reading) but not seeing" effect. Consequently, inadequate paraphrases emerged despite the subjects' grasping (or even confirming their knowledge of) the idiomatic sense. One of the frequently occurring errors was the attribution of the "increasingly crowded cap" not to the Virgin company, but to Sting, e.g., *Sukces Stinga był tylko początkiem jego rosnącej popularności* 'Sting's success was only the beginning of his increasing popularity'; *Sukces Stinga był jedynie początkiem jego spektakularnej kariery* 'Sting's success was merely the beginning of his spectacular career'; *It meant that Sting could still achieve something more as he had great potential for achieving greater success; The success that Sting achieved at the beginning of his career was only a drop in the sea of his future achievements.*

To sum up, what were the causes of such disappointing results of reading in the "context only" condition? It seems that non-canonical forms of low-familiarity idioms had thrown the students into confusion. Whatever vague idea of the dictionary versions they might have had, the elaborate context effectively blurred this already feeble awareness, so much so that linking the original and the modified meaning bordered on the impossible. In one case, the complexity of the idiomatic expression was heightened by the absence of usable contextual clues and the students' failure to evoke the appropriate schemata of their world knowledge. Moreover, the contextual clues in the remaining fragments allowed only imprecise guesses at the meaning of the idiom alluded to, and without it the sense of the underlined fragment was hardly retrievable. Simultaneous actualisation of the idiomatic and the literal reading was a further complicating factor: those who did not recognise idiomaticity took the sentence to be literal. Finally, the students' inclination to find the Polish equivalent resulted in negative transfer. On the whole, context did not prove to be a sufficient means of repairing the comprehension breakdown in the situation under discussion.

Research question 1b: *Is context alone a reliable predictor of meaning: How accurate are the inferences concerning the canonical meaning of idioms?*

In view of the students' poor comprehension of contextualised idioms, it would have been unrealistic to expect Group A to infer more than rough approximations of their canonical meaning without any external guidance whatsoever. Awareness of what constituted the idiom was heavily influenced by the neighbouring text, which invariably fused with the target expressions. Accordingly, the average score in the definition task was nearly half the mean in the paraphrase task in Group A, and the cued recall of the form fared only slightly better. The recalled forms being inextricably mixed with context, comprehension did not remain unaffected. By way of illustration, let us consider a selection of the more interesting definitions.

Focus on *merely* and *one* that modified *a feather in one's cap* resulted in explanations that might be dubbed "one element out of many", as evidenced by *one thing out of plenty; to be one of many; be only one example out of a large group of similar events/actions/occurences; jeden z wielu kamyczków w bogatym dorobku* 'one of the numerous pebbles in one's considerable output'. The inferred "commonness" notion was sometimes tinged with "disparagement", as in *one unimportant thing among many others*; *to be merely an element in a larger group*; *to be unimportant*; *to be a small thing when compared to all needed things; just another thing that is not necessary because we already have many of those.* As a result, the positive aspect of the experience, whenever mentioned, was often automatically diminished, e.g., *to be but one good thing among other possible felicitous events.* At times "oneness" was over-extended to imply "insufficiency", expressed, among others, by means of the idiom *kropla w morzu potrzeb* 'a drop in the ocean of needs'; *zbyt mało w stosunku do innych* 'too little in comparison with others'. At the other pole we have the isolated definitions where *one* amounts to *unique*, e.g., *Kiedy mówimy, że ktoś wyróżnia się z tłumu* 'When we say that someone stands out in a crowd'; *to be exceptional*, or even *igła w stogu siana* 'a needle in a haystack', completely out of place here. Those students who concentrated on *an increasingly crowded cap*, took the idiom to mean "the beginning of something", e.g., *być zapowiedzią, początkiem czegoś ważnego, dużego* 'be a prelude to something important, big'; *początek sukcesu* 'the beginning of success'. Among the more fanciful explanations were: *być wierzchołkiem góry lodowej* 'be the tip of the iceberg', *as w rękawie* 'an ace up your sleeve', and *zmieniać zdanie* 'change one's mind', the last one probably resulting from a distant association of a feather with a small flag from the Polish *być jak chorągiewka na wietrze/dachu* (literally, 'be like a small flag in the wind/on the roof/a weathercock'), meaning 'be a changeable person'.

In the case of the idiom *be tarred with the same brush*, where *the same* had been replaced by the contextually specific *colonial*, there was no chance for the subjects to guess the canonical form. At most, the students were able to arrive at *be tarred with a (colonial) brush*, the verb *tar* connoting negatively (as a result of its literal meaning and/or *shouldn't* preceding it) to invoke vague definitions such as: *być przez coś nękanym* 'be plagued with something', *to be bothered with sth; być czymś zagrożonym* 'be in danger of sth; be put in trouble; odczuć coś boleśnie* 'feel something painfully'; *run into problems; napotykać coś trudnego* 'encounter something difficult'. Numerous interpretations drew directly on the contents of the text by highlighting "involvement" and (lack of) "interference" as major semantic components of the idiom in question, e.g., *to be involved in colonial arguments; one should not meddle in the inappropriate matters; not to be interested in sb else's mess; zostać wplątanym w konflikt* 'be embroiled in a conflict'; *wchodzić w ciemne konszachty* 'enter into secret dealings'. Somewhat more detached from the context seem the explanations that mention a sort of "influence", occasionally alternating with the more specific "dependence", e.g., *to be influenced by something on a great scale, to be dependant and compliant to sb; to be influenced in a negative way by something that should not have a "spoiling" effect; be touched/affected by sth; być pod czyjąś kontrolą* 'be controlled by someone'. Due to the subjects' impression of "subordination" underlying the sense of the idiom, a few definitions mention the treatment that the inferior receive, e.g., *to be treated in a harsh and rude way; to ignore sb, być traktowanym protekcjonalnie* 'be patronised'; *insult or offend sb; to ignore sb; treat sb/sth as inferior; to be treated badly because of being of lesser importance.* Other explanations concentrated on the effect that such a treatment has on reputation, e.g., *to blacken sb; to adulterate sth or sb's good conduct with a taint of sth rather inglorious; zeszmacić kogoś, oczernić* 'drag someone through the mud, blacken'; *być zbrukanym/mieć naruszoną reputację sprawami kolonialnymi* 'have one's reputation tarnished by colonial matters'. Several definitions represented the highest level of abstraction and thus were closest to the canonical meaning, e.g., *treated the same way; traktować* *coś/kogoś w jakiś sposób* 'treat something/somebody somehow'; *mierzyć kogoś tą samą miarą*,[18] literally 'measure sb with the same measure'. There were also several random guesses, such as *carry a burden that is specified by the type of the "brush"*; *pobrudzić sobie ręce* 'soil one's hands'; *mieć chorą ambicję* 'be overly ambitious'; *być przestraszonym* 'be afraid'; *skorzystać, otrzeć się o coś* 'take advantage of sth, to come across sth'.

The integrity of the idiom *throw the book at sb* being impaired by adjectival or adverbial modifiers and a prepositional phrase, most of the definitions included a varying amount of context information, e.g., *to throw legal books at sb*; *to throw every legal book from one's library*, *to throw a book in one's library*; *to throw every book in a library at sb*, *to throw one's every possible book in one's rich library at sbd*; *to throw every considerable book at sb*. One subject quoted the whole sentence instead of an idiom: *He threw at her every legal book he had in his astonishing library*. The clue *he would go purple in the face* directly preceding the idiom, as well as its literal meaning, allowed the subjects to surmise that the sense of the idiom was 'being angry' or 'any behaviour accompanying the state of being angry'. Hence we have: *to go mad at somebody about something*; *get furious and throw abuses*; *wściekać się na kogoś* 'be furious with someone', and the far-fetched: *zdenerwować się do tego stopnia, że nie panować nad sobą i zrobić wszystko, by się odegrać – tonący brzytwy się chwyta* 'become so angry as to lose one's temper and do everything to get even – clutch at straws'. Another foothold for the interpretations were "the legal books", to most respondents a metonymy of the law, legal action, rules or knowledge in general, used against someone. This understanding has been captured in the largest number of explanations such as: *wykorzystywać kruczki prawne znane sobie* 'exploit the legal loopholes that one knows'; *to use rules, regulations to fight sb*; *find evidence in the codes that sb's actions are illegal*; *to take to court*; *udowadniać przy pomocy litery prawa* 'prove by means of the letter of the law"; *to "hide" behind the law*. There were also students who interpreted "throwing books" as *quoting fragments from books, pelting sb with definitions, very bookish knowledge*. The definitions most abstracted from the context referred to criticism or accusations, for instance: *to criticise sb, to attack sb, rzucać oskarżenia pod czyimś adresem* 'make accusations against someone'. Some answers were completely unrelated, e.g., *to ask a lot of questions, to sacrifice all the things you have to get sth else*; *zademonstrować coś, pokazać* 'demonstrate something, show something'.

The students fared reasonably well in the case of the idiom *have an axe to grind*, whose form was least entangled in context. Despite the intervening modifier *technological*, the integrity of this idiom was for most students easy to perceive. Although the determiner *own* was often treated as part of the idiom, the adjective *technological* was usually skipped. Two recurring interpretations were: "a problem to overcome" and "an individual approach (to problems)". Examples of the former are: *to tackle some difficult problems, cope with sth*; *dużo problemów do rozwiązywania* 'a lot of problems to solve'; *zmierzyć się z czymś, znosić coś* 'bear something'. Just as with paraphrases, some negative transfer occurred when the idiom was translated as *mieć twardy/trudny orzech do zgryzienia* 'have a hard nut to crack'. The "approach" explanation is present in, for instance: *to have one's own methods/ways to achieve the goal*; *to deal with the problem individually, in one's specific way*; *każdy działa według swoich własnych zasad* 'everyone acts according to their own rules';

---

[18] Unlike the English idiom, this Polish phraseologism is not restricted to the context of ascribing negative features to someone on the basis of the behaviour of their associates.

mieć swój sposób działania 'have one's own way of acting'; *to have one's own way in dealing with things.* Finally, there are the nearly correct explanations such as: *to have one's own profits in mind, to have one's own interest in sth; not being willing to compromise; to have one's own business, take care of one's own business; dbać o własny interes* 'care about one's business'; *mieć jakiś własny interes w czymś i dlatego nie być obiektywnym* 'have a vested interest in something, and, therefore, not to be objective'. The last group consists of idiosyncratic guesses, e.g., *be in need of a financial or technological jump forwards; to have interest in different field; wtrącać swoje pięć groszy* 'put/shove one's oar in'; *one needs to prepare and develop; to have not an easy task to do in order to gain sth; mieć swoje zalety do wykorzystania* 'have one's advantages to use'; *używać odpowiednich środków do wybranego celu* 'use means adequate to the aims'; *spełniać wymogi* 'meet the requirements'.

To conclude, the chances that ESL students will infer the canonical meaning of idiomatic expressions from their modified versions are slim, and to a large extent depend on the degree of contextual transformation. The ubiquity of context elements in the idiomatic forms recalled and in the ensuing definitions not only substantiates the "mental effort hypothesis"[19], but it also conveys the impression that advanced learners – aware of the multitude of English idiomatic expressions and sensitised to their "rigidity" by years of instruction – would rather quote too much than accidentally tamper with the structure or meaning of a possibly existing idiom.

Research question 2 has been dealt with at 5.7.4, 5.7.5 and 5.7.6.

Research question 3: *What were the trouble spots in the case of failed consultation acts: poor findability or misinterpretation of the entry?*

Only three per cent of the searches were not completed successfully, which confirms the assumption that advanced students are experienced dictionary users. The proportion of look-up failures being negligible, it is nonetheless interesting to look at their reasons. One person looked for Idiom2 under non-existing base-forms *tare, tarry.* Another failure to locate the same idiom cannot be explained, as the subject did not report the headword under which he/she searched, but only wrote *tarred with the colonial brush* and put a cross under "no information". Whether they had expected to find the quoted form in the dictionary, or really could not find the idiom, is debatable, but comparison of written protocols with definitions and paraphrases points to the latter possibility as more plausible. As far as the idiom *have an axe to grind* is concerned, one subject looked up *grind,* found a cross-reference, which he/she acknowledged by marking "information partly found", then, surprisingly, went on to the headword *have,* and, finally, abandoned the search by stating "no information". The only sensible explanation of this extraordinary behaviour is that the subject read as far as "see also have an axe to grind", but failed to notice (AXE[1] (4)), which, unlike the idiom, was not in bold print. The other three subjects, for unclear reasons, did not follow

---

[19] According to this hypothesis, the deeper new words are processed, the better they will be remembered; the idea originated from "depth of processing" proposed by Craik and Lockhart (1972, cited in Tono 2001: 26).

the cross-reference under *grind*, which had probably been noticed, judging from the box "information partly found" and even "information found" being marked.

Success in locating the target items and moderate improvement in paraphrase quality after look-up indicates that the information was not exploited to the full. Leaving the aforementioned interfering context factor aside, the peculiar formulation of two entries was one of the chief culprits responsible for underachievement. Let us compare the definitions of *be/get tarred with the same brush (as sb)* as presented in learner's dictionaries.

CIDE	*Because they were so close John was* **tarred with the same brush** *as* (= thought to have similar faults to) *Tim.*
COBUILD2	If some people in a group behave badly and if people falsely think that all of the group is equally bad, you can say that the whole group is tarred with the same brush.
LDOCE3	to be blamed for sb else's faults or crimes
MEDAL	if all the people or things in a group are tarred with the same brush, you think or say they are all bad because you know some of them are bad
OALD5	having or considered to have the same faults as sb

Of the five, COBUILD2 and MEDAL are perhaps most successful in conveying the sense of the idiom in that they spell out the connection one forms between the negative features of people/things in a group and a person/thing associated with them. CIDE captures this point by stating the close relationship between John and Tim, the faults of the latter being transferred to the former in people's minds. OALD5 is less explicit about the cause of "tarring", and LDOCE3's definition leaves the reader at a loss as to the reasons for "blaming someone for somebody else's faults or crimes". Consequently, some subjects took the definition at face value and understood the situation as that of a person getting away with a crime and someone else being charged with it. This gross misinterpretation is evidenced by the disappointingly large number of inadequate corrections of Paraphrase2, e.g., *The US should not be blamed for the crimes and faults committed by GB as a colonial power; US shouldn't be blamed for the colonial times; US should not be blamed for crimes of colonialism; The USA shouldn't be blamed for colonial policy of the British; The US should not be blamed for all colonial mistakes; Stany Zjednoczone nie powinny być obwiniane za kolonialne zbrodnie/błędy* 'The United States shouldn't be blamed for colonial crimes/mistakes'.

Another example of unfortunate wording is the LDOCE3 definition of *have an axe to grind*: "to do or say something again and again because you want to persuade people to accept your ideas or beliefs: *I have no political axe to grind*". By emphasising the repetitiveness of someone's actions or words (only a means of bringing others around), it diverts the reader's attention from the essential semantic component of the target expression, that is, the reason for being so persevering, which, however, is explicitly stated in the corresponding definitions in other learner's dictionaries:

CIDE	If you **have an axe to grind** you have a personal, sometimes secret, reason for wanting something to happen, or a particular idea or belief that you are always trying to persuade other people to agree with, or a good reason for complaining about something: *Environmentalists have no political axe to grind – they just want to save the planet. He's always grinding his axe about avoiding sexism and racism. Tim certainly has an axe to grind now that his salary has been reduced.*

COBUILD2   If you say that someone **has an axe to grind**, you mean their reason for doing something in a particular situation is motivated by selfishness; an informal expression. *Mr Rollins, who according to Mr Perot was fired, may be suspected of having an axe to grind.*

OALD5   to have private reasons for being involved in sth: *She had no particular axe to grind and was only acting out of concern for their safety.*

The peculiarity of phrasing in LDOCE3 led several subjects to believe that *have an axe to grind* means 'be persuasive' or 'repeat oneself', such an interpretation being reflected, e.g., in the following pseudo-corrections: *Each vendor has to be as persuasive as far as the technological values are concerned; Każdy sprzedawca ma tendencję do powtarzania się, gdyż zależy im do przekonania innych do swoich pomysłów* 'Every vendor has a tendency to repeat himself/herself because they care deeply about bringing others round to their ideas'; *Każdy sprzedawca musi powtarzać w kółko to samo* 'Every vendor has to repeat things again and again'.

Remarkably, it was not the incomprehensible metalanguage or complex definition format, but tricky formulation that confused whatever accurate notions the students may have had before consultation. Lack of illuminating examples only exacerbated the problem. Evidently, sacrificing precision to user-friendliness or economising on space in the case of idiom entries turns out to have a detrimental effect on comprehension.

Research question 4: Does a successful consultation act guarantee success in the comprehension task? (To what extent do learners apply the newly acquired information to verify their initial hypotheses about the meaning of the passage?)

The disproportion between the number of successful searches and mean improvement in the paraphrase task clearly demonstrates that finding the required information does not guarantee success in the comprehension task. 22% of "no improvement" paths corroborates Müllich's (1990, cited in Nesi and Haill 2002: 288) observation of the sham use of dictionaries. Some students attempted to save their inference by attaching a fragment of the definition to it, which represents a more sophisticated version of sham use, e.g.,

(1)   *The fact that Sting's songs were top hits was only one factor to bring him fame, and next were to come. → Sting's songs were only one of many things he could be proud of.*

(2)   *Sting's success was too small to be taken seriously in the music business. → Sting's success was too small to be proud of.*

Instead of checking the retrieved information against the contextual form and the surrounding sentences, the subjects preferred to quote whole or fragmented definitions, with little or no effort at adjustment.[20] Examples of the sense thus distorted can be found in the following paraphrases: *Wilson should be proud of his cooperation with Sting; The USA shouldn't be blamed for crimes or faults of others; Mr Simpson would charge him with as many offences as possible; Each vendor was saying sth again and again because they wanted to persuade others to accept their ideas.*

---

[20]   Cf. category-three errors in Nesi and Haill (2002: 299).

The motivation behind such behaviour is unclear: was it genuine inability to incorporate the dictionary meaning into context, inability to paraphrase the meaning, or simply a desire for a compromise between one's reluctance to complete the task and a sense of duty? More importantly, do the subjects tend to dismiss the context after dictionary consultation while reading at their leisure?

Research question 5: *What are the results of processing contextual and dictionary information during reading as reflected in the definitions of standard idiomatic meaning?*

The use of the dictionary did not wipe out the effects of intense context processing, of which more or less distinct traces (in the form of the inclusion of the subject matter of the paragraphs in definitions) were registered in 14% of the total number of answers (in 25 definitions of Idiom1, 9 definitions of Idiom3 and 5 definitions of Idiom5), e.g., *one thing among many others, to be one of the many, to be just one part of sth bigger, more important* (Idiom1); *react angrily, violently, to act offensively, use arguments from a book, to use legal expertise to stop somebody* (Idiom3). Usually fragments of the dictionary definition and context were combined, e.g., *one of numerous successes; one more thing to be proud of* (Idiom1); *to find every possible argument (a legal one) to punish sb* (Idiom3). This type of linguistic evidence validates the prediction made in Chapter 3 that innovative modifications of idioms are processed like novel expressions.

Ideally, the subjects should have reconsidered the text after consultation not only to generate the context-specific meaning, but also to keep potential misinterpretations of the entry in check. Unfortunately, this was rarely the case, as translations and paraphrases (but not direct quotations) of dictionary definitions reveal, e.g., *być obarczanym za winy innych* 'be burdened with responsibility for others' faults'; *to punish sb severely for sb else's crime or offence* (Idiom2); *to be blamed for and burdened with the responsibility for a crime committed by somebody else; mieć dar przekonywania* 'have great powers of persuasion'; *mówić o czymś "w koło Macieju" żeby przekonać innych do swojego punktu widzenia* 'talk about something over and over again in order to bring others round to your point of view' (Idiom5); *to say sth many times in order to persuade sb to do sth.*

All in all, despite the fact that the dictionary meaning did not totally override the correctly or incorrectly inferred contextual meaning, and the contextual information did not always rectify the effects of misreading the entry, exposure to dictionary information significantly enhanced the subjects' awareness of the difference between the canonical and contextual form and meaning of idioms, as the results of the recall and definition task in Group A and B demonstrate.

5.9. Concluding remarks

Statistical analysis reveals a positive picture of the usefulness of the monolingual learner's dictionary in the reading situation under discussion. As was expected, the dictionary turned out to be essential to the successful completion of the paraphrase task as a source of the hardly inferable canonical meaning of idioms. However, despite a 50% rise in scores after consultation, in only two cases – of the idiom least detached from its canonical version (*have an axe to grind*) and the most familiar one (*throw the book at*) – was the difference between the dictionary and no-dictionary condition statistically significant.

Several factors seem to have reduced the overall positive influence of the dictionary on reading comprehension performance of advanced learners. First and foremost, the peculiar formulation of two definitions led the students astray and induced curious paraphrases and definitions. The subjects themselves, though expert in picking out the idioms from the macro- and microstructure, exhibited less satisfactory skills in handling the correctly located definition. Some, lacking in flexibility in processing the dictionary information, tended to take the contents of the entry for granted, which led to misinterpretations of the confusingly formulated definitions. In the absence of verbalisations of learners' thoughts, it is impossible to be very specific about strategies responsible for comprehension errors. Nonetheless, certain general trends of dictionary-user behaviour emerge from the accumulated material.

Some of the responses discussed in section 5.8. could be taken for signs of the learners' reliance on selected aspects of the definition stemming from difficulties in integrating its components in one meaning. To this category belong those paraphrases and definitions of *have an axe to grind* that prioritise the "incessant talking" or "being persuasive" as the core of its meaning. Unexpectedly, a similar trend is observable in the "no-dictionary" group's use of context, to be exemplified with the "one element out of many" or "the beginning of something" interpretations of *a feather in one's cap*. Also, despite information to the contrary, many subjects were intent on providing a Polish idiom (e.g., *a feather in one's cap* = *kropla w morzu potrzeb* 'a drop in the ocean of needs', *igła w stogu siana* 'a needle in a haystack', *wierzchołek góry lodowej* 'the tip of the iceberg, *as w rękawie* 'an ace up your sleeve'; *throw the book at* = *tonący brzytwy się chwyta* 'clutch at straws'; *have an axe to grind* = *mieć twardy orzech do zgryzienia* 'have a hard nut to crack', *wtrącać swoje pięć groszy* 'put one's oar in').

These findings are consonant with the unpleasant suspicion voiced, among others, by Wingate (2002: 222), that in their use of a monolingual dictionary, at least intermediate learners "are still guided by the habits of bilingual dictionary use, seeking equivalents for the unknown words instead of trying to derive the word meaning from the whole definition". Old habits die hard, although in the case of advanced learners this tendency is more veiled and, interestingly, not restricted to definitions. Instead of simply taking the fragment of a definition for a target, they would rather use the former as a basis for a more elaborate process of building a synonymous expression. A small-scale study could help to delve into this "quasi-kidrule" problem deeper.

The predominant feature of the answers, however, was excessive concentration on one source of information and simultaneous rejection of the other, most obvious in the sham use of dictionaries, which in the present study was responsible for 22% of sustained incorrect ideas. The other side of the coin was the dismissal of context after consultation. The subjects, as if complacent about finding the target item, were quite content to quote parts of the definitions with minimal or crude adjustments – hence a wide discrepancy between the scores in the paraphrase and definition task after dictionary consultation. Disregarding the context was not confined to the after-look-up stage: whereas the more difficult contexts were, on the whole, read carefully, the overinformative context invited perfunctory reading, which also spurred incorrect paraphrases.

The ultimate obstacle to comprehension was the complexity of the context. On one occasion it turned out to be so obscure that it blocked the positive effect of dictionary consultation almost completely. The degree of contextual transformation was not without significance, either: the least changed Idiom5 had the highest rate of improvement. At times, the modification was so disconcerting to the students that even the recognition of the idiom as familiar could not help in capturing the instantiated sense. In other words, knowing the idiom did not guarantee the comprehension of its one-off version. The subjects, accustomed to treating idioms as fossilised chunks, were apparently taken aback by their innovative applications. One person volunteered a comment: "To mi nie wygląda na idiom" ["This doesn't look like an idiom to me"]. There were also isolated cases when the idiom had evidently been located, but the self-report said "not found", as if the contextual form had been expected in the dictionary.

Finally, the results might have been affected by the design of the task booklet. The need to register searches and other self-reports undoubtedly consumed the subjects' energy and distracted their attention, which otherwise might have been directed at reconsidering the context. Nonetheless, the accuracy and consistency of the data remained remarkably high, pointing to the students' alertness and capability of managing multiple linguistic and meta-linguistic tasks.

Conclusions and implications for further research

The present study aimed to explicate how advanced students approach a complex comprehension task with a monolingual dictionary at hand, and to expose the factors underlying their success or failure.

As Chapter 1 demonstrated, the highly relevant subject of dictionary use for receptive purposes requires a great deal of methodological rigour of the researcher. Above all, the effort involved in keeping track of the subjects' pre- and post-consultation decisions is worthwhile. Accounting for the potential yet unexecuted consultations as well as the successfully completed yet not efficiently exploited ones, rather than simply comparing the scores of the experimental and control group, ensures a far more realistic picture of the effectiveness of dictionary use. Moreover, bearing in mind the limitations of questionnaires, experiments and observations, it is advisable to optimise the reliability of the results by combining various data-collecting methods. Careful scrutiny of the contents of the entry, the subjects' reported and actual consultation behaviour as well as the scores should normally provide ample evidence for the factors impeding smooth performance, such as flaws in entry design or/and deficiencies in the learners' reference skills. In other words, by adopting a comprehensive approach to the issue of dictionary use, i.e., a simultaneously product- and process-oriented perspective, one can not only establish individual results with considerable precision but also – which is of more lasting value to lexicographers and teachers – explain them. Pooling the available data on the sources of underachievement in dictionary-assisted reading might constitute a useful databank – a basis for developing explicit instruction in reference skills as well as the grounds for improving selected aspects of dictionary description. Last but not least, future researchers might benefit from being sensitised to frequent design defects.

Although, as Chapter 1 postulated, the pre-search stages of the consultation act should receive due attention, this study, unlike most of its predecessors, did not stress the role of context in predicting meaning. Instead, the significance of considering context after consultation so as to accommodate the information gleaned from the dictionary was emphasised. Chapter 2 presented a revision of arguments commonly put forward in favour of inference, exposing their weaknesses. Given the limitations of this interpretation strategy, the implementation of the top-down model of reading in the form of "banishing" the dictionary from the L2 classroom must be viewed as misguided. Although guessing from context is part and parcel of reading, it is not to be relied upon as a foolproof strategy. Rather, it is a preliminary to dictionary consultation, the latter acting as a safeguard against inaccurate guesses.

In the light of the characteristics of idiom variation and psycholinguistic views on idiom interpretation analysed in Chapter 3, context – distorting the canonical form – cannot offer reliable clues as to the meaning of modified idioms. The role of context will, at best, boil down to indicating the idiomaticity of the phrase and sending the reader on a search for the source of the transformation. Under these circumstances, the recommendation to process the contextual and dictionary information in tandem becomes an imperative. Only through careful back-and-forth matching of the entry against the contextual form can the reader approach the writer's meaning. The reanalysis of context after consultation is crucial to the successful completion of the comprehension task.

Chapter 4 was an attempt to assess the role of the monolingual learner's dictionary in the task of decoding idiom variants. Inevitably, its potential helpfulness will be diminished. The most obvious reason is poor findability – limited due to the form of the expression being non-canonical and occasionally incomplete cross-referencing. However, it seems that the information, even when located in the entry, may turn out to be insufficient for the reader to grasp the meaning. Possible obstacles to full comprehension are: restricted defining vocabulary often resulting in simplistic inaccurate definitions that fail to give justice to complex idiomatic meaning, lack of examples (especially of contextually modified idioms) and pragmatic notes. All in all, the usefulness of the MLD for the task was predicted to be moderate.

The actual role of the learner's dictionary in decoding idiom transformations was tested in the experiment reported in Chapter 5. In order to account for the effect of dictionary use on performance, control was exerted over the subjects' familiarity with the targeted items, consultation decisions, the number of actually located targets, as well as the degree of satisfaction with the dictionary. Ultimately, it was established that dictionary use positively affected comprehension in 28% of all instances of successfully completed searches.

The results corroborate earlier findings in this field that advanced students are competent dictionary users as long as user skills are defined as extracting the targets from the macro- and microstructure. Unfortunately, success in locating the desired information does not automatically translate into high scores in the comprehension task. The fact that students in the dictionary group recalled the canonical form and definition of idioms significantly better than they were able to apply this knowledge when paraphrasing their context-embedded versions brings out the well-known truth that "[t]he dictionary does not really 'give' the student the meaning of a word. The reader has to 'negotiate' that according to the context" (Bensoussan 1983: 345). It is those "negotiating" skills that crown the consultation act or, if they are lacking, spoil it. In other words, whereas the inability to locate a multi-word item may indeed be responsible for underachievement in the case of intermediate learners, advanced users' failure is ascribable rather to insufficient attention being directed at the proper understanding and application of the information retrieved. Apparently, with an increase in language proficiency, negative strategies, though largely eradicated from the macro- and microstructure search, linger on at the final stages of consultation to prevent successful exploitation of the located definition.

To elaborate on the matter of advanced users' consultation behaviour, its prevalent feature was the tendency to minimise mental effort when processing the dictionary information, reflected in, for example, sham use of the dictionary as well as few or no alterations in the shape of definitions, whose fragments were sometimes uncritically inserted into paraphrases. This is a striking thing to observe in proficient learners, to whom explanations couched in a restricted set of 2000 common words certainly could not have presented comprehension problems. Moreover, awkwardness in assimilating the meaning showed in synonymous expressions conceived on the basis of selected elements of the definition or context that, one might speculate, appeared somehow conspicuous or important to the subjects. In addition, Polish equivalents were supplied by dint of obscure associations or formal analogy. Little more can be said on learner interpretation strategies; a separate small-scale investigation using a think-aloud protocol as a methodological tool could shed some light on this issue. In brief, such behaviour conveys an impression of learners taking short cuts by adopting a somewhat superficial attitude towards the information accessed, be it of a dictionary or contextual type, and putting forth only a minimal amount of effort to integrate the two.

However, one might argue, had the students been more aware of idiom flexibility, the difficulty with bridging the gap between the canonical and variant versions might have been alleviated. Thus, the present study points up a need for raising awareness of the productivity potential in idioms, for example, by means of corpus-based exercises, in which students manipulate idioms and comment on the meaning thus obtained.

Another factor responsible for the reduction of the overall positive effect of the monolingual dictionary on comprehension performance was the imprecise description of meaning. Obviously, idioms, being semantically complex and culturally specific, as well as infrequent, require particularly careful lexicographic treatment. On the other hand, this study provokes questions about the definability of idioms in the monolingual learner's dictionary. As was mentioned, abstract idiomatic meaning escapes the rigours of analytical definition and does not lend itself easily to paraphrasing, which "dilutes" it and never conveys the "feeling" it has for native speakers. In particular, the feasibility of transmitting the subtleties of idiomatic meaning in terms of a limited set of defining vocabulary is debatable. The learners' occasionally perfunctory and fragmentary reading of definitions could have stemmed from their inability to synthesise the meaning, or from tiredness or laziness. However, it is also likely that simplified texts of definitions do not invite careful reading and lower readers' attentiveness. McCreary and Dolezal (1999: 134) invoke McKeown's (1993) idea of developing a special "learner's dictionary" for native speakers, to help them learn unfamiliar words. To reverse this idea, perhaps the time has come for a "native speaker's dictionary" for advanced foreign learners, devoid of infantile style and yet equipped with the encoding information characteristic of MLDs. Ultimately, the problem boils down to what is more irksome (or beneficial) for advanced learners: hunting for the elusive meaning in five learner's dictionaries and still being unable to pin it down, or having to look up one or two additional words from a definition written in a non-restricted defining vocabulary (and incidentally enriching one's lexicon). It would certainly be intriguing to probe users' preferences in this field, and to test the actual effect of both types of explanations on advanced users' comprehension performance.[1]

A related but even more general issue that this study raises is whether the monolingual dictionary is in fact the optimal solution for reading. In view of the outcome of the reported experiment, distraction caused by the break devoted to reassembling the analytically presented meaning, the futility of the invested effort (i.e., failure to come up with the right meaning), the costs of resorting to the monolingual dictionary during reading seem to outweigh its advantages. Under the circumstances, one feels inclined to agree with Humblé (2001: 65) that "for decoding purposes, bilingual dictionaries would be more suited if they had the same coverage as monolingual dictionaries". Should transfer play a role in idiom

---

[1] In part, this would constitute a follow-up to the study by MacFarquhar and Richards (1983). Although their intermediate and advanced subjects preferred definitions written in the defining vocabulary, it is unclear whether the proficiency level of advanced foreign students from Asia and the Pacific enrolled in courses at the English Language Institute at the University of Hawaii is comparable with that of English-majoring students at a Polish university.

interpretation (Irujo 1986a) (and learners search L2 definitions mainly for synonyms that would help them to arrive at equivalents), analogy, rather than analysis, sounds more of a key word in rendering idiom meaning, this approach being advocated, for example, by Lattey (1986). In the absence of an exact L1 match, it is naturally easier to exploit the closest near-equivalent and point out the differences than define the meaning of an unfamiliar idiom from scratch. Also, the analogy-based entry can be enriched by idiomatic "false friends" and cross references to existing synonyms, antonyms or reverses.

In conclusion, in the light of this study, comprehension of dictionary information and its active integration with the context deserves particular attention as a weak link in the chain of advanced learners' procedures directed at the retrieval of the writer-intended meaning. More tentative conclusions can be drawn concerning the features of the monolingual learner's dictionary that diminish its effectiveness for highly proficient students. As was suggested, the traditional analytical definition, which reduces meaning to a paraphrase, is likely to deplete the sense of an idiom. Moreover, defining vocabulary, introduced to stave off circularity and facilitate intermediate learners' access to language, might be too crude a tool for rendering the semantic subtleties of infrequent, specialised and complex items such as idioms. These observations, however, rest on too small a sample of dictionary material to be deemed definitive. A more systematic research, directed specifically at the comparison of the usefulness of, firstly, analogy-based idiom entries and, secondly, idiom entries written in a non-restricted vocabulary, with those from the monolingual learner's dictionary, would be a valuable extension and verification of the claims of this study.

References

Cited Dictionaries

CIDE = CAMBRIDGE INTERNATIONAL DICTIONARY OF ENGLISH. Ed. Paul Procter. Cambridge: Cambridge University Press 1995.

COBUILD2 = COLLINS COBUILD ENGLISH DICTIONARY. Ed. John M. Sinclair. London: HarperCollins Publishers ²1995 [¹1987 Ed. John M. Sinclair].

LDOCE1 = LONGMAN DICTIONARY OF CONTEMPORARY ENGLISH. Ed. Paul Procter. Harlow: Longman ¹1978.

LDOCE3 = LONGMAN DICTIONARY OF CONTEMPORARY ENGLISH. Ed. Della Summers. Harlow: Longman ³1995 [¹1978 Ed. Paul Procter]

MEDAL = MACMILLAN ENGLISH DICTIONARY FOR ADVANCED LEARNERS. Ed. Michael Rundell. Oxford: Macmillan Publishers 2002.

OALD5 = OXFORD ADVANCED LEARNER'S DICTIONARY OF CURRENT ENGLISH. Ed. Jonathan Crowther. Oxford: Oxford University Press (⁵1995) [¹1948 Comp. A. S. Hornby].

ODCIE = OXFORD DICTIONARY OF CURRENT IDIOMATIC ENGLISH. Vol. 2: Phrase, clause and sentence idioms. Eds. Anthony P Cowie/Ronald Mackin/Isabel R. McCaig. Oxford: Oxford University Press 1983.

Other Literature

Alexander, Richard J. (1978): *Fixed expressions in English: A linguistic, psycholinguistic, sociolinguistic and didactic study.* Trier: University of Trier.

– (1992a): "Fixed expressions, idioms and phraseology in recent English learner's dictionaries." – In: Hannu Tommola et al. (eds.) 1, 35–42.

– (1992b): "Fixed expressions, phraseology and language teaching: A sociosemiotic perspective." – *Zeitschrift für Anglistik und Amerikanistik* 3, 238–249.

– (1998): "Really spoilt for choice? Fixed expressions in learners' dictionaries of English." – In: Thierry Fontenelle et al. (eds.) 2, 535–543.

Alvar Ezquerra, Manuel (ed.) (1992): *Euralex'90 proceedings: Actes del IV Congreso International.* Barcelona: Biblograf/VOX.

Anderson, Peter/Richard C. Freebody (1981): "Vocabulary knowledge." – In: John T. Guthrie (ed.), 77–117.

Arnaud, Pierre J. L./Sandra J. Savignon (1997): "Rare words, complex lexical units and the advanced learner." – In: James Coady/Thomas Huckin (eds.), 157–173.

Atkins, B. T. Sue (ed.) (1998): *Using dictionaries: Studies of dictionary use by language learners and translators.* Tübingen: Niemeyer (Lexicographica. Series Maior 88).

Atkins, B. T. Sue/Krista Varantola (1998a): "Language learners using dictionaries: The final report on the EURALEX / AILA research project on dictionary use." – In: B. T. Sue Atkins (ed.), 21–81.

– (1998b): "Monitoring dictionary use." – In: B. T. Sue Atkins (ed.), 83–122.

Atwood, Margaret (1969): *The edible woman.* Toronto: McClelland – Bantam, Inc.

Bartlett, Frederic C. (1932; 1995): *Remembering: A study in experimental and social psychology.* Cambridge: Cambridge University Press.

Béjoint, Henri (1981): "The foreign student's use of monolingual English dictionaries: A study of language needs and reference skills." – *Applied Linguistics* 2, 207–222.

– (1994): *Tradition and innovation in modern English dictionaries.* Oxford: Clarendon Press.

Bensoussan, Marsha (1983): "Dictionaries and tests of EFL reading comprehension." – *ELT Journal* 37, 341–345.

Bensoussan, Marsha/Batia Laufer (1984): "Lexical guessing in context in EFL reading comprehension." – *Journal of Research in Reading* 7, 15–32.

Bensoussan, Marsha/Donald Sim/Razelle Weiss (1984): "The effect of dictionary usage on EFL test performance compared with student and teacher attitudes and expectations." – *Reading in a Foreign Language* 2, 262–276.

Bogaards, Paul (1996): "Dictionaries for learners of English." – *International Journal of Lexicography* 9, 277–320.

Braasch, Anna/Claus Povlsen (eds.) (2002): *Proceedings of the Tenth Euralex International Congress.* Copenhagen: Center for Sprogteknologi. 2 vols.

Cacciari, Cristina (1993): "The place of idioms in a literal and metaphorical world." – In: Cristina Cacciari/Patrizia Tabossi (eds.), 27–55.

Cacciari, Cristina/Sam Glucksberg (1991): "Understanding idiomatic expressions: The contribution of word meanings." – In: Greg B. Simpson (ed.), 217–240.

Cacciari, Cristina/Patrizia Tabossi (1988): "The comprehension of idioms." – *Journal of Memory and Language* 27, 668–683.

Cacciari, Cristina/Patrizia Tabossi (eds.) (1993): *Idioms: Processing, structure and interpretation.* Hillsdale, NJ: Lawrence Erlbaum Associates.

Carrell, Patricia L. (1983): "Three components of background knowledge in reading comprehension." – *Language Learning* 33, 183–205.

– (1988): "Some causes of text-boundedness and schema interference in ESL reading." – In: Patricia L. Carrell/Joanne Devine/David E. Eskey (eds.), 101–113.

Carrell, Patricia L./Joanne Devine/David E. Eskey (eds.) (1988): *Interactive approaches to second language reading.* Cambridge: Cambridge University Press.

Carrell, Patricia L./Joan C. Eisterhold (1988): "Schema theory and ESL reading pedagogy." – In: Patricia L. Carrell/Joanne Devine/David E. Eskey (eds.), 73–92.

Carter, Ronald (1987; [2]1998): *Vocabulary: Applied linguistic perspectives.* London: Routledge.

Carter, Ronald/Michael McCarthy (eds.) (1988): *Vocabulary and language teaching.* London and New York: Longman.

Chodkiewicz, Halina (2000): *Vocabulary acquisition from the written context: Inferring word meanings by Polish learners of English.* Lublin: Maria Curie-Skłodowska University Press.

Cignoni, Laura/Stephen Coffey (2000): "A corpus study of Italian proverbs: Implications for lexicographical description." – In: Ulrich Heid et al. (eds.), 2, 549–555.

Coady, James (1993): "Research on ESL/EFL vocabulary acquisition: Putting it in context." – In: Thomas Huckin/Margot Haynes/James Coady (eds.), 3–23.

Coady, James/Thomas Huckin (eds.) (1997): *Second language vocabulary acquisition: A rationale for pedagogy.* Cambridge: Cambridge University Press.

Coffey, Stephen (2001): "Disturbing the form-meaning nucleus of multiword units: Data and issues." – *Studi Italiani di Linguistica Teorica e Applicata* 30, 215–228.

Cowie, Anthony P. (ed.) (1998): *Phraseology: Theory, analysis and applications.* Oxford: Clarendon Press.

Craik, F./R. Lockhart (1972): "Levels of processing: A framework for memory research." – *Journal of Experimental Psychology* 104, 268–284.

Cronk, Brian C./Susan D. Lima/Wendy A. Schweigert (1993): "Idioms in sentences: Effects of frequency, literalness, and familiarity." – *Journal of Psycholinguistic Research* 22, 59–82.

Cronk, Brian C./Wendy A. Schweigert (1992): "The comprehension of idioms: The effects of familiarity, literalness, and usage." – *Applied Psycholinguistics* 13, 131–146.

Davis, James N. (1989): "Facilitating effects of marginal glosses on foreign language reading." – *Modern Language Journal* 73, 41–48.

Delabastita, Dirk (ed.) (1997): *Traductio. Essays on punning and translation.* Manchester: St. Jerome.

Diab, Turki (1990): *Pedagogical lexicography: A case study of Arab nurses as dictionary users.* Tübingen: Niemeyer (Lexicographica. Series Maior 31).

Eskey, David E. (1988): "Holding in the bottom: An interactive approach to the language problems of second language readers." – In: Patricia L. Carrell/Joanne Devine/David E. Eskey (eds.), 93–100.

Everaert, Martin/Erik-Jan van der Linden/André Schenk/Rob Schreuder (eds.) (1995): *Idioms: Structural and psychological perspectives*. Hillsdale, NJ: Lawrence Erlbaum Associates.

Fernando, Chitra (1978): "Towards a definition of idiom, its nature and function." – *Studies in Language* 2.3, 313–343.

– (1996): *Idioms and idiomaticity*. Oxford: Oxford University Press.

Finn, P. (1977–1978): "Word frequency, information theory, and cloze performance: A transfer feature theory of processing in reading." – *Reading Research Quarterly* 13, 508–537.

Flores d'Arcais, Giovanni B. (1993): "The comprehension and semantic interpretation of idioms." – In: Cristina Cacciari/Patrizia Tabossi (eds.), 79–98.

Fontenelle, Thierry/Philippe Hiligsmann/Archibald Michiels/André Moulin/Siegfried Theissen (eds.) (1998): *Actes EURALEX'98*. Liège: Universite de Liège. 2 vols.

Forrester, Michael A. (1995): "Tropic implicature and context in the comprehension of idiomatic phrases." – *Journal of Psycholinguistic Research* 24, 1–22.

Freebody, P./R. C. Anderson (1983): "Effects on text comprehension of differing propositions and locations of difficult vocabulary." – *Journal of Reading Behavior* 15, 19–39.

Gellerstam, Martin/Jerker Järborg/Sven-Göran Malmgren/Kerstin Norén/Lena Rogström/Catarina Röjder Papmehl (eds.) (1996): *EURALEX'96 proceedings: Papers submitted to the 7th EURALEX International Congress on Lexicography in Göteborg, Sweden*. Göteborg: Göteborg University. 2 vols.

Gibbs, Raymond W., Jr. (1985): "On the process of understanding idioms." – *Journal of Psycholinguistic Research* 14, 465–472.

– (1990): "Psycholinguistic studies on the conceptual basis of idiomaticity." – *Cognitive Linguistics* 1–4, 417–451.

– (1993): "Why idioms are not dead metaphors." – In: Cristina Cacciari/Patrizia Tabossi (eds.), 57–77.

– (1995): "Idiomaticity and human cognition." – In: Martin Everaert et al. (eds.), 97–116.

Gibbs, Raymond W., Jr./Dinara Beitel (1995): "What proverb understanding reveals about how people think." – *Psychological Bulletin* 118, 133–154.

Giora, Rachel (1999): "On the priority of salient meanings: Studies of literal and figurative language." – *Journal of Pragmatics* 31, 919–929.

Giora, Rachel/Ofer Fein (1999): "On understanding familiar and less-familiar figurative language." – *Journal of Pragmatics* 31, 1601–1618.

Gläser, Rosemarie (1998): "The stylistic potential of phraseological units in the light of genre analysis." – In: Anthony P. Cowie (ed.), 125–143.

Glucksberg, Sam (1991): "Beyond literal meanings: The psychology of allusion." – *Psychological Science* 2, 146–152.

– (1993): "Idiom meanings and allusional content." – In: Cristina Cacciari/Patrizia Tabossi (eds.), 3–26.

Goodman, Kenneth S. (1970): "Reading: A psycholinguistic guessing game." – In: Doris V. Gunderson (ed.), 107–119.

Götz, Dieter (1986): "Idioms and real texts." – *Arbeiten aus Anglistik und Amerikanistik* 11, 83–93.

Grabe, William (1988): "Reassessing the term 'interactive.'" – In: Patricia L. Carrell/Joanne Devine/David E. Eskey (eds.), 56–70.

Gunderson, Doris V. (ed.) (1970): *Language and reading. An interdisciplinary approach*. Washington, DC: Center for Applied Linguistics.

Guthrie, John T. (ed.) (1981): *Comprehension and teaching: Research reviews*. Newark, DE: International Reading Association.

Halevy, Rivka (1996): "Contextual modulation of lexical meaning." – In: Edda Weigand/Franz Hundsnurscher (eds.), 223–231.

Hartmann, Reinhard R. K. (2001): *Teaching and researching lexicography*. Harlow, England: Longman.

Hartmann, Reinhard R. K. (ed.) (1984): *LEXeter'83 proceedings: Papers from the International Conference on Lexicography at Exeter*. Tübingen: Niemeyer (Lexicographica. Series Maior 1).

Hartmann, Reinhard R. K./Gregory James (1998): *Dictionary of lexicography*. London: Routledge.

Hatherall, Glyn (1984): "Studying dictionary use: Some findings and proposals." – In: Reinhard R. K. Hartmann (ed.), 183–189.

Haynes, Margot (1993): "Patterns and perils of guessing in second language reading." – In: Thomas Huckin/Margot Haynes/James Coady (eds.), 46–64.

Heid, Ulrich/Stefan Evert/Egbert Lehmann/Christian Rohrer (eds.) (2000): *Proceedings of the Ninth EURALEX International Congress*. Stuttgart: Institut für Maschinelle Sprachverarbeitung, Universität Stuttgart. 2 vols.

Herbst, Thomas (1996): "On the way to the perfect learners' dictionary: A first comparison of OALD5, LDOCE3, COBUILD2 and CIDE." – *International Journal of Lexicography* 9, 321–357.

Herbst, Thomas/Kerstin Popp (eds.) (1999): *The perfect learners' dictionary (?)*. Tübingen: Niemeyer (Lexicographica. Series Maior 95).

Hobbs, John (1979): "Metaphor, metaphor schemata and selective inferencing", *Technical note no. 204 SRI International,* Menlo Park, CA.

Honeyfield, John (1977): "Word frequency and the importance of context in vocabulary learning." – *RELC Journal* 8, 35–42.

Hosenfeld, Carol (1977): "A preliminary investigation of the reading strategies of successful and nonsuccessful second language learners." – *System* 5, 110–123.

Howarth, Peter A. (1996): *Phraseology in English academic writing: Some implications for language learning and dictionary making*. Tübingen: Niemeyer (Lexicographica. Series Maior 75).

– (1998): "Phraseology and second language proficiency." – *Applied Linguistics* 19, 24–44.

Huckin, Thomas/Joel Bloch (1993): "Strategies for inferring word-meanings in context: A cognitive model." – In: Thomas Huckin/Margot Haynes/James Coady (eds.), 153–176.

Huckin, Thomas/Margot Haynes/James Coady (eds.) (1993): *Second language reading and vocabulary learning*. Norwood, NJ: Ablex.

Hudson, Jean (1998): *Perspectives on fixedness applied and theoretical*. Lund: Lund University Press (Lund Studies in English 94).

Hulstijn, Jan H. (1993): "When do foreign-language readers look up the meaning of unfamiliar words? The influence of task and learner variables." – *Modern Language Journal* 77, 139–147.

Hulstijn, Jan H./B. T. Sue Atkins (1998): "Empirical research on dictionary use in foreign-language learning: Survey and discussion." – In: B. T. Sue Atkins (ed.), 7–19.

Hulstijn, Jan H./Merel Hollander/Tine Greidanus (1996): "Incidental vocabulary learning by advanced foreign language students: The influence of marginal glosses, dictionary use, and reoccurrence of unknown words." – *Modern Language Journal* 80, 327–339.

Humblé, Philippe (2001): *Dictionaries and language learners*. Frankfurt am Main: Haag und Herchen.

Irujo, Suzanne (1986a): "Don't put your leg in your mouth: Transfer in the acquisition of idioms in a second language." – *TESOL Quarterly* 20, 287–304.

– (1986b): "A piece of cake: Learning and teaching idioms." – *ELT Journal* 40, 236–242.

Johnson-Laird, Philip N. (1993): "Foreword." – In: Cristina Cacciari/Patrizia Tabossi (eds.), vii–x.

Katz, Albert N./Cristina Cacciari/Raymond W. Gibbs, Jr./Mark Turner (eds.) (1998): *Figurative language and thought*. New York and Oxford: Oxford University Press.

Katz, Albert N./Mark Turner/Raymond W. Gibbs, Jr./Cristina Cacciari (1998): "Counterpoint commentary." – In: Albert N. Katz et al. (eds.), 158–192.

Knight, Susan (1994): "Dictionary use while reading: The effects on comprehension and vocabulary acquisition for students of different verbal abilities." – *Modern Language Journal* 78, 285–299.

Kövecses, Zoltan (1989): *Minimal and full definitions of meaning*. Duisburg: University of Duisburg.

Lakoff, George (1993): "The contemporary theory of metaphor." – In: Andrew Ortony (ed.), 202–251.

Lakoff, George/Mark Johnson (1980): *Metaphors we live by*. Chicago: Chicago University Press.

Lattey, Elsa (1986): "Pragmatic classification of idioms as an aid for the language learner." – *IRAL* 24: 217–233.

Laufer, Batia (1993): "The effect of dictionary definitions and examples on the use and comprehension of new L2 words." – *Cahiers de lexicologie* 63, 131–142.

– (1997): "The lexical plight in second language reading: Words you don't know, words you think you know, and words you can't guess." – In: James Coady/Thomas Huckin (eds.), 20–34.

Laufer, Batia/Donald D. Sim (1985): "Taking the easy way out: Non-use and misuse of clues in EFL reading." – *ELT Forum* 23, 7–10.

Leppihalme, Ritva (1997): *"Culture bumps": An empirical approach to the translation of allusions.* Clevedon, UK: Multilingual Matters (Topics in Translation 10).

Lew, Robert (2002a): "Questionnaires in dictionary use research: A reexamination." – In: Anna Braasch/Claus Povlsen (eds.) 1, 267–271.

– (2002b): "A study in the use of bilingual and monolingual dictionaries by Polish learners of English: A preliminary report." – In: Anna Braasch/Claus Povlsen (eds.) 2, 759–763.

Lewandowska-Tomaszczyk, Barbara (1983): "Convention and creativity in natural language." – *Studia Anglica Posnaniensia* 16, 97–105.

Li, Xiaolong (1988): "Effects of contextual cues on inferring and remembering meanings of new words." – *Applied Linguistics* 9, 402–413.

Liontas, John (2002): "Context and idiom understanding in second language." – *EUROSLA Yearbook* 2, 155–185.

McCarthy, Michael (1992): "English idioms in use." – *Revista Canaria de Estudios Ingleses* 25, 55–65.

McCreary, Don R./Fredric T. Dolezal (1999): "A study of dictionary use by ESL students in an American university." – *International Journal of Lexicography* 12, 107–145.

MacFarquhar, Peter D./Jack C. Richards (1983): "On dictionaries and definitions." – *RELC Journal* 14, 111–124.

McGlone, Matthew S./Sam Glucksberg/Cristina Cacciari (1994): "Semantic productivity and idiom comprehension." – *Discourse Processes* 17, 167–190.

McKeown, Margaret (1993): "Creating effective definitions for young word learners." – *Reading Research Quarterly* 28.1, 16–31.

Miller, George A./Patricia M. Gildea (1987): "How children learn words." – *Scientific American* 257, 94–99.

Mitchell, Evelyn (1983): *Search-do reading: Difficulties in using a dictionary.* Aberdeen: Aberdeen College of Education (Formative Assessment of Reading, Working Paper 21).

Mondria, Jan-Arjen/Marijke Wit-de Boer (1991): "The effects of contextual richness on the guessability and retention of words in a foreign language." – *Applied Linguistics* 12, 249–267.

Moon, Rosamund (1988): "'Time' and idioms." – In: Mary Snell-Hornby (ed.), 107–115.

– (1992): "'There is reason in the roasting of eggs': A consideration of fixed expressions in native-speaker dictionaries." – In: Hannu Tommola et al. (eds.) 2, 493–502.

– (1996): "Data, description, and idioms in corpus lexicography." – In: Martin Gellerstam et al. (eds.) 1, 245–256.

– (1998a): *Fixed expressions and idioms in English: A corpus-based approach.* Oxford: Clarendon Press.

– (1998b): "Frequencies and forms of phrasal lexemes in English." – In: Anthony P. Cowie (ed.), 79–100.

– (1999): "Needles and haystacks, idioms and corpora: Gaining insights into idioms, using corpus analysis." – In: Thomas Herbst/Kerstin Popp (eds.), 265–281.

– (2001): "The distribution of idioms in English." – *Studi Italiani di Linguistica Teorica e Applicata* 30, 229–241.

Müllich, Harald (1990): *'Die Definition ist blöd!' Herübersetzen mit dem einsprachigen Wörterbuch. Das französische und englische Lernerwörterbuch in der Hand der deutschen Schüler.* Tübingen: Niemeyer (Lexicographica. Series Maior 37).

Na, Liu/I. S. P. Nation (1985): "Factors affecting guessing vocabulary in context." – *RELC Journal* 16, 33–42.

Nation, Paul/James Coady (1988): "Vocabulary and reading." – In: Ronald Carter/Michael McCarthy (eds.), 97–110.

Nattinger, James (1988): "Some current trends in vocabulary teaching." – In: Ronald Carter/Michael McCarthy (eds.), 62–82.

Nerlich, Brigitte/David D. Clarke (2001): "Ambiguities we live by: Towards a pragmatics of polysemy." – *Journal of Pragmatics* 33, 1–20.

Nesi, Hilary (2000): *The use and abuse of EFL dictionaries: How learners of English as a Foreign Language read and interpret dictionary entries*. Tübingen: Niemeyer (Lexicographica. Series Maior 98).

Nesi, Hilary/Richard Haill (2002): "A study of dictionary use by international students at a British university." – *International Journal of Lexicography* 15, 277–305.

Nesi, Hilary/Paul Meara (1991): "How using dictionaries affects performance in multiple-choice EFL tests." – *Reading in a Foreign Language* 8, 631–643.

Neubach, Abigail/Andrew D. Cohen (1988): "Processing strategies and problems encountered in the use of dictionaries." – *Dictionaries* 10, 1–19.

Nippold, Marilyn A./Stephanie T. Martin (1989): "Idiom interpretation in isolation versus context: A developmental study with adolescents." – *Journal of Speech and Hearing Research* 32, 59–66.

Nippold, Marilyn A./Mishelle Rudzinski (1993): "Familiarity and transparency in idiom explanation: A developmental study of children and adolescents." – *Journal of Speech and Hearing Research* 36, 728–737.

Nippold, Marilyn A./Catherine L. Taylor (1995): "Idiom understanding in youth: Further examination of familiarity and transparency." – *Journal of Speech and Hearing Research* 38, 426–433.

Norrick, Neal R. (1985): *How proverbs mean: Semantic studies in English proverbs*. Berlin: Mouton.

Nuccorini, Stefania (1988): "The treatment of metaphorical and idiomatic expressions in learners' dictionaries." – In: Mary Snell-Hornby (ed.), 149–160.

– (1992): "Monitoring dictionary use." – In: Hannu Tommola et al. (eds.) 1, 98–102.

– (2001): "When a torch becomes a candle: Variation in phraseology." – *Studi Italiani di Linguistica Teorica e Applicata* 30, 193–198.

Omaggio, Alice C. (1986): *Proficiency-oriented instruction*. Boston: Heinle and Heinle.

Ortony, Andrew (ed.) (1979; ²1993): *Metaphor and thought*. Cambridge: Cambridge University Press.

Padron, Yolanda N./Hersholt C. Waxman (1988): "The effect of ESL students' perceptions of their cognitive strategies on reading achievement", in: *TESOL Quarterly* 22, 146–150.

Paretsky, S. (1987): *Bitter medicine*. London: Gollancz.

Piotrowski, Tadeusz (1994): *Z zagadnień leksykografii*. Warszawa: Wydawnictwo Naukowe PWN.

Popiel, Stephen J./Ken McRae (1988): "The figurative and literal senses of idioms, or all idioms are not used equally." – *Journal of Psycholinguistic Research* 17, 475–487.

Redfern, Walter (1997): "Traduction, puns, clichés, plagiat." – In: Dirk Delabastita (ed.), 261–269.

Samuels, S. Jay/Michael L. Kamil (1988): "Models of the reading process." – In: Patricia L. Carrell/Joanne Devine/David E. Eskey (eds.), 22–36.

Schatz, Elinore Kress/R. Scott Baldwin (1986): "Context clues are unreliable predictors of word meanings." – *Reading Research Quarterly* 21, 439–453.

Schmitt, Norbert/Michael McCarthy (eds.) (1997): *Vocabulary: Description, acquisition and pedagogy*. Cambridge: Cambridge University Press.

Scholfield, Phil (1982): "Using the English dictionary for comprehension." – *TESOL Quarterly* 16, 185–194.

– (1997): "Vocabulary reference works in foreign language learning." – In: Norbert Schmitt/Michael McCarthy (eds.), 279–302.

– (1999): "Dictionary use in reception." – *International Journal of Lexicography* 12, 13–34.

Schraw, Gregory/Woodrow Trathen/Ralph E. Reynolds/Richard T. Lapan (1988): "Preferences for idioms: Restrictions due to lexicalization and familiarity." – *Journal of Psycholinguistic Research* 17, 413–424.

Schweigert, Wendy A. (1991): "The muddy waters of idiom comprehension." – *Journal of Psycholinguistic Research* 20, 305–314.

Simpson, Greg B. (ed.) (1991): *Understanding word and sentence*. Amsterdam: North-Holland (Advances in Psychology 77).

Snell-Hornby, Mary (ed.) (1988): *ZüriLEX'86 Proceedings. Papers Read at the EURALEX International Congress*. Tübingen: Francke.

Stanovich, Keith E. (1980): "Towards an interactive-compensatory model of individual differences in the development of reading fluency." – *Reading Research Quarterly* 16, 32–71.

Statman, Stella (1987): "Obstacles to access: An investigation into the perceptual strategies of the non-native learner of English." – *System* 15, 289–301.

Stein, Mark J. (1993): "The healthy inadequacy of contextual definition." – In: Thomas Huckin/Margot Haynes/James Coady (eds.), 203–212.

Stoller, Fredricka L./William Grabe (1993): "Implications for L2 acquisition and instruction from L1 vocabulary research." – In: Thomas Huckin/Margot Haynes/James Coady (eds.), 24–45.

Stroop, John R. (1935): "Studies of interference in serial verbal reactions." – *Journal of Experimental Psychology* 18, 643–662.

Summers, Della (1988): "The role of dictionaries in language learning." – In: Ronald Carter/Michael McCarthy (eds.), 111–125.

Swaffar, Janet K. (1988): "Readers, texts, and second languages: The interactive processes." – *Modern Language Journal* 72, 123–149.

Swanepoel, Piet H. (1992): "Linguistic motivation and its lexicographical application." – In: Manuel Alvar Ezquerra (ed.), 291–314.

Teliya, Veronika/Natalya Bragina/Elena Oparina/Irina Sandomirskaya (1998): "Phraselogy as a language of culture: Its role in the representation of a collective mentality." – In: Anthony P. Cowie (ed.), 55–75.

Titone, Debra A./Cynthia M. Connine (1999): "On the compositional and noncompositional nature of idiomatic expressions." – *Journal of Pragmatics* 31, 1655–1674.

Tomaszczyk, Jerzy (1979): "Dictionaries: Users and uses." – *Glottodidactica* 12, 104–119.

Tommola, Hannu/Krista Varantola/Tarja Salmi-Tolonen/Jürgen Schopp (eds.) (1992): *Euralex'92 proceedings I-II: Papers submitted to the 5th EURALEX International Congress on Lexicography.* Tampere: Yliopisto. 2 vols.

Tono, Yukio (2001): *Research on dictionary use in the context of foreign language learning: Focus on reading comprehension.* Tübingen: Niemeyer (Lexicographica. Series Maior 106).

Van Parreren, Carel F./Carolien Schouten-van Parreren (1981): "Contextual guessing: A trainable reader strategy." – *System* 9, 235–241.

Veisbergs, Andrejs (1997): "The contextual use of idioms, wordplay, and translation." – In: Dirk Delabastita (ed.), 155–176.

Weigand, Edda/Franz Hundsnurscher (eds.) (1996): *Lexical structure and language use. Proceedings of the International Conference on Lexicology and Lexical Semantics, Münster, September 13-15, 1994.* Tübingen: Niemeyer.

West, Michael (1953): *A general service list of English words.* London: Longman.

Wierzbicka, Anna (1972): *Semantic primitives.* Frankfurt: Athenäum.

– (1999): *Język – umysł – kultura.* Warszawa: Wydawnictwo Naukowe PWN.

Wilde, Oscar (1983): *The importance of being Earnest.* Harlow, Essex: Longman. [First published 1899.]

Wingate, Ursula (2002): *The effectiveness of different learner dictionaries. An investigation into the use of dictionaries for reading comprehension by intermediate learners of German.* Tübingen: Niemeyer (Lexicographica. Series Maior 112).

Wittrock, M./C. Marks/M. Doctorow (1975): "Reading as a generative process." – *Journal of educational psychology* 67, 484–489.

Appendices

Appendix 1

A sample of 40 idiom entries in five learner's dictionaries

	LDOCE3	OALD5	COBUILD2	CIDE	MEDAL
1) at the drop of a hat	Used to say that you would do something immediately if you had the opportunity: I'd go to the Far East at the drop of a hat.	Without delay or hesitation or without good reason: You can't expect me to move my home at the drop of a hat.	If you say that you are ready to do something at the drop of a hat, you mean that you are willing to do it immediately, without hesitating. India is one part of the world I would go to at the drop of a hat. PHRASES PHR after v	She expected me to find the book for her at the drop of a hat (= unreasonably quickly)	Immediately or in a way that shows that you have no doubts about doing something.
2) blow hot and cold	To keep changing your attitude towards someone or something: I can't tell what he wants – he keeps blowing hot and cold.	(infml) to keep changing one's opinions about sth: He blows hot and cold about getting married.	If someone blows hot and cold, they keep changing their attitude towards something or someone, sometimes being very enthusiastic and at other times expressing no interest at all. The media, meanwhile, has blown hot and cold on the affair. PHRASES V inflects, Oft PHR on/ Over/about n	If a person blows hot and cold about something, they are very interested in it at one time, but soon after do not seem interested in it: He's been blowing hot and cold about the trip to Holland ever since I first suggested it.	To have positive and then negative opinions or feelings about something or someone again and again: The government has blown hot and cold on this bill, and we just don't know where they stand now.

	LDOCE3	OALD5	COBUILD2	CIDE	MEDAL
3) carry the can	BrE informal to be blamed or punished for something that is someone else's fault as well as your own: Why am I always left to carry the can?	(infml) to accept the responsibility or blame for something: He left the company and I had to carry the can for all his bad decisions.	If you have to carry the can, you have to take all the blame for something; used mainly in informal British English. We have a luxury restaurant and if people have a bad experience, we have to carry the can. PHRASES V inflects = take the rap	(Br infml) If you carry the can for something you take the blame for it: As usual, I was left to carry the can.	BrE informal to be the person considered responsible for something
4) twist/turn the knife	To say something that makes someone more upset about a subject they are already unhappy about	To make sb who is already suffering sufer even more	If you twist the knife or if you turn the knife in someone's wound, you do or say something to make an unpleasant situation they are in even more unpleasant. Even as Mrs Thatcher is fighting to survive fellow EC leaders have been turning the knife in her wounds... It is the turn of Latvia to twist the knife. V inflects	If you twist/turn the knife (in the wound), you make someone who is annoyed, anxious or upset feel even worse: Just to turn the knife a little, he told me he'd seen my old girlfriend with her new man.	To make a bad situation even worse.

	LDOCE3	OALD5	COBUILD2	CIDE	MEDAL
5) give sb the slip	Informal to manage to escape from someone who is chasing you: Bates gave the police the slip.	(infml) to escape or get away from sb who is following or chasing one: I managed to give him the slip by hiding behind a wall.	If you give sb the slip, you escape from them when they are following you or watching you; an informal expression He gave reporters the slip by leaving at midnight.	If you give someone the slip you escape from them: If you're not interested in a bloke you can always give him the slip in a bar as crowded as that.	To escape from someone who is following or chasing you.
6) be on your mettle	To be ready to try as hard as possible because your abilities are being tested: You have to be on your mettle in the oral exam.	Encouraged or forced to do one's best. The team will be on their mettle for the big match.	If you are on your mettle, you are ready to do something as well as you can, because you know that you are being tested or challenged The added competition keeps them on their mettle. PHRASE: V-link PHR, PHR after v	Both players were on their mettle (=playing as well as they could) in the final round.	----------- (show your mettle)

	LDOCE3	OALD5	COBUILD2	CIDE	MEDAL
7) find your feet	To get used to a new situation, especially one that is difficult at first: Matt's only been at the school two weeks and he hasn't found his feet yet.	To become able to act independently and confidently. I only recently joined the firm so I'm still finding my feet.	If you say that someone is finding their feet in a new situation, you mean that they are starting to feel confident and deal with things successfully I don't know anyone in England but I'm sure I will manage when I find my feet... Once he had found his feet he was able to deal with any problem. V inflects = cope	Did it take you long to find your feet (=become familiar with your new surroundings and be able to do things on your own with confidence) when you started your new job?	To become confident and feel that you know what to do in a new situation: It's bound to take a bit of time to find your feet.
8) fly by the seat of your pants	Informal to do something by guessing how to do it because you have very little knowledge or experience.	By the seat of one's pants – relying on instinct rather than careful thought or skill.	If you fly by the seat of your pants or do something by the seat of your pants, you use your instincts to tell you what to do in a new or difficult situation rather than following a plan or relying on equipment V inflects.	----------	(flying) by the seat of your pants – using only your judgement and skill when you are doing something new and you cannot rely on your previous experience: We started the business in 1996, and for the first couple of years we were flying by the seat of our pants.

	LDOCE3	OALD5	COBUILD2	CIDE	MEDAL
9) lead sb a (merry) dance	Informal to make someone feel worried and confused, especially because they do not know what you are going to do next: Once they were married, Gwen led her poor husband a hell of a dance.	To cause sb a lot of trouble, esp by making them follow from place to place.	If someone leads you a merry dance, they make you do things over a period of time which cause you problems and do not benefit you in any way; used in British English PHRASE: V inflects	(infml) to lead someone a (merry) chase/dance is to cause them a lot of trouble, esp. by getting them to do a lot of things that are not necessary.	BrE to treat someone badly over a period of time; for example by making them do things that are not necessary or by telling them things that are not true.
10) kick over the traces	To stop following the rules of a social group and do what you want	(of a person) to refuse suddenly to accept discipline or control from parents, etc.	----------	(dated) If someone kicks over the traces they behave badly and show no respect for authority: It was no wonder that soldiers who risked death every day tended to kick over the traces on their evenings off.	---------
11) go against the grain	If something that you have to do goes against the grain, you do not like doing it, because it is not what you would naturally do: It went against the grain for her to be so strict.	(be/go) against the grain – (to be) contrary to one's nature or instinct: It really goes against the grain to have to go into the office at weekends (i.e. I do not like it)	If you say that an idea or action goes against the grain, you mean that it is very difficult for you to accept it or do it, because it conflicts with your previous ideas, beliefs or principles. Privatisation goes against the grain of their principle of opposition to private ownership of industry. PHRASE: V inflects	(fig) It really goes against the grain for Sarah (=it is not typical of her and she does not like) to admit that she's wrong) (fig) These actions go against the grain (=principles) of the party.	To be completely different from what you feel is right, natural, or normal for you.

	LDOCE3	OALD5	COBUILD2	CIDE	MEDAL
12) have sb over a barrel	To put someone in a situation in which they are forced to accept or do what you want: The manager had us over a barrel – either we worked on a Saturday or we lost our jobs.	(Get/have sb) over a barrel (infml) (to put/have sb) in a position in which they must do what one wants them to do: Since we needed them to lend us money, they've got us over a barrel.	If someone has you over a barrel, they have put you in a difficult situation where you have little choice but do what they want you to do: an informal use. V inflects	(infml) If someone has you over a barrel they have put you in a very difficult situation in which you have no choice about what to do: She knows I need the work so she's got me over a barrel in terms of what she pays me.	Over a barrel informal If someone has you over a barrel, they know that you are in a difficult situation and that you will have to do what they want.
13) make no bones about (doing) sth	To not feel nervous or ashamed about doing or saying something: We made no bones about our commitment to Marxism.	To be frank about sth; to admit sth; not to hesitate to do sth: He made no bones about telling her husband she wanted a divorce.	If you make no bones about something, you talk openly about it, rather than trying to keep it a secret. Some of them make no bones about their political views. V inflects, Usu PHR about -ing	To make no bones about (doing) something is not to try to hide your feelings: He made no bones about his dissatisfaction with the sentence.	To talk about or do sth in a very open way without feeling ashamed or embarrassed: He makes no bones about the fact that he wants my job.
14) cramp sb's style	To prevent someone from doing something they want to do, especially by going with them when they do not want you: He left Helen in the ski lodge. He didn't want anyone cramping his style on the slopes.	(infml) to prevent sb from doing sth freely, or as well as they can: It cramps my style to have you watching over me all the time.	If someone or something cramps your style, their presence or existence restricts your behaviour in some way; an informal expression. Like more and more women, she believes wedlock would cramp her style. PHRASE: V inflects	To cramp someone's style means to limit what someone is able to do, esp. what they do for pleasure: Having his leg in plaster rather cramped his style on the dance floor.	To make someone feel that they cannot behave in the way they want

	LDOCE3	OALD5	COBUILD2	CIDE	MEDAL
15) cut your teeth on sth	To get your first experience of doing something by practising on something simple	To gain experience from something	If you say that someone cut their teeth doing a particular thing, at a particular time, or in a particular place, you mean they began their career and learned some of their skills doing that thing, at that time, or in that place ...Director John Glen, who cut his teeth on Bond movies... He cut his teeth in the sixties as director of Edinburgh's Traverse Theatre V inflects, PHR prep, PHR –ing	------------	To get your first experience in a particular job by doing something: Actors who cut their teeth on low-budget films.
16) Drive a wedge between	To do something that makes people disagree or start to dislike each other: Lisa's lies drove a wedge between the couple.	(sb and sb) to make people quarrel with or start disliking each other.	If someone drives a wedge between two people who are close, they cause ill feelings between them in order to weaken their relationship. I started to feel Toby was driving a wedge between us. PHRASES V inflects Usu PHR Between pl-n	(under drive) To drive a wedge between two people or two groups means to damage the good relationship that they have: It would be silly to let things which have happened in the past drive a wedge between us now.	To cause two people or groups to disagree or be unfriendly to one another, especially in order to gain an advantage for yourself.

	LDOCE3	OALD5	COBUILD2	CIDE	MEDAL
17) drop a clanger/brick	BrE to say something socially embarrassing	(Brit infml) to say or do sth that causes offence or embarrassment without realizing that it does.	If you say that you have dropped a clanger, you mean that you have done or said something stupid or embarrassing. PHRASE V and N inflect	To drop a brick/(Br also) a clanger is to do or say something which makes you feel embarrassed: I dropped a real clanger asking about her boyfriend – I had no idea they weren't going out any longer!	Clanger – Br informal an embarrassing mistake, especially while you are talking. To drop a clanger means to make an embarrassing mistake like this.
18) not see sb for dust	Br E informal If you do not see someone for dust, they leave a place very quickly in order to avoid something: Tell him it's his turn to pay for the drinks and you won't see him for dust	--------------------	--------------------	--------------------	You would not see sb for dust Br E informal Used for saying that someone would leave a place very quickly in order to avoid trouble or responsibility.
19) be out on your ear	Informal to be forced to leave a job, organisation etc. especially because you have done something wrong. You'd better start working harder, or you'll be out on your ear.	Suddenly dismissed, forced to leave, etc.	If someone says that you will be out on your ear, they mean that you will be thrown out or dismissed suddenly and unpleasantly. We never objected. We'd have been out on our ears looking for another job if we had. N inflects v-link PHR	(slang) One minute I was in a good job and the next I was out on my ear (= suddenly dismissed).	Informal to be suddenly removed from your job or your place in an organisation

	LDOCE3	OALD5	COBUILD2	CIDE	MEDAL
20) give sb the elbow	Br E informal to tell someone that you no longer like them or want them to work for you and that they should leave	Give sb/get the elbow – (to dismiss or reject sb/to be dismissed or rejected: She gave me the elbow when she started going out with Roger.	-----------------	(Br infml) If you give someone the elbow, you end your relationship with them: When she discovered what had happened, she soon gave him the elbow.	BrE informal to end your relationship with someone
21) sit on the fence	To avoid saying which side of an argument you support: The Liberals prefer to sit on the fence while the other parties fight it out.	To fail or refuse to decide between two proposals, courses of action, etc eg because one is afraid or does not want to offend sb.	If you sit on the fence, you avoid supporting a particular side in a discussion or argument. They are sitting on the fence and refusing to commit themselves... He's not afraid of making decisions and a man who never sits on the fence. V inflects	You can't sit on the fence (= delay making a decision) any longer – you have to make a decision.	Sit/be on the fence To refuse to support either side in an argument
22) send sb off with a flea in their ear	To talk angrily to someone, especially because they have done something you disapprove of	With a flea in one's ear – With severe and clearly expressed anger and disapproval from sb: He interrupted the board meeting and got sent away with a flea in his ear.	-----------------	(infml) You'll get a flea in your ear (= an annoying or angry remark) if you do that again.	BrE to criticize someone severely
23) flog sth to death	Esp Br E informal To repeat a story, complaint, idea etc so often that people become bored with it	(infml) to repeat sth so often or continue sth for so long that other people lose interest in it.	-----------------	(infml) That idea has been absolutely flogged to death (= has been repeated so often that it is no longer interesting).	Informal to talk about something so much that that no one else wants to hear any more about it.

	LDOCE3	OALD5	COBUILD2	CIDE	MEDAL
24) move the goalposts	Br E informal to change the rules, limits etc while someone is trying to do something, and make it more difficult for them	(Brit infml) to change the accepted conditions within which a particular matter is being discussed or a particular action taken.	If you accuse someone of moving the goalposts, you mean that they have changed the rules in a situation or an activity, especially to benefit themselves and to make the situation or activity harder for everyone else involved; used showing disapproval. They seem to move the goal posts every time I meet the conditions which are required. PHRASE V inflects PRAGMATICS	Under move (position) (Br and Aus infml) We'd almost signed the contract when the other guys moved the goalposts (= changed the conditions of the agreement) and said they wanted more money.	Move/shift the goalposts – to change the rules and make it difficult for people to achieve something or to know what to do.
25) get sb's goat	Spoken to make someone extremely annoyed: I'll tell you another thing that really got my goat.	(infml) to irritate or annoy sb greatly.	------------------	(infml) That sort of attitude really gets her goat/(Aus) gets (on) her goat (= annoys her greatly).	Informal – to annoy someone: It really gets my goat – the way she keeps interrupting all the time.
26) play gooseberry	Br E informal to be the unwanted third person who is with two people who are having a romantic relationship and want to be alone together	Gooseberry (Brit infml) – a third person present when two people (esp lovers) wish to be alone together: I didn't want to play gooseberry so I left them together.	------------------	Under play (ACT) (Br) To play a gooseberry (Am be a third wheel) is to be an unwanted third person who is present when two other people, esp. two lovers, want to be alone.	Be a gooseberry/play a gooseberry BrE informal to be with two people who love each other and would prefer to be alone together.

	LDOCE3	OALD5	COBUILD2	CIDE	MEDAL
27) kick sb upstairs	To move sb to a job that seems to be more important than their present one but actually means that they have less influence	(infml) to promote sb to a position that seems more important but in fact is less so.	------------------	If you say that someone has been kicked upstairs you mean that they have been moved to a job which although it seems better than the one they had, in fact has less power: In Britain important politicians are given a peerage and kicked upstairs to the House of Lords.	Under kick 1 (no cross refer from upstairs) Be kicked upstairs Informal to be given a job or position that seems more important but has less power.
28) put/throw a spanner in the works	BrE informal to unexpectedly do somethin that prevents a plan or process from continuing or succeeding: He won't lend us the money? Well, that really puts a spanner in the works.	(throw) a spanner in the works (Brit infml) (to cause) a delay or problem in a plan, process, etc.	In British English, if someone throws a spanner in the works, they prevent something happening smoothly in the way that it was planned, by causing a problem or difficulty. The American expression is to throw a wrench or throw a monkey wrench into something. A bad result is sure to throw a spanner in the works. PHRASE: V inflects	(Br and Aus) To put/throw a spanner in the works (Am throw a (monkey) wrench in something) is to be the cause of spoiling a plan: The train strike has really thrown a spanner in the works – we'll never be able to deliver the goods on time now.	Br informal – to do something that suddenly stops a process or plan

	LDOCE3	OALD5	COBUILD2	CIDE	MEDAL
29) not cut the mustard	To not be good enough for a particular job: He'll never cut the mustard as a manager.	--------------------	If someone does not cut the mustard, their work or their performance is not as good as it should be or as good as it is expected to be; an informal expression. PHRASES V inflects Usu with neg PRAGMATICS	Under cut (deal with) – Cut it/cut the mustard Am to be able to deal with problems or difficulties satisfactorily. If he can't cut it, then we'll get someone else to do the job.	[usually in negatives] informal to reach the expected or necessary standard: He just can't cut the mustard any more.
30) the thin end of the wedge	Esp Br E spoken An expression meaning something that you think is the beginning of a harmful development: These job cuts are just the thin end of the wedge.	(esp Brit) an event, an action or a demand that seems unimportant but is likely to lead to others that are much more important or serious: Newspaper editors regard the government's intention to regulate the press as the thin end of the wedge.	If you say that something is the thin end of the wedge, you mean that it appears to be unimportant at the moment, but that it is the beginning of a harmful development. I think it's the thin end of the wedge when you have armed police permanently on patrol round a city. v-link PHR, PHR after v	Under thin (not thick) no cross-references (Br) It's the thin end of the wedge means that something bad can be started by something quite small: Identity cards for football supporters could be the thin end of the wedge – soon everyone might have to carry identification.	Something that is not important by itself but will have serious, usually bad, effects in the future
31) born on the wrong side of the blanket	Humorous to have parents who were not married when you were born	Dated Br euph Born from parents who were not married to each other; ILLEGITI-MATE	--------------------	--------------------	-------------------

	LDOCE3	OALD5	COBUILD2	CIDE	MEDAL
32) keep the wolf from the door	To earn just enough money to buy the basic things you need: Between us, we earn just enough to keep the wolf from the door.	To have enough money to avoid hunger and need: I earn enough to keep the wolf from the door.	If you keep the wolf from the door, you succeed in providing food and other necessary things for yourself or your family; an informal expression. A lot of the lads took small jobs to help keep the wolf from the door.	If you keep the wolf from the door, you have just enough money to be able to eat and live: As a student, he took an evening job to keep the wolf from the door.	To manage to earn enough money to buy food and other essential thing.
33) keep one's eyes peeled/skinned /open	Spoken to watch carefully for something Keep your eyes peeled for a campsite.	To watch constantly and carefully; to be very careful to notice sb/sth: She walked along slowly, keeping her eyes peeled/skinned for any unusual flowers.	If you tell someone to keep their eyes peeled for something, you are telling them to watch very carefully for it; an informal expression.	(infml) If you keep an/your eye out for something, or if you keep your eyes open/peeled (Br) skinned for something, you look for it: When you're shopping, keep your eye out for something we can give John as a birthday present.	To keep looking for something that you hope to find: Keep your eyes open for a petrol station. -- (used for telling someone to look carefully so that they notice someone or something.)
34) butter would not melt in one's mouth	Used to say that someone seems to be very kind and sincere but is not really	To appear innocent, kind, gentle, etc although one is probably not	------------------	Tommy looked as if butter wouldn't melt in his mouth (= he looked as if he would never do anything wrong, although you feel certain he would).	Used for saying that although someone looks as if they are not capable of doing bad things, they are in fact capable of doing them.

	LDOCE3	OALD5	COBUILD2	CIDE	MEDAL
35) make hay while the sun shines	Do something while the conditions are favourable	(saying) to make good use of opportunities, favourable conditions, etc while they last.	If you say that someone is making hay or is making hay while the sun shines, you mean that they are taking advantage of a situation that is favourable to them while they have the chance to. We shared a prescience of the coming war, and were determined to make hay while we could.	If you make hay while the sun shines you make good use of an opportunity.	To do something while a situation allows you to, because the situation may not last very long
36) bark up the wrong tree	Informal to have a wrong idea, especially about how to get a particular result: You're barking up the wrong tree if you think Sam can help you.	(esp in the continuous tenses) to pursue a course of action or line of thought that is wrongly directed: If you think that, you're barking up the wrong tree altogether.	If you say that someone is barking up the wrong tree, you mean that they are following the wrong course of action because their beliefs or ideas about something are incorrect; an informal expression. Scientists in Switzerland realised that most other researchers had been barking up the wrong tree.	(infml) If you are barking up the wrong tree, you are wrong about something, or you will not be successful in what you are trying to achieve: Chris suspects Mark of stealing her watch, but I reckon she's barking up the wrong tree. I think the researchers are barking up the wrong tree.	Informal doing something that will not get the result you want

	LDOCE3	OALD5	COBUILD2	CIDE	MEDAL
37) live by one's wits	To get money by being clever or dishonest, and not by doing an ordinary job	To earn money by clever and sometimes dishonest means	-------------------	Someone who lives by/on their wits makes money by deceiving people rather than by working honestly.	To have no real job but make the money you need by being clever or dishonest - to be very poor but manage to get the things you need to live by being very clever
38) laugh on the other side of one's face	-------------------	(infml) to be forced to change from feeling joy or satisfaction to disappointment, annoyance or regret: He'll be laughing on the other side of his face when he reads this letter.	-------------------	If someone laughs on the other side of their face/(Am also) laughs out of the other side of their mouth they were pleased at first but now they are upset or disappointed, esp. because something does not happen as they planned: She's pleased with her promotion but she'll be laughing on the other side of her face when she sees the extra work.	Spoken used for telling someone that something is going to happen to stop them feeling so happy about a situation

	LDOCE3	OALD5	COBUILD2	CIDE	MEDAL
39) not have a leg to stand on	Informal to be in a situation where you cannot prove or legally support what you say: If you didn't sign a contract, you won't have a leg to stand on.	(infml) to have nothing to support one's opinion or justify one's actions.	If you say that someone does not have a leg to stand on, or hasn't got a leg to stand on, you mean that a statement or claim they have made cannot be justified or proved; an informal expression. It's only my word against his, I know. So I don't have a leg to stand on.	This leaves us without a leg to stand on/We haven't got a leg to stand on (= we have no good arguments to support our case).	Informal to not have any way of proving that you are right about something
40) play/be devil's advocate	To pretend that you disagree with something so that there will be a discussion about it	Devil's advocate – a person who speaks against sb/sth simply to encourage discussion or to make sb justify a view or an argument: Play devil's advocate	If you say that you are playing devil's advocate in a discussion or debate, you mean that you are expressing an opinion which you do not agree with in order to make the argument more interesting. If you say that someone else is playing devil's advocate, you mean that you disapprove of them because they are pretending to hold an unpopular opinion in order to make an argument more interesting.	In an argument or discussion, a devil's advocate is a person who supports an unpopular or opposite argument in order to make people think seriously about the matter, and question the truth of the most widely held belief: Joe didn't really believe the things he was saying in the meeting, he was just playing devil's advocate.	To pretend to disagree with someone in order to start an argument or interesting discussion.

Appendix 2

Pragmatic information in the idiom entry in five learner's dictionaries

1) drag one's feet	LDOCE3 informal to take too much time to do something because you do not want to do it: The authorities are dragging their feet over banning cigarette advertising. OALD5 to be deliberately slow in doing sth or in making a decision: I want to sell the house, but my husband is dragging his feet. COBUILD2 If you drag your feet or drag your heels, you delay doing something or do it very slowly because you do not want to do it. The government, he claimed, was dragging his feet, and this was definitely threatening moves towards peace. CIDE If you drag your heels/feet, you do something slowly because you do not want to do it: I suspect the government is dragging its heels over this issue. MEDAL to do something very slowly because you do not really want to do it
2) you can't have your cake and eat it	LDOCE3 spoken used to tell someone that that they cannot have the advantage of something without its disadvantages OALD5 (infml) (usu in negative sentences) to enjoy the benefits from two different courses of action, etc when only one or the other is possible: He wants a regular income but doesn't want to work. He can't have his cake and eat it! COBUILD2 If you think that someone wants the benefits of doing two things when it is only reasonable to expect the benefits of doing one, you can say that they want to have their cake and eat it; used showing disapproval. What he wants is a switch to market economy in a way which does not reduce people's standard of living. To many this sounds like wanting to have his cake and eat it. PRAGMATICS. CIDE To have more local services but also to pay less tax is to want to have your cake and eat it (=have/do two things that it is impossible to have/do together). MEDAL to have all the benefits of a situation when, in fact, having one thing means that you cannot have the other: He wants to stay with his wife but still see his girlfriend – talk about having your cake and eating it!
3) make a mountain out of a molehill	LDOCE3 to treat a problem as if it was very serious when in fact it is not OALD5 (derog) to make a very unimportant matter seem important COBUILD2 If you say that someone is making a mountain out of a molehill, you are critical of them for making an unimportant fact or difficulty seem like a serious one. The British press, making a mountain out of a molehill, precipitated an unnecessary economic crisis. PRAGMATICS CIDE I think you're making a mountain out of a molehill (= making something unimportant seem important). MEDAL to treat a minor problem as if it were a very serious problem

116

4) wash one's hands of sth	LDOCE3 to refuse to be responsible for something anymore: I've washed my hands of the whole affair. OALD5 to refuse to be responsible for or involved with sb/sth: I've washed my hands of the whole sordid business. COBUILD2 If you wash your hands of someone or something, you refuse to be involved with them any more or to take responsibility for them. He seems to have washed his hands of the job. CIDE If you wash your hands of something that you were previously responsible for, you intentionally stop being involved in or connected with it in any way: She couldn't wait to wash her hands of the whole project. MEDAL to say or show that you do not want to be involved with someone or something and that you are not responsible for them: I've decided to wash my hands of her.
5) put the cart before the horse	LDOCE3 to do things in the wrong order OALD5 to put things in the wrong order, eg by saying that sth is the cause of an event when it is really the result of what happened. COBUILD2 If you say that someone is putting the cart before the horse, you mean that they are doing things in the wrong order; an informal expression. This puts the cart before the horse; elections should follow, not precede, agreement on a constitution. CIDE Aren't you putting the cart before the horse (= doing things in the wrong order) by deciding what to wear for the wedding before you've even been invited to it? MEDAL to do one thing before another thing that you should have done first.
6) scrape the bottom of the barrel	LDOCE3 Informal to have to use something even though it is not very good because there is nothing better available OALD5 to use the worst items or people because they are the only ones available: It's really scraping the barrel when you have to bring players out of retirement to make up a team. COBUILD2 If you say that someone is scraping the barrel, or scraping the bottom of the barrel, you disapprove of the fact that they are using or doing something of extremely poor quality; an informal use. PRAGMATICS CIDE To scrape (the bottom of) the barrel is to use the worst people or things because that is all that is available: Richard's in the team? – You really are scraping the barrel! MEDAL informal to use or do something that you know is not very good, because you do not have anything better
7) wash dirty linen in public	LDOCE3 to discuss something unpleasant or embarrassing in public OALD5 (derog) to discuss or argue about one's personal affairs in public. COBUILD2 In British English, if you say that someone washes their dirty linen in public, you disapprove of them discussing or arguing about unpleasant or private things in front of other people. The usual American expression is wash your dirty laundry in public. The spectacle of the former naval officers washing their dirty linen in public was distinctly embarrassing... We shouldn't wash our dirty laundry in public and if I was in his position, I'd say nothing at all. PRAGMATICS CIDE (disapproving) People who wash their dirty linen in public discuss or allow to be discussed in public, matters which should be kept private. MEDAL to discuss private subjects or problems in public: Washing football's dirty linen in public does nothing for the game.

8) put all one's eggs into one basket	LDOCE3 to depend completely on one thing or one course of action in order to get success OALD5 to risk everything one has on the success of one plan, eg by putting all one's money into one business. COBUILD2 If someone puts all their eggs in one basket, they put all their effort or resources into doing one thing so that, if it fails, they have no alternatives left. The key word here is diversify; don't put all your eggs in one basket. CIDE (infml) If you put all your eggs in one basket, you depend on a single plan of action or person for success: I'm applying for several jobs because I don't really want to put all my eggs in one basket. MEDAL to depend completely on just one idea, plan, or person so that you have no other possibilities if things go wrong
9) fan the flames of sth	LDOCE3 fan 2. To make someone feel an emotion more strongly ... | fan the flames A pro-vocative article in The People's Daily only served to fan the flames of rebellion. OALD5 to make emotions, etc stronger or activity more intense: Her wild behaviour merely fanned the flames of his jealousy. COBUILD2 If someone or something fans the flames of a situation or feeling, usually a bad one, they make it more intense or extreme in some way. He accused the Tories of 'fanning the flames of extremism'. CIDE In the 1960s his speeches fanned the flames of racial tension (= made it worse). MEDAL fan 3. Formal to make a feeling or belief stronger... ♦fan the flames of sth a speech which fanned the flames of hatred
10) rock the boat	LDOCE3 informal to cause problems for other members of a group by criticising something or trying to change the way something is done: A lot of people didn't really agree with the policy, but they didn't want to rock the boat. OALD5 (infml) to do sth that upsets a delicate situation and causes difficulties: Things are progressing well – please don't (do anything to) rock the boat. COBUILD2 If you say that someone is rocking the boat, you mean that they are upsetting a calm situation and causing trouble. I said I didn't want to rock the boat in any way. CIDE (infml) If you rock the boat, you do or say something that will upset people or cause problems: A small number of MPs are determined to speak out against the bill, even if this means rocking the boat. MEDAL informal to cause problems by changing a situation that is considered satisfactory: I realise I'm new here and I don't want to rock the boat.

Appendix 3

Texts used in the experiment

1) Sting, as a songwriter, had been signed to Virgin by the head of the publishing division, Carol Wilson. It was Wilson who had "discovered" the singer as an unknown in his native Newcastle... Under her direction, and with Virgin money, Sting had recorded a series of demos which had led to his association with the Police, a recording contract with A&M and, ultimately, the hit parade. The arrangement Sting had signed with Virgin had been for a 50-50 split, rising to 60-40 in Sting's favour after two years. It was a standard contract for an unknown songwriter, but as the Police began to enjoy enormous success, so Sting's value in the market-place rose... Sting and Carol Wilson had remained friends throughout the negotiations. In fact it was she who had advised him to get a second opinion on the matter from a lawyer... For Wilson, *Sting's success,* and the prodigious royalties it had earned for Virgin, *was merely one feather in an increasingly crowded cap.*

British National Corpus World Edition. Source description: Text id FNX; Richard Branson: the inside story. Brown, M, Headline Book Publishing plc, London (1989), 157–303. Sample containing about 42225 words from a book (domain: applied science).

Native speakers' interpretation:

It was just one more honor among the many successes she had already achieved.

Sting's high ratings was only one of many lucrative contracts.

Sting's success was for Wilson only one more accomplishment in a host of successes.

2) In their dispute with Iran the British set out to close off all outlets for Iranian oil. American oil companies (fearful of the knock-on effects to themselves in the Middle East if Iranian radicals were seen to succeed) proved more enthusiastic allies than the State Department. The British, however, remained suspicious of American motives, and resentful of their advice. Eden's private secretary, Shuckburgh, thought it "very offensive" when, following an unsatisfactory meeting on Anglo-American policy towards Iran, he was told by Acheson that the British had to learn to live in the world as it was. Yet Acheson's remarks were hardly surprising when his department was receiving so many reports of the strength of Arab feeling against the British. By 1952 he was becoming all the more determined that *the United States should not be tarred with the colonial brush.*

British National Corpus World Edition. Source description: Text id HY8; The special relationship. Bartlett, C J, Longman Group UK Ltd, Harlow (1992), 1–124. Sample containing about 46090 words from a book (domain: world affairs).

Native speakers' interpretation:

The U.S. [as a former colony] should not be accused of colonialism.

The U.S. should not be tainted by accusations of being imperialistic.

The U.S. should not be identified as having the same outlook on the world as the colonizing countries.

3) ...However, this remarkable literary work -- even given an army of fans as keen as his niece -- would not have brought in very much income, nor would the journalism, and it was to be assumed the trust provided the rest. What he was also wondering was whether Harriet had received any letters of the kind received by Tom Fearon and if so, whether she had kept them? But he had little reason yet to ask for a search warrant and *Mr Simpson would* go purple in the face and *throw every legal book in his considerable library at him* if he so much as tried. But it would be worth making contact with Miss Frances Needham-Burrell when she arrived and asking her -- when sorting out her cousin's effects -- to keep an eye open for letters with a threatening or abusive content.

British National Corpus World Edition. Source description: Text id CEB; A season for murder. Granger, Ann, Headline Book Publishing plc, London (1991), 21–134. Sample containing about 37282 words from a book (domain: imaginative).
Native speakers' interpretation:
Mr Simpson, who had much experience in litigation, would introduce every legal obstacle he could.
Mr Simpson would fly into a rage and oppose him on all legal grounds.
Mr Simpson would try every legal challenge possible and he had a lot of options open to him

4) I can clearly remember that night, the hush that fell over the audience after the first song. They were amazed at this big, big voice coming out of this tiny girl. By this time, Sinead had already linked up with Farelly in Dublin... Record company talent scouts in Dublin had already expressed an interest in her, but not the rest of the band. Today ex-manager Farelly claims he is not bitter about the split but says he is annoyed about the things Sinead has said about that period: "The only thing that rankles me is what she says about Ireland. She's rewritten her own biography, and is very touchy about her past". *He wants Sinead to put her commitment where her mouth is.* She could be such a positive force for the organisations she purports to feel for, such as CARE, a charity for abused children.
British National Corpus World Edition. Source description: Text id CEK; Today, News Group Newspapers Ltd., London (1992–12). Sample containing about 124295 words from a periodical (domain: social science).
Native speakers' interpretation:
He wants Sinead to take positive action on behalf of the causes that she speaks about.
He wants Sinead to show where she stands by actions and not mere words.
He wants Sinead to do something about the causes that she professes, not merely talk about them.

5) Lee Rothstein, director of Southport, Connecticut-based market research firm New Science Associates Inc's advanced network computing service, takes umbrage with a lot of current thinking on open systems. He says that much of his firm's research showed, at an early stage, that open systems concepts "weren't going to cut it"; moreover, that many "were a myth". In theory, guidelines for open systems are formulated when a committee of vendors come to some sort of agreement over architectural definitions and create a standard. "However, in reality, *each vendor has its own technological axe to grind* and the results miss the mark", says Rothstein. The committees "never get to the leading edge because large companies usually don't understand new technology, so they drag their feet on the committees until they are able to catch up."
British National Corpus World Edition. Source description: Text id CTM; Unigram x. APT Data Services Ltd. (1993-04/1993-05). Sample containing about 8042 words from a periodical (domain: applied science).
Native speakers' interpretation:
Each vendor is interested in promoting its own type of technology.
Each sales agent has his/her own personal motive in promoting a particular product.
Each seller wants to promote the advantages of its own open system, especially the specific technology that it incorporates.

120

Appendix 4

Task booklet[1]

A1 ....No ....
Read carefully each text (they all come from different sources) and write English or Polish para-
phrases of the underlined fragments in the space provided. You may disregard the formal accuracy
(i.e., spelling, grammar) of your paraphrases.
Text 1)
Text 2)
Text 3)
Text 4)
Text 5)

***

A2 ....No ....
Write the idiomatic expressions that appear in the underlined fragments. State your familiarity of the
idiom before this test by circling one of the numbers 1–5: 1 – very well known, 2 – well known, 3 –
vaguely familiar, 4 – rather unfamiliar, 5 – completely unfamiliar.
Text 1)
Text 2)
Text 3)
Text 4)
Text 5)
1..1 - 2 - 3 - 4 - 5
2..1 - 2 - 3 - 4 - 5
3..1 - 2 - 3 - 4 - 5
4..1 - 2 - 3 - 4 - 5
5..1 - 2 - 3 - 4 - 5

***

A3 ....No ....
Use the cues to build idiomatic expressions; if necessary, add articles, prepositions or other missing
words. Then define the idiom (in English or in Polish). You may disregard the formal accuracy (i.e.,
spelling, grammar) of your definitions.
1.   feather, cap
idiom: ....
definition: ....
2.   tar, brush
idiom: ....
definition: ....
3.   book, throw
idiom: ....
definition: ....
4.   put, mouth
idiom: ....
definition: ....
5.   axe, grind
idiom: ....
definition: ....

---

[1] The original Polish instructions have not been provided here so as to economise on space.

***

B1 ....No.......
Read carefully each text (they all come from different sources) and circle any words/phrases that you
would like to look up in the dictionary. Then write English or Polish paraphrases of the underlined
fragments in the space provided. You may disregard the formal accuracy (i.e., spelling, grammar) of
your paraphrases.

Text 1)
Text 2)
Text 3)
Text 4)
Text 5)

***

B2 ....No ....
You may consult the dictionary now if you wish. Register every consultation in the table: what you
are looking for, under which headword, whether you have found the desired information. If you think
your first paraphrase is faulty, there is space for corrections under the table. (Please do not add anything to the first part of the test.)

	Word/phrase looked up	Headword looked up	Information		
			Present	Partly Present	Absent
1					
2					
3					

Possible changes in the paraphrases:
1. ....
2. ....
3. ....
4. ....
5. ....

Please circle one option that is true in your case:
1.At home I use   a) the same   b) a different   dictionary.
Point 2 concerns people who have circled 1b.
2.Using the dictionary other than my own made arriving at the desired information
a) extremely   b) rather   c) slightly   d) not at all   difficult.

***

B3 ....No......
Fill in the table with the idioms that appear in the underlined fragments. Tick (√) the appropriate
column.

Text 1)
Text 2)
Text 3)
Text 4)
Text 5)

Idiom	I knew the idiom so I did not look it up.	I knew the idiom but I looked it up.	I didn't know the idiom so I looked it up.	I didn't know the idiom but I did not look it up.

***

B4 ....No......

Use the cues to build idiomatic expressions; if necessary, add articles, prepositions, and other missing words. State your familiarity of the idioms before this test by circling one of the numbers 1–5: 1 – very well known, 2 – well known, 3 – vaguely familiar, 4 – rather unfamiliar, 5 – completely unfamiliar. Then define the idiom (in English or in Polish). You may disregard the formal accuracy (i.e., spelling, grammar) of your definition.

1.   feather, cap
idiom: ....1 - 2 - 3 - 4 - 5
definition: ....
2.   tar, brush
idiom: ....1 - 2 - 3 - 4 - 5
definition: ....
3.   book, throw
idiom: ....1 - 2 - 3 - 4 - 5
definition: ....
4.   put, mouth
idiom: ....1 - 2 - 3 - 4 - 5
definition: ....
5.   axe, grind
idiom: ....1 - 2 - 3 - 4 - 5
definition: ....

Thank you for your cooperation,
Renata Szczepaniak

Appendix 5

Paraphrases in Group A and B (before and after consultation)

Paraphrase 1 A

1. Sting was one of many successful artists.
2. Fame he achieved (his world-wide fame) was one of the things he was proud of
3. Sting was only one of many artists signed to Virgin (who) that were successful (and the number of such artists was growing).
4. Sting's success was only one of the contributions Wilson made for Virgin.
5. Sukces Stinga był jedynie małą częścią powiększającego się źródła dochodów.
6. Sukces, który odniósł Sting był jednym z licznych dokonań
7. Sukces Stinga był kolejnym udanym przedsięwzięciem w jej karierze.
8. Sukces osiągnięty przez Stinga był jedynie małą częścią całego dorobku C. Wilson.
9. Sukces Stinga był jedynie kroplą w rosnącym morzu.
10. Sting's success was just the begining of something bigger.
11. Sting's success was only one of many examples of success
12. Success of Sting was only one small thing, a part of great number of many other needed successes
13. The underlined text says that for Virgin Sting's success was just a drop in the bucket. Carol was also popular (probably because of Sting) as a head of publishing division and she promoted other pop stars too.
14. For Wilson, Sting's success was just a one minor success among many others. Wilson's account of succes was becoming bigger and bigger.
15. Osiągnięcie Stinga było zaledwie jednym spośród wielu sukcesów.
16. Sting's achievement was just few among many
17. His success was one of the many issues, matters the Virgin was dealing with
18. For Carol Wilson Sting's career was just another success in the music industry – it meant less to her than it meant for the artist (Sting) himself.
19. Sting's success was only one of many successful results she knew (for her it wasn't as important as for him)
20. Sting becoming famous and rich he was not much with comparison to the crowded show-business.
21. Wilson mógł wliczyć sukces Stinga w rosnącą liczbę swoich sukcesów.
22. The fact that Sting achieved success was at best only one element of a still growing company.
23. Even though Sting's success contributed to Virgin budget, it wasn't that beneficial for the company as many other singers earned a lot of money for Virgin.
24. Sting was only one of many, who Virgin earned money on.
25. Sting's success was one of many more on the music market.
26. Sukces Stinga był jednym z wielu, do których przyczyniła się Wilson.; był tylko jednym z wielu w nieustannie powiększającym się...
27. This success was only one out of many many more she had had.
28. Sting' success was just one of the many that Virgin had.
29. Sting's becoming successful was only the tip of an iceberg.
30. Sting being successful was just a small part of the booming business.
31. The success Sting achieved was just one of the many successes that Wilson contributed to.
32. Sting's achievement was only one of Sting's numerous successes.
33. Sukces Stinga to jeden z wielu, które nagromadziły się przez lata.
34. Sting was one of many people who succeeded.
35. Sting's success was only one of many , which Wilson has ever contributed to.

36. Sting's achievement was just a begining.
37. growing popularity of Sting was one of many successful contracts with other artists.
38. Sting's success was only one exception among many singers on the market.
39. Sting was only one of many artists who wanted to negotiate better contract conditions.
40. Sting had become popular and his popularity was only a small beginning step in his further career.
41. Sting's success was one of many among other artists signed to Virgin
42. ----------------------------
43. Wzrost popularności Stinga był dopiero początkiem jego dalszych osiągnięć.
44. one case of many
45. Sukces Stinga był jednym piórkiem w rosnącej zatłoczonej czapce.
46. his contribution to the income of the firm was not substantial (he was merely an element of the bigger body)
47. Sting was not the only artist working for the Virgin who was successful and brought the company good name and fortune.
48. Sting was only one out of many artists who provided Virgin with income coming from their successful career.
49. The success achieved by Sting was not an isolated phenomenon in Wilson's company; in fact, it was one among myriad others.
50. Sukces Stinga był jednym z wielu, które miały nadejść.
51. Sting's success was only one many.
52. Sting's triumph was only one stage of a very long distance (był jednym etapem długiej drogi)
53. The revenue that Wilson had from Sting's success was only a part of the huge fortune that she could gain from the music business.
54. Sukces Stinga był tylko kroplą w morzu dla Virgin (w porównaniu do ich całkowitych obrotów i ilości ludzi, którzy dla nich pracowali)
55. Sting was just one of many singers whose success brought income to Virgin label.
56. Sting was just one of the many successful to-be performers (and the number of them constantly rose) that Virgin had taken under their wing
57. Sting's success was just one out of many Virgin experienced. Virgin had a lot of successful artists, artists they promoted, who brought them money.
58. Sting's success was rather insignificant in view of what was to come.
59. Sukces Stinga był jedynie zapowiedzią "tłustych lat" dla Virgin.
60. Sting was one of many talented people signed to Virgin who could bring lucrative profits.
61. Sukces Stinga był zaledwie małą drobiną w coraz bardziej powiększającej się grupie osób, z którymi podpisywała kontrakty.
62. His success was only small percentage of what she eventually gained.
63. Carol Wilson depreciated Sting's success and said it was only a small sum of money.
64. Sukces, który odniósł Sting był zaledwie początkiem jego przyszłej kariery.
65. Sukces Stinga był tylko/zaledwie małą cząstką jej osiągnięć.
66. that Sting became popular/a star didn't influence her much , because she dealt with many other stars.
67. Sukces Stinga był zaledwie jednym z wielu w branży muzycznej.
68. Sukces Stinga był tylko jednym z wielu w jej bogatym dorobku.
69. Sukces Stinga spowodował duże zyski.
70. the fact that Sting succeeded was one of many successes
71. Sukces Stinga był jedynie kroplą w morzu (sukcesów)
72. Sukces Stinga był zaledwie piórkiem we wzrastającym, był zaczątkiem czegoś większego.
73. Sukces Stinga był jednym z coraz liczniejszej grupy
74. Sting's success and the money he earned , although it was quite much, was little in comparison with the multitude of other singers on the market
75. Sting's career due to his talent and a little bit of others' support was just one of the many such like artists (young, talented)

Paraphrase 2 A

1. The USA should remain independent from British decisions.
2. The US should learn to live in the world without any „colonial history memories", not paying attention to the fact that Britain once ruled the USA (colony of Britain)
3. The United States should not have colonies.
4. The United States should not be one of the aims of the British colonial foreign policy.
5. Colonial states' policy shouldn't affect the United States policy
6. Stany Zjednoczone nie powinny się mieszać w sprawy państw kolonialnych
7. Stany Zjednoczone nie powinny mieszać się w sprawy państw kolonialnych
8. Amerykanie nie powinni być mierzeni tą samą miarą, co Brytyjczycy.
9. Stany Zjednoczone nie powinny być mieszane do kolonialnych konfliktów.
10. The US should not get into the British-Iranian conflict.
11. The US should not get involved in the British – Iranian conflict.
12. The US should not get involved in the conflict in colonies
13. It means that the US should not interfere with the colonial issues
14. The United States should not be influenced by „the colonial brush" – the British empire any more.
15. ----------------
16. The US shouldn't participate in colonialism
17. US should not be bothered, annoyed with the British colonial matters, arguments.
18. US should not take part in colonialism
19. USA should not take part in collonial matters; the USA should not take any kind of colonial affairs/events into consideration while making their decisions.
20. USA nie powinny być zasmolone niepotrzebnymi zasobami kolonialnymi
21. Nie mam pojęcia
22. The USA should not take the business of the post-colonial politics.
23. US shouldn't involve in the affairs b-n Britain & its colonies
24. The US shouldn't be influenced by the British policy.
25. The United States should not interfere into the British colonies' matters.
26. The US shouldn't be treated as one of the colonies/as less important than the British.
27. The USA should not be treated the same way as the British.
28. US should not bother with the British problems and resenments.
29. The United States shouldn't be treated as non-important
30. The United States ought not to be in any way affected by the influence of Great Britain.
31. The United States should resent the tendency towards the policy of colonialism – Stany Zjednoczone nie powinny skłaniać się ku polityce kolonizacyjnej.
32. the US should not be touched by the colonial dislike.
33. Stany nie powinny wchodzić w interesy z Brytolami
34. the US shouldn't be under the British control
35. The US should not be looked down by Britain as if it (US) was inferior, just like former colonies used to be.
36. The US won't be probably bothered by the Middle East/Iran.
37. The US shouldn't be interrupted in its politics by the ex-colonial empire, Great Britain
38. The United States should not try to impose their authority over other nations
39. The USA shouldn't be offended by the British – again, my guess, based on the context and the knowledge of the verb "to tar"
40. There are no longer any ties between GB and the US, so the attitude towards the Americans should nnot be the same as towards the British.
41. The US shouldn't be perceived/treated as a former colony anymore.
42. The United States shouldn't be afraid of what is happening in Iran.
43. Stany Zjednoczone nie powinny być utożsamiane z koloniami ani w ten sposób traktowane.
44. US shouldn't engage in conflicts
45. Stany Zjednoczone nie powinny być

126

46. past rules (political) should not be imposed on American policy (Americans should not be limited in their actions with British options)
47. The United States should not be..... by the British.
48. The United States should not try to question overseas countries' policies, but should pay attention to their internal affairs.
49. the foreign policy of the British concerning their former colonies should not bother the USA or influence its own policy.
50. Stany Zjednoczone nie powinny się mieszać do kolonialnych tarć.
51. The USA should not concentrate on themselves only.
52. that the US should remain free from the colonial brush; that the US should be/remain untouched by the colonial brush.
53. the United States should not get involved in the colonial matters
54. Stany Zjednoczone nie powinny być zbrukane kolonijnymi.
55. the US reputation should not be tarnished by associating its politics with that of G Britain
56. the USA ought to avoid and resent treating other countries the way the UK used to.
57. The USA shouldn't behave the same as the British, Ameryka nie powinna ulec wpływom Brytanii.
58. The United States should not get tainted by the colonial mentality.
59. Kolonialne zaszłości nie powinny mieć wpływu na politykę Stanów Zjednoczonych.
60. The United States shouldn't interfere with British problems.
61. Stany Zjednoczone nie powinny (?) sugerować się/stosować się do czegoś/mając na uwadze/wpływem/wpływ/dominacją/dominację na/ nad resztą świata
62. The US shouldn't be frightened of those feelings.
63. The United States should not meddle in the colonial affairs.
64. Stany Zjednoczone nie powinny być winione za kolonialne sytuacje.
65. the US States should not be economically influenced/dependent by England.
66. The US should not be obliged to comply to the UK (siedzieć pod pantoflem)
67. -----------------------
68. .. że USA nie powinny mieć udziału w koloniach
69. The USA shouldn't be omitted by the colonial brush.
70. The US should not be treated as a colony
71. Stany Zjednoczone nie powinny
72. Stany Zjednoczone nie powinny być czyszczone (?) kolonialną miotłą – nie powinny być traktowane jednakową miarą
73. ------------------
74. The United States should not get involved in the British policy towards its colonies, because it can damage the United States' image.
75. The US is no longer a British colony, but an independent country with its international policy (not depending on the UK)

Paraphrase 3 A

1. would try to find any possible accusation.
2. Mr Simpson used to go purple; provide scientific explanation
3. Mr Simpson would protest against a search on the grounds of it being illegal
4. Mr Simpson would use all his legal knowledge against him
5. Mr Simpson uczyniłby wszystko, użyłby całej dostępnej wiedzy prawniczej, aby mu udowodnić, że jest w błędzie
6. Pan Simpson odwołałby się do wszystkich znanych mu przepisów prawnych
7. Pan Simpson odwołałby się do wszystkich znanych mu przepisów prawnych
8. Mr Simpson would go mad at him and resort to all legal regulations known to him
9. Pan Simpson rzucił w niego każdą prawniczą książką ze swojej obszernej biblioteczki
10. Pan Simpson zaatakowałby go każdą z prawniczych książek ze swojej obszernej biblioteki
11. Mr Simpson would do everything to prevent him from doing it

12. Mr Simpson would sacrifice everything he had most valuable
13. It means that Mr Simpson would prove it illegal if „somebody" got into his house with a search warrant.
14. Mr Simpson would become very angry and would disapprove of his action – he would criticise him
15. Pan Simpson byłby wściekły, rozłościłby się, (pokazałby mu) rzuciłby mu każdą książkę prawniczą ze swojej bogatej biblioteki ?
16. Mr Simpson would get furious
17. Mr Simpson would go mad, become furious
18. Mr Simpson would refuse , not allow
19. Mr Simpson would refuse
20. Mr simpson would get angry and tell him he had no right to ask her such things
21. Pan Simpson sięgnąłby po wszelkie znane sobie kruczki prawne, a było ich wiele
22. Mr Simpson would use any possible legal means against him
23. Mr Simpson would take him to court.
24. Mr Simpson would go furious at him
25. Mr Simpson would oppose him & present all legal arguments he would find in his library to support his own opinion.
26. ---------------
27. Mr Simpson could find a lot of reasons to sue him
28. Mr Simpson would leaf through every legal book just to find some „kruczki prawne" that could be used against him
29. Mr Simpson used to ... and try to assure him that the law was on his side
30. Mr Simpson would do his best to protect himself from unjust accusations
31. Pan Simpson rzuciłby w niego każdą książkę z zakresu tematyki prawnej, która znajdowała się w jego pokaźnej bibliotece.
32. Mr Simpson used to protest fiercely
33. Simpson by się zezłościł i zasypał go kruczkami prawnymi (które by uniemożliwiły wykonanie nakazu)
34. Mr Simpson would try to explain it wasn't legal
35. she would become furious ansd throw invectives at him
36. Mr Simpson had a tendency/used to quote every book that he had in his huge library.
37. Mr Simpson was ready to ... abuse
38. Mr Simpson would become angry with him
39. Mr Simpson would use legal ways to achieve sth; go to court
40. Mr Simpson would get furious. (?)
41. Mr Simpson would use all legal means to prevent him from getting a search warrant.
42. would criticise him by supporting his arguments with the law
43. would criticise him heavily
44. he would use his weaknesses to defeat him
45. Pan Simpson rzucałby w niego każdą legalną książkę w swojej okazałej bibliotece
46. he would go through all the books concerning law problems available in his library
47. In his profound knowledge of the subject, Mr Simpson would point out the inappropriacy of such an act in a very violent manner.
48. Mr Simpson would reject his request for a search warrant on the legal grounds.
49. he would dress him down
50. Pan Simpson użyłby wszelkich możliwych prawniczych środków przeciwko niemu.
51. Mr Simpson would use every legal way to stop him (from trying)
52. Mr Simpson would use every (legal) rule/law
53. Mr Simpson used to look for some legal ways to get this search warrant
54. Mr Simpson mógł wejść na drogę sądową, pozwać go do sądu (znaleźć wiele haczyków prawnych na niego)
55. Mr Simpson would resort to every legal trick at his disposal to fight him
56. Mr Simpson would make use of every means that was in his possession

57. Mr Simpson would "hide behind the law" (do his best, everything he can) not to let the author of the text search for letters
58. Mr Simpson would provide him in a rather aggressive manner with legal considerations in this matter
59. Pan Simpson gotów byłby oskarżać go o wszystko, co możliwe.
60. Mr Simpson would use all possible legal solutions to stop the man's actions.
61. Mr Simpson znalazłby powód aby oskarżyć go o...
62. Mr Simpson would be angry at him
63. ----------------
64. Pan Simpson rzuci w niego każdą książkę prawniczą, jaką ma w bibliotece (zrobi mu awanturę w bibliotece)
65. Mr Simpson would quote many legal rules/laws which state he cannot search his house.
66. Mr Simpson would point him out that he had no right to do that
67. Mr Simpson rzuciłby w niego każdą książkę prawniczą ze swojej pokaźnej biblioteczki.
68. Mr Simpson wyciągnąłby wszystkie znane mu kruczki prawnicze ze swojego bogatego zasobu.
69. Pan Simpson zaczerwieniłby się i rzuciłby w niego jakąkolwiek legalną książkę z jego poważanej biblioteki.
70. threw every legal book in his big library at him
71. Pan Simpson rzuciłby go każdy z książek z jego zasobnej biblioteki
72. Pan Simpson rzuciłby każdą legalną książkę
73. Mr Simpson robił się czerwony i rzucał prawniczymi książkami w niego w swojej dużej bibliotece.
74. Mr Simpson would use all his knowledge of the law (as he probably is a lawyer) to use against him (that is the writer)
75. argue that he knows law.

Paraphrase 5 A

1. Each vendor has its own standards.
2. There's always some more explanation to one problem
3. Each vendor has its own technology that is not up-to-date, thus slowing the whole project.
4. Each vendor has a separate technological advancement he wants to promote
5. Każdy uczestnik przedsięwzięcia ma wytyczone własne cele.
6. Każdy ma swoje własne technologiczne problemy.
7. Każdy musi rozwiązać problem technologiczny na swój sposób
8. Każdy ...musi uporać się z własnymi problemami technologicznymi
9. Each vendor has his own way
10. Each vendor has it's own ways, standards.
11. Each vendor has his/ her own point of view.
12. Each vendor has its own technological approach, the field he is interested in and wants to examine it.
13. It means that each vendor has an idea which he/she wants to get support for
14. Each vendor has its own approach to technology – that's why there are so many musunderstandings.
15. -------------
16. Everybody has their standards they must conform to
17. In reality, each merchandiser has its own technological idea, solution
18. Each company has its own idea/concept which they use
19. Each vendor has his/ her own concept or theory or privet matters which he/she wants to push – so no agreement is possible
20. Technology is moving so fast forward that it is very hard to catch up with it and keep even pace with it
21. Nie mam pojęcia
22. Each company has its technology to improve

23. They have their own intrests in it
24. Every new technology has to come through a series of problems
25. Each vendor has his/her own opinion on technology
26. Each vendor has its own technological "interests" and is not interested in getting into new technologies
27. Każdy vendor ma pewną niedoskonałość/haczyk do pokonania, do rozwiązania
28. Each vendor has some problem that has to be overcome
29. Each vendor deals with different aspects of these architectural definitions
30. Each vendor has its own "technological" bill to pass/each vendor has its own aims to achieve
31. Każdy... ma własny orzech do zgryzienia (techniczny problem do rozwiązania)
32. Every ... has its own technological hindrance to cope with
33. Każdy Handlowiec ma swoje własne technologiczne zalety, które chce wykorzystać
34. for each vendor there are different architectural requirements
35. each vendor is only interested in his own business, and doesn't care for a mutual agreement
36. Each group of people has their/its own principles, rules by which they follow.
37. Wants his/her project to be the leading one
38. Each vendor has its own criteria
39. Each vendor has its own methods/ways of doing things they must do – again, it's my guess, normally at this point I would use a dictionary
40. Each vendor has its own technological problems to solve
41. Each vendor should be supported with technology which is most suitable
42. Each vendor has something technological that should be corrected or fixed, there are some technological drawbacks in each vendor
43. Each member of committee has its own ideas concerning new technology and wants it to be used
44. Has sth to say about the subject
45. Każdy właścicie ma swoje własne technologiczne do mielenia
46. Własny problem do zgryzienia
47. each vendor has its own technological methods or tools to make the material get the satisfying shape (to achieve his/her goal)
48. each vendor has its own point of view and comes up with its own solutions
49. each member of the committee has his/her own field in which s/he is well informed & which s/he is able to examine & face problems connected with sth.
50. każdy członek komisji ma swój własny twardy przech do zgryzienia (?)
51. each committee member has different guidelines
52. each vendor has its own technological task/problem to solve
53. ----------------
54. każdy sp
55. each vendor has to do some catching up on technology in view of their particular drawbacks
56. each vendor has its own individual technological problems as well as different ways dealing with it
57. each vendor has its own field of interest
58. Each company has its own way in advancing new technologies
59. Każdy sprzedawca ma swoje własne cele, jeśli chodzi o technologię
60. Depending on a committee, standards can be different
61. Każdy członek komisji ? ma swój pogląd/sposób na przeprowadzenie danych rzeczy
62. Each seller has its own technological requirements to fulfil
63. Each vendor has its own way to introduce himself in the market
64. Każdy udziałowiec miał swój własny pomysł
65. Each vendor has its own idea and tries to persuade the others to accept it and sticks to it
66. Each vendor says a different thing
67. ------------
68. Każdy kupujący preferuje własne technologie.
69. Każda osoba decyzyjna ma swoje narzędzie, aby...
70. Each vendor has its own new technology to force
71. Każdy ma swój własny sposób

72. Każdy działa we własnym interesie
73. Każdy ma
74. Each vendor has its own problems, different from others.
75. Each ? has it's own technological problem to solve.

Paraphrase 1B

1. Sukces Stinga był tylko początkiem,
2. Początkowy sukces Stinga był jedynie zapowiedzią jego późniejszej kariery.
3. Sting's Success was only one among many successful investements of Virgin.
4. He (Sting) in a way made Virgin more popular, but he just started the process of the company getting to be popular. He wasn't the only one to make Virgin known.
5. Sukces Stinga był tylko początkiem jego rosnącej popularności.
6. Sukces Stinga był zaledwie jednym z wielu, które wtedy miały miejsce.
7. Sting's success was too small to be taken seriously in the music business.
8. The fact the Sting's song's were top hits was only one factor to bring him fame, and next were to come.
9. Te success of Sting as a singer was only one element of the success of Virgin.
10. The fact that Sting became popular was not a problem/was beneficial for both sides.
11. Sting was only one of the many who contributed to Wilson's career as a pop manager.
12. Sting's success was just a part of a weathy corporation
13. Sukces Stinga był jednym z wielu (sukcesów).
14. Sukces Stinga był zaledwie kroplą w morzu.
15. Sukces Stinga był zaledwie jednym z wielu temu podobnych zjawisk w wytwórni muzycznej Virgin.
16. Sukces Stinga był tylko kroplą w morzu zysków wytwórni Virgin.
17. His success was one of the many achievements of Virgin.
18. It meant that Sting could still achieve something more as he had great potential for achieving greater success.
19. Wilson had discovered many prosperous-to be songwriters, Sting being only one of those who brought high profits for Virgin.
20. Sukces Stinga był zaledwie „kroplą w morzu" (morzu utalentowanych innych artystów).
21. Sukces Stinga był tylko jednym z wielu i tak rosnących źródeł dochodów.
22. Sting's getting to the top was one of the things he was to encounter in his career.
23. Sting was only one of many (perhaps one of the first) stars whose success brought money for Virgin.
24. For W. the fact that Sting has succeeded was simply the beginning of the great career.
25. Sting's success was only one of many to which she contributed.
26. Sukces Stinga nie był jedynym sukcesem wytwórni Virgin.
27. Sting's success was something not exceptional.
28. Sting's fame was not that extraordinary.
29. Sting was just one in many artists who achieved success.
30. Sting's popularity ...one of many other similar things.
31. Sukces Stinga był jedynie jednym z wielu, których ciągle przybywało.
32. Sting's success was not outstanding or extraordinary in an increasingly crowded songwriters' market.
33. Sukces Stinga był tylko „piórkiem w rozrastającym się pióropuszu" (był częścią rosnącego sukcesu Virgin).
34. Sting's success was ony one of many others.
35. Sting's success was just one of her many victories in the music business.
36. Sting's sucess was only one out of many other achievements of Wilson as the head of the publishing division.
37. Sting's great achievements was in fact nothing in comparison to what else can be achieved in this business.

38. He was one out of many young/unknown singers she's helped to gain faith and thus has the right to be proud of.
39. Sting's success was for Wilson yet another successful discovery of a new singer; she didn't care about his money.
40. Sting's success (although enormous) was not so outstanding if placed among other singers' success.
41. The success that Sting achieved at the beginning of his career was only a drop in the sea of his future achievements.
42. Sting's success was one of many successful enterprises for C. Wilson.
43. Powodzenie Stinga było kroplą w morzu.
44. The situation was only one of the successes she achieved.
45. Stinng was one of many who succeeded thanks to Virgin.
46. Sting's success was just one out of many she participated in.
47. Sukces Stinga był tylko małym fragmentem w rosnącym i przeładowanym rynku muzycznym.
48. Sukces Stinga był zaledwie jednym spośród wielu osiągnięć Carol Wilson.
49. His success was one of many others.
50. Sting's successful cooperation with Wilson resulting in new records was one step forward in his career.
51. Sukces Stinga z (met.): był jedynie czubkiem góry lodowej.
52. Sting's becoming so popular ... was something of lesser importance than real values he presented with himself.
53. Sting's success – Sting's fame and stardom – didn't matter that much, wasn't of great importance.
54. The singer's popularity was an implication of great success.
55. The singer's achievements was only one out of many careers discovered.
56. Sting's success was hardly meaningful concidering the whole
57. The popularity of Sting was just one of many other of the kind.
58. Sukces Stinga/was one of the many others.
59. Sukcesy Stinga były zaledwie kroplą w morzu potrzeb.
60. Sukces Stinga był zaledwie początkiem jego spektakularnej kariery.
61. For her it was nothing but one another artist who has become successful in the market place in (on) which there were many other successful artists.
62. Sting's success was not exceptional/Sting's success was yet another achievement among many others.
63. Sukces Stinga był zaledwie jednym z wielu innych osiągnięć pani Wilson.
64. (...) Sting only began an avalanche of success, which first was his small molehill, but arose to a mountain.
65. Songwriter's success wasn't of great importance, she had a lot of such discoveries.
66. The success Sting achieved was just one of the elements of (reasons for) Wilson's (and Virgin's) success.
67. Sting was one of very many people who owed their success to Wilson.
68. Sukces Stinga był zaledwie jednym piórkiem we wzrastająco zatłoczonym

Corrections to Paraphrase 1B

1. ------------
2. -------------
3. -----------
4. Wilson should be proud of his cooperation with Sting
5. -----------
6. Sukces Stinga był zaledwie jednym z wielu, z których Wilson może być dumny
7. Sting's success was too small to be proud of it.
8. Sting's songs were only one of many things he could be proud of.
9. ----------

132

10. the incomes were a great success, reason for pride for all of them, the record company, for Wilson and Sting
11. ----------
12. ----------
13. sukces Stinga był zwyczajnie powodem do dumy
14. Sukces Stinga był zaledwie jednym z wielu sukcesów/osiągnięć.
15. Był czymś, z czego powinien być dumny
16. -----------
17. ----------
18. Sting's success was something he should be proud of
19. -----------
20. Sukces Stinga był jedną z tych rzeczy, z których firma powinna być dumna
21. Sukces Stinga był tylko jednym z wielu przysparzających (im) chwały.
22. ....was one of the positive things
23. Sting was only one of many stars who owe their success to Virgin
24. -------------
25. ------------
26. -----------
27. Sting's success was one of the many things Wilson prided in.
28. ---------
29. -----------
30. Another of her many successes
31. -----------
32. ---------
33. ---------
34. ---------
35. ---------
36. ---------
37. Sting's great achievement was just one of the things he can be proud of
38. ----------
39. ----------
40. ----------
41. -----------
42. ----------
43. było jednym z wielu jej licznych sukcesów
44. ----------
45. ---------
46. jeden z wielu powodów do dumy
47. -----------
48. Sukces Stinga był zaledwie częścią szerokiego wachlarza jej osiągnięć
49. His success was one more thing she could be proud of/of many others she could be...
50. ----------
51. ---------
52. was so successful
53. it was just one more thing she could be proud of
54. it was only one thing among other that she could be proud of
55. was only one things out of many to be proud of
56. Sting's success was merely a one thing from the whole she should be proud of
57. Sukces Stinga to coś, z czego można być dumnym
58. Sukces Stinga był czymś z czego powinno być się dumnym
59. Sukcesy Stinga były zaledwie wstępem do czegoś jeszcze znakomitszego.
60. -------
61. For Wilson it was merely another thing that she was successful in/she has succeeded in among many others (nothing really surprising really)
62. ---------

63. ----------
64. ----------
65. ----------
66. Sting's success is just one (of many) of things Wilson can be proud of.
67. Sting's success was only one of Wilson's achievements
68. Sukces Stinga był zaledwie jedną rzeczą z której mogła być dumna.

Paraphrase 2 B

1. ------------
2. The United States shouldn't be bothered with the problems of other countries.
3. US shouldn't suffer the consequences of colonialism.
4. The USA shouldn't be affected by the opinion of Great Britain.
5. The US should not act imperialistically.
6. USA nie powinny być powiązane ze sprawami Wielkiej Brytanii.
7. The United States should not be bothered by the colonial battles.
8. The United States shouldn't....
9. The United States were not on the British side, sided with the colonies.
10. The US should be treated separately, as acting in a different way than UK with its colonial past.
11. The US should stay away from the colonies' struggle for independence.
12. The United States should not try to colonize this territory.
13. Stany Zjednoczone nie powinny posługiwać się koloniami w załatwianiu swoich interesów.
14. Stany Zjednoczone nie powinny dać się powalać colonialnym naleciałościom.
15. Ozdabiany kolonialnymi farbami (= ......)
16. Stany Zjednoczone nie powinny być traktowane przez pryzmat swojej kolonialnej przeszłości.
17. The US should not be influenced (in its policy on Iran) by the British.
18. The United States should be prevented from becoming a colonial power.
19. US should not be allowed to interfere in the affairs between Britain and Iran. ?
20. The United States nie powinny czuć się związane z opinią UK (faktem bycia kolonią brytyjską)
21. Że Stany Zjednoczone nie będą marionetką w rękach kolonialistów.
22. The United States should not be despised by the British colonies.
23. The USA should not follow the British, who still regard themselves (their country) as the colonial empire.
24. It would be better for the USA not to be associated/connected with the British policy.
25. ----------------
26. Stany Zjednoczone nie powinny się wtrącać w nieswoje sprawy.
27. The USA should not be affected by the British – Arab antagonism.
28. The US shall not be worried by their allies.
29. The US should not have a patronising attitude towards other countries.
30. The US should not be involved in colonial policies, because it would destroy the country's reputation.
31. Should not be allowed to interfere in colonial matters.
32. The United States will not suffer because of the tensions in colonial regions.
33. The US should not be allowed to interfere too much in colonial matters.
34. The United States should not be treated as if it was still a British colony.
35. The United States is not badly influenced by the post-colonial conflicts.
36. The US, with its strong position in the world's policy, have to be taken into account and not just follow what G. B. says.
37. That the United States should not be blamed for the colonies.
38. The US shouldn't be perceived through the prism of British colonialism, since as a nation that evolved after the colonialism they have no common grounds with colonial UK.
39. The US should not get involved in the matters which would make it look like it were a colonial country (like Britain and its empire).
40. The Arab countries should not put pressure on America.

41. The States should not get involved in the colonial affairs.
42. The US should not interfere with the post-colonial countries.
43. , że Stany Zjednoczone nie powinny być traktowane jako jeszcze jedna kolonia brytyjska
44. Britain should change its attitude.
45. The US should not be treated the same as the British.
46. The US should not be associated with any shady business.
47. Stany Zjednoczone nie powinny być zaangażowane w kwestie kolonialne.
48. Stany Zjednoczone nie powinny ponosić konsekwencji z powodu kolonialnej przeszłości Anglii.
49. ----------------
50. United States should not exert too strong influence/impact on Iran.
51. Stany Zjednoczone nie powinny być wciągane w kolonialne „porachunki".
52. The US was to avoid being manipulated like other colonies.
53. The United States should not interfere with the conflicts concerning British overseas territories and Great Britain.
54. The United States should stay away from the colonies.
55. The United States should not get involved in colonial matters.
56. The US should not be worried with the colonial brush
57. The USA should not be treated on the basis of its expancy of the colonial kind
58. The United States should not be ignored in any way.
59. Stany Zjednoczone nie powinny być ignorowane.
60. Stany Zjednoczone nie powinny psuć szyku Brytyjczykom.
61. That the US shouldn't care much about what the UK thinks about certain matters/about the UK's stand on certain things.
62. The US should not gain profits to the British detriment
63. Stany Zjednoczone nie powinny ingerować (mieszać się) w wydarzenia/sprawy, w które zaangażowane są Wielka Brytania i jej dawne kolonie
64. (...) the US should not be influenced by the colonial history of Britain
65. the United States shouldn't depend on the British policy
66. --------------
67. The United States shouldn't be engaged in/connected with (?)/interfere with/Anglo-Iranian matters
68. The USA shouldn't be concerned with British – Iranian dispute.

Corrections to Paraphrase 2B

1. Nie można winić Stanów Zjednoczonych za kolonialną politykę Brytyjczyków.
2. The United States shouldn't be blamed for the faults of the British and their former colonies
3. -------
4. the USA shouldn't be blamed for G. B's faults
5. USA nie powinny być obwiniane za kolonialne błędy
6. USA nie powinny być obwiniane za przestępstwa/winy popełnione przez Wk Bryt.
7. The United States should not be blamed for the colonial faults
8. The United States should't be blamed for the British faults
9. The US shouldn't be blamed for the actions of Iran
10. Zaznacza się tu trend by oddzielić Stany Zjednoczone od Wk Brytanii by Stany nie nosiły piętna kolonializmu.
11. ----------
12. The United States should not be burdened with Great Britain's faults.
13. Stany Zjednoczone nie powinny być obwiniane za błędy kolonialne.
14. Stany Zjednoczone nie powinny być obarczane winą za kolonialne winy
15. Ponosić konsekwencje nie swoich błędów
16. St. Zjednoczone nie powinny być traktowane przez pryzmat kolonialnej przeszłości W. Brytanii
17. The US should not be blamed for the faulty Iran policy of Britain
18. The US should not be blamed for the crimes and faults committed by GB as a colonial power

19. The Americans should not be blamed for the British failure
20. USA nie powinno być winione za błędy UK (mniej więcej o to mi chodziło w cz. I)
21. Że Stany Zjednoczone nie powinny być obarczane za winy kolonialistów
22. ... by the British colonies, because of the Brits.
23. The USA shouldn't be blamed for colonial policy of the British.
24. & be blamed for the British/policy, actions.
25. -----------
26. Stany Zjednoczone nie powinny być obwiniane za błędy kolonialne
27. USA should not be responsible for British failures
28. The US shall not be blamed for the Arab „crimes"
29. The US should not be blamed for the faulty (colonial) British policy towards Arab countries.
30. The US should not be blamed for Britain's policy
31. Should not be accused of colonial aspirations
32. ----------
33. The US shouldn't be blamed for all colonial mistakes.
34. The United States should not be blamed for the colonial faults
35. The United States should not be on the same side of the post-colonial conflicts as Great Britain (should not be accused of being enemies of Iran etc. like the British)
36. The US should not be blamed for GB's faults
37. --------
38. ----------
39. the US should't be blamed for Britain's faults as a colonial country.
40. America should not be blamed for colonialism
41. The States should not be blamed for the consequences of the British colonial policy
42. Stany Zjednoczone nie powinny „brudzić" swojej reputacji mieszając się w sprawy byłych państw kolonialnych
43. Że nie powinny być winione za błędy kolonializmu brytyjskiego
44. US should not be blamed for crimes of colonialism
45. ----------
46. ----------
47. Stany Zjednoczone nie powinny winić się za kolonialny zamęt
48. Stany Zjednoczone nie powinny ponosić konsekwencji z powodu kolonialnych ambicji Anglii
49. US should't be blamed for the colonial times.
50. -----------
51. ----------
52. was not to be talked into
53. the US should not interfere with the conflicts between British colonies and Great Britain unless it should be held responsible for the British overseas politics' errors.
54. The United States should not be blamed for the colonial brush
55. The United States should not be blamed for the colonial faults
56. The US should not be blamed for the colonial faults
57. The USA should not be judged on the basis of their colonial expansion
58. The United States shouldn't be blamed for someone else's faults or crimes
59. Stany Zjednoczone nie powinny być obwiniane za kolonialne zbrodnie/błędy
60. Stany Zjednoczone nie powinny być obwiniane za cudze przewinienia
61. That the US shouldn't be blamed for the crimes or faults of the UK
62. ------------
63. Stany Zjednoczone nie powinny być obwiniane za wydarzenia związane z kolonializmem.
64. ------------
65. ----------
66. the US shouldn't be blamed for colonies' faults/mistakes
67. the US shouldn't be blamed for the faults of the colonies
68. the USA shouldn't be blamed for crimes or faults of others

Paraphrase 3B

1. Pan Simpson
2. Mr Simpson would make all possible accusations.
3. Mr Simpson would react violently.
4. Mr. Simpson would be angry.
5. Mr. Simpson znalazłby (wytknąłby) wszelkie możliwe zarzuty
6. Pan Simpson powołałby się na wszystkie możliwe akty prawne, gdyby ktoś ośmielił się przyjść z nakazem rewizji/dosł. : Pan Simpson rzuciłby w niego każdą książkę prawniczą ze swej ogromnej biblioteki.
7. Mr. Simpson would accuse him, underrate Tom Fearson's credibility.
8. Mr Simpson would make accusations on him.
9. He would envoke any law.
10. Mr Simpson was sure to... Mr Simpson would use all legal arguments available in his books to reject the idea of asking for a search warrant.
11. Mr Simpson would accuse him of every possible wrongdoing that he knows about.
12. Mr Simpson would try to find every possible loophole.
13. Rzucał oszczerstwami
14. Pan Simpson rzuciłby mu w twarz wszystkie prawnicze książki, jakie posiada w swojej znacznej bibliotece.
15. Oskarżał by go w swojej bibliotece.
16. Pan Simpson pozwałby go z każdego paragrafu jaki tylko istnieje.
17. Mr Simpson would make every possible accusation against him, which should be feared as he knows the law very well.
18. He would use all possible means which would be within his reach.
19. She would use all the possible means against him
20. Pan Simpson podałby/wynalazłby/odszukałby każdy z możliwych zarzutów aby go ukarać
21. Pan Simpson stwarzałby mu wszelkie możliwe trudności.
22. Pan Simpson zastosowałby każdy możliwy paragraf przeciw niemu.
23. Mr Simpson would not agree to his request for he thought it would be against the law
24. Mr Simpson would be extremely angry with him
25. Mr Simpson would put all possible charges against him
26. Obrzuciłby go wyzwiskami/zrobiłby awanturę
27. Mr Simpson would threaten him with legal action.
28. Mr Simpson would do everything that is possible to stop him.
29. Mr Simpson would bring up all the possible legal arguments.
30. Mr Simpson would use legal arguments, threaten with a lawsuit act.
31. He would use every possible way to prevent him from doing so.
32. Mr Simpson would make any possible charges against him.
33. Pan Simpson użyłby wszelkich możliwych legalnych środków przeciwko niemu, oskarżyłby go.
34. Mr Simpson wouldn't let him do it.
35. Mr Simpson would use one of his many legal methods against him.
36. Mr Simpson would never agree to give him a search warrant.
37. Mr Simpson would accuse him of being deceitful.
38. She'd go to any lengths to punish (make him take legal responsibility) him for resorting to a search warrant.
39. Mr Simpson would accuse him of every crime possible.
40. Mr Simpson would show (reveal to) him adequate regulations.
41. Mr Simpson (a knowledgeable person) would make all possible accusations of his decisions.
42. Mr Simpson would get angry.
43. Pan Simpson mógłby i użyłby wszelkich środków, aby
44. Would find legal regulations making such action impossible.
45. Mr Simpson would throw every accessible book in his huge library at him
46. Would go to any lenghts to prove his point
47. Pan Simpson byłby bardzo zdenerwowany na niego

48. Pan Simpson byłby oburzony
49. He wouldn't let them look for the letters on the baisi of his knowledge of law
50. Mr Simpson (here the boss – supervisor) will be angry and will punish him
51. Pan Simpson ostro skrytykowałby go (kieruję się tu znajomością idiomu „throw books at sb", jednak nie wiem, co zrobić z resztą)
52. Mr Simpson used to consult every source of legal nature
53. Mr Simpson was bound to/certain/sure to give vent to his anger/wrath openly on him
54. He would be offended, get angry, show the content of his impressing collection
55. He could get angry; toss each legal book at his direction
56. Mr Simpson would throw every book in his direction from the library
57. Pan Simpson rzuciłby każdą książkę w swojej bibliotece na niego
58. Mr Simpson might/rzuciłby każdą książkę w swojej bibliotece w niego
59. Pan Simpson byłby nawet w stanie poświęcić książki swojej imponującej biblioteczki by rzucić nimi w niego.
60. Pan Simpson użyłby wszystkich dostępnych mu środków
61. Mr Simpson would give him all the possible reasons against doing this (i.e. issuing the search warrant)
62. Would use arguments based on law literature to oppose him/to defend himself
63. Pan Simpson rzuciłby każdą księgę prawniczą w swej bogatej bibliotece
64. (...) Mr Simpson would give vent to his anger with the help of a book from his library.
65. Harriet would not accept any of his opinions
66. Mr Simpson is likely to treat him with legal books from his large library (but I guess that this sentence has an idiomatic meaning which I don't know)
67. Mr Simpson użyłby wszelkich możliwych argumentów przeciwko niemu
68. Mr Simpson would show him books without threatening or abusive content as proper ones

Corrections to Paraphrase 3B

1. --------------
2. --------------
3. --------------
4. Mr Simpson would punish him.
5. -----------
6. -------------
7. Mr Simpson would charge him.
8. Mr Simpson would punish him severely.
9. ----------
10. ----------
11. ----------
12. Mr Simpson would go mad and behave very aggressive.
13. Ukarałby go surowo (lub moja wersja w I części testu)
14. Pan Simpson wykorzystałby każdy najdrobniejszy przepis prawny by go ukarać/by pokazać gdzie jego miejsce
15. Ukarał go
16. ---------
17. ----------
18. He would charge him with all possible offences.
19. --------
20. --------
21. Pan Simpson wytaczałby przeciwko niemu wszelkie możliwe oskarżenia.
22. ---------
23. Mr Simpson would charge him for searching his house.
24. Would punish him
25. ---------

26. zarzuciłby go jak największą ilością oskarżeń
27. Mr Simpson would put blame for as many things as possible on him
28. Mr Simpson would punish him severely using as much offence as possible
29. Mr Simpson would charge him with every possible offence
30. --------
31. ---------
32. ---------
33. ---------
34. --------
35. ----------
36. --------
37. ----------
38. ---------
39. ---------
40. Mr Simpson would punish him.
41. ---------
42. ---------
43. --------
44. ---------
45. Mr Simpson would punish him severely.
46. ---------
47. ----------
48. Pan Simpson zareagowałby gwałtownym protestem./gwałtownie by zaprotestował
49. He would charge him with any legal accusation he could think of
50. ----------
51. ----------
52. talk persuasively
53. ----------
54. Mr Simpson would punish him as severely as possible
55. Punish him as severely as possible for his offences
56. Mr Simpson charged him with as many offences as possible
57. Pan Simpson zastosowałby wszelkiego rodzaju sposoby prawne, by go ukarać
58. Mr Simpson would punish him as severely as possible or charge him with as many offences as possible
59. ---------
60. pan Simpson uciekłby się do wszelkich dostępnych mu form kary
61. ---------
62. ----------
63. Mr Simpson would charge him with as many offences as possible
64. -------
65. ---------
66. ----------
67. ----------
68. ---------

Paraphrase 5 B

1. -----------
2. Each vendor has to struggle with technological problems himself.
3. Vendors have different opinions and different interests.
4. Each sales representative use its own method to get through to the market, its niche.
5. Każdy specjalista ma swoją działkę/każdy sprzedawca ma swój sposób na przekonanie (klienta o kupnie).

6. Każdy członek komisji ma "swoją technologiczną działkę" (zakres działań), z której musi się rozliczyć/z którą musi się zmierzyć.
7. Każdy ..... ma swoje własne problemy technologiczne, z którymi musi się zmagać.
8. Each sellman has to find the optimal solution
9. Each vendor wants sth else, sth different
10. Each vendor has their own technology/idea about technology.
11. Each firm wants its own technology to be the standard.
12. Each producer would like to promote their technology
13. Każdy komputerowiec chce, aby jego rozwiązanie technologiczne "przeszło"/zostało zaakceptowane.
14. Każdy sprzedawca ma swój pomysł na technologiczne przecieranie szlaków.
15. Ma swoją metodę na podcięcie = obalenie (jakiegoś pomysłu?
16. Every vendor has to struggle with technological difficulties on his own.
17. Vendors differ on how technology should be applied
18. Each vendor has his own approach and method.
19. There's no agreement reached as every single vendor is interested in his own business; not working together, convince others to accept your ideas.
20. Każdy ma swoje trzy grosze do dodania
21. Każdy z członków komitetu posługuje się własnym żargonem
22. Each vendor has to –on its own – try and check new technologies
23. Each vendor defends his own technology and doesn' t want to give an inch.
24. Every single vendor has got his own particular viewpoint.
25. ------------
26. Każdy ma swoje włąsne technologiczne rozwiązania.
27. Each vendor has its own ideas and visions concerning technological solutions.
28. Each vendor has its own objectives to meet
29. Each vendor disagree on the technological details
30. Each vendor wants to achieve their goals by influencing the standard
31. Each has its own theory or way of doing things
32. Each vendor develops his own particular technology
33. Each vendor has its own idea concerning the technological solution
34. Each vendor is different
35. Each vendor has its own way of doing things (technologically) or: each vendor has its own technological objectives
36. Each vendor has its own concept of the system in terms of technology as it's used in reality
37. Each vendor has its own ideas on various matters to voice
38. There is a problem with each member, and each should deal with it on its own instead of influencing others.
39. Each vendor wants to follow his own technological ideas/projects.
40. Each vendor has its own conception
41. Each vendor cares only about their own technological development. Vendors do not cooperate.
42. Each vendor has its own technological problem to deal with.
43. Każdy kontrahent ma własny orzech do zgryzienia
44. Everyone has their own motives
45. Each vendor judges according to his own criterion
46. Each vendor is concerned mostly with their own case, which is an obstacle to reach a coherent plan
47. Każdy członek komisji posiada swoją własną teorię, którą się podpiera
48. Everything works differently
49. -----------
50. each vendor has its own opinion – view; another interpretation – rządzi się swoimi prawami
51. każdy z naukowców kładzie nacisk na inny aspekt technologiczny
52. each vendor has its technological ground of specialty
53. each vendor has his own idea how to do it/what should be done
54. each vendor has its own way of dealing with the concept

55. every contribution presents its own device to deal with
56. each vendor has its own problems to deal with
57. każdy (specjalista) ma własne sposoby technologiczne
58. every specialist/seller has its own way of thinking/point of view/technological possibilities, propositions
59. każdy sprzedawca ma swoje własne technologiczne podejście
60. każdy realizuje to we właściwy sobie sposób
61. that – in reality – it's very difficult for the committee of vendors to reach an agreement/to work some common solution that would satisfy everybody.
62. Each vendor has its own way/idea/method to be used/applied
63. Każdy sprzedawca popiera daną technologię
64. Each vendor has its own weaknesses
65. Each vendor is connected with a particular technological path
66. -----------
67. Każdy sprzedawca ma swoje indywidualne, technologiczne koncepcje (?)
68. Każdy .... ma swoją własną techniczną siekierę do mielenia (dosłownie)

Corrections to Paraphrase 5B

1. Każdy sprzedawca ma swój sposób przekonywania i namawiania.
2. Each vendor has to be as persuasive as possible as far as the technological values are concerned.
3. Each seller talks continuously only about his own technological issue
4. Each sales representative , vendor repeats sth to encourage consumers to buy.
5. -------
6. Każdy sprzedawca chce/musi przekonać innych do swojej technologii.
7. Każdy sprzedawca
8. Each sellman wants to persuade people to accept his beliefs
9. Each vendor wants to get sth and
10. Each vendor has their own point of view and so they fail to agree.
11. ---------
12. Each producer would try to promote their technology whenever possible.
13. Każdy sprzedawca
14. Każdy sprzedawca chce narzucić innym/przekonać innych do swojej technologii
15. Metody na przekonanie
16. -------
17. Vendors do not seek compromise, but try to persuade others to accept their own ideas
18. Each vendor has sth to say to persuade others and change their beliefs.
19. -------
20. każdy próbuje przeforsować swoją opcję/wizję
21. Każdy ze sprzedawców forsuje własną technologię
22. Each vendor has to support and talk about their new technologies.
23. Each vendor praises his own technology and wants to persuade others to his idea/technology.
24. Every single salesman has got his own particular way of persuading people.
25. ---------
26. ...., o których za wszelką cenę chce przeciwną stronę przekonać.
27. ....to defend.
28. Each vendor/seller persuades others by repeating things over and over again
29. Each vendor wants to promote its own technology
30. Each vendor promoted their own solutions (forcibly, without listening to the others)
31. All fighted to have things there own way
32. ----------
33. Each vendor tries to persuade people to sell its own technological solutions
34. Each vendor wants others to accept its own technological system
35. Each vendor tries to persuade others to use his technologies

36. Each vendor has its own concept and tries to persuade others to accept it.
37. Do everything to persuade others to their ideas
38. Each vendor has to persuade customers to buy his product.
39. Each vendor wants people to accept its beliefs, not compromise.
40. Each vendor insists on its own conception
41. Each vendor wants to persuade other people to believe in their own idea of technological development
42. -------
43. ---------
44. ---------
45. ---------
46. usilnie przekonywać
47. Każdy sprzedawca ma swoją technologiczną metodę którą się posługuje
48. ---------
49. each seller repeated his/her technological standard trying to persuade others
50. -------
51. Każdy ze sprzedawców nakłania do innego rozwiązania technologicznego
52. To work hard on
53. Each salesman has his own idea what should be done and insists on it
54. Each seller is in favor of his own idea that he/she wants to popularize
55. Every seller has his own method to persuade others to buy his product
56. Each vendor has its own technological reasons
57. Każdy sprzedawca powtarza pewne rzeczy aby przekonać ludzi do tego o czym mówi
58. Every seller has its own way of persuading others.
59. Każdy sprzedawca ma tendencje do powtarzania się, gdyż zależy im do przekonania innych do swoich pomysłów
60. Każdy we właściwy sobie sposób traktuje technologię
61. Each vendor was saying sth again and again bec. they wanted to persuade others to accept their ideas
62. -------
63. --------
64. ---------
65. ---------
66. each seller wants to convince others that his choice (of the system) was right
67. Każdy sprzedawca próbuje na wszelkie sposoby przekonać innych do swojego zdania (on open systems)
68. Każdy sprzedawca musi powtarzać w kółko to samo

142

Appendix 6

Form and definition in Group A and B

Idiom 1 A

	Form		Definition
1	A feather in a crowded cap	1	Jedna z wielu rzeczy, którą można się pochwalić
2	A feather in one's cap	2	A feature which makes one proud
3	Be a feather in one's cap	3	Be an asset, something that one can boast with
4	To be a feather in a crowded cap	4	Być tylko małą częścią czegoś większego (nieistotną)
5	To be a feather in one's cap	5	Być czyimś osiągnięciem, oznaką odniesionego sukcesu
6	To be another feather in one's cup	6	Być kolejnym czyimś sukcesem
7	To have another feather in one's cup	7	Odnieść kolejny sukces
8	A feather in an increasingly crowded cap	8	Kropla w morzu osiągnięć
9	To be one feather in a crowded cup	9	Być częścią czegoś dużego
10	Be one feather in a crowded cap	10	Być zapowiedzią, początkiem czegoś ważnego, dużego
11	To be merely a feather in a considerably growing cap	11	Tylko jedna z wielu rzeczy
12	To be merely a feather in a crowded cap	12	To be a small thing when compared to the all needed things
13	Another feather in one's cap	13	Just another thing that is not necessary because we already have many of those
14	To be a one feather in one's (increasingly) crowded cap	14	To be a piece of a crowded whole
15	One feather in a cap	15	Kropla w morzu
16	Feather in a filled cap	16	Very few among many
17	One feather in a cap	17	Kropla w morzu, one of many problems, issues
18	One feather in a cap	18	To be one of many
19	One feather in a cap	19	To be one of many
20	One feather in a crowded cap	20	Kropla w morzu
21	To be another feather in one's crowded cap	21	Kolejny sukces w paśmie innych sukcesów
22	To be a feather in a cap	22	To be of little importance
23	To be a feather in a (crowded) cap	23	One thing out of plenty
24	One feather in a cap	24	Only one thing amongst many others
25	(to be) a feather in one's cap	25	One of the many things
26	Another feather in a crowded cap	26	Jeszcze jedno osiągnięcie, sukces w i tak już wspaniałej karierze
27	Feather in a crowded cap	27	One out of many
28	To be a feather in a cap	28	To be one of the many
29	To be one feather in a crowded cap	29	Być tylko początkiem czegoś

	Form		Definition
30	A feather in a crowded cap	30	One unimportant thing among many others
31	A feather in onc's cap	31	As w rękawie
32	The feather in one's cap	32	Sth to be proud of; coś (zasługa), z której jest się dumnym
33	To be a feather in a cap	33	Być jednym z wielu
34	To be a feather in a crowded cap	34	Być jednym z wielu
35	To be a feather in a cap	35	Być drobiazgiem, mało istotnym elementem wśród innych podobnych elementów
36	A feather in a crowding cap	36	Początek sukcesu
37	Only one feather in the cap	37	Kropla w morzu
38	To be one feather in a crowded cap	38	Kiedy mówimy, że ktoś wyróżnia się z tłumu
39	Be a feather in a crowded cap	39	Be only one example out of a large group of similar events/actions/occurrences
40	To be one feather in a crowded cap	40	To be only part of sth larger
41	One feather in a cap	41	Nic specjalnego, jedno z wielu
42	Be one feather in a cap	42	?-------------------------------
43	One feather in a crowded cap	43	Początek, wstęp do czegoś większego
44	To be a single feather in a crowded cap	44	Być wierzchołkiem góry lodowej
45	To be a feather in a cap	45	Zmieniać zdanie
46	A feather in a cap	46	To be merely an element in a larger group
47	To be merely one feather in an (increasingly) crowded cap	47	To be merely one of the many
48	To be one feather in an increasingly crowded cap	48	To be merely one out of many
49	One feather in an increasingly crowded cap	49	One small "thing" among many others
50	One feathe in an increasingly crowded cap	50	Jeden z licznych mających nadejść (sukcesów)
51	To be only one feather in a cap	51	Być jednym z wielu
52	Be one feather in a (crowded) cap	52	To be only one part of a greater deal, probably not a very significant part
53	Be only a feather in an increasingly crowded cap	53	Być kroplą w morzu
54	To be a feather in a crowded cap(sth is only a feather in an (increasingly) crowded cap)	54	Jest tylko kroplą w morzu
55	To be a feather in sb's cap	55	To be an affective but unnecessary addition
56	To be a feather in one's cap	56	To be just one of the many things that one has, etc.
57	To be one feather in a cap	57	To be exceptional
58	To be a feather in a cap	58	To be but one good thing among the possible other felicitous events
59	One feather in a crowded cap	59	Zapowiedź dobrego biznesu
60	To have many feathers in a cap	60	To have many options to choose from
61	To have one feather in one's own cap	61	Mieć profit z czegoś jednocześnie mając jeszcze inne wpływy

	Form		Definition
62	Just one feather in an increasingly ... cap	62	Początek sukcesu, jeden z pasma sukcesów
63	One feather in increasingly crowded cap	63	Zbyt mało w stosunku do innych
64	It is a feather in the crowded cap	64	To tylko fragment całości, początek czegoś
65	One feather in a cap	65	One thing among many others (positive ones)
66	A feather in a cap	66	Jeden z wielu
67	A feather in a crowded cap	67	Kolejna rzecz wśród wielu, jedna z wielu
68	A feather in one's increasingly crowded cap	68	Jeden z wielu kamyczków w bogatym dorobku
69	To be one feather in a cap	69	Być niewielką częścią w czymś
70	One feather in a crowded cap	70	One of many
71	One feather in the increasingly crowded cap	71	Kropla w morzu potrzeb
72	To be (merely) a feather in the crowded cap	72	Igła w stogu siana
73	To be a feather in a cap	73	---
74	To be a feather in a cap	74	Kropla w szklance wody
75	Only one feather in a cap	75	Jeden z wielu elementów

Idiom 2 A

	Form		Definition
1	To tar with the (colonial) brush	1	Pod wpływem kolonialnym
2	To tar with a brush	2	?---
3	Be tarred with a brush	3	Carry a burden that is specified by the type of the "brush"
4	To be tarred by sbd's brush	4	Być częścią czyjegoś planu, aktywności
5	To be tarred with the brush	5	Być przez coś nękanym
6	To be tarred with the brush	6	Mieszać się do czegoś
7	To be tarred with a brush	7	Mieszać się do czegoś
8	To tar sb with sb's own brush	8	Mierzyć kogoś tą samą miarą
9	To be tarred with the colonial brush	9	Zostać wplątanym w konflikt
10	Be tarred with the colonial brush	10	Nie wtrącać się
11	To be tarred with a brush	11	Pobrudzić sobie ręce
12	To be tarred with brush	12	To take part in something
13	To be tarred with a brush	13	To be treated in a harsh and rude way
14	To be tarred with a (colonial) brush	14	To be influenced (badly) by sth in a negative sense
15	To tar off a brush ?	15	---
16	Be tarred with a .... brush	16	To get involved in something
17	To tar with a brush	17	To make angry, to bother
18	To be tarred in the brush	18	To be interested in
19	To be tarred in the brush	19	To be interested in
20	To be tarred with colonial brush	20	Zaśmiecone
21	To be tarred with a brush	21	Nie wiem

	Form		Definition
22	To be tarred with a brush	22	To be troubled or involved
23	To be tarred with a brush	23	To be bothered with sth
24	To be tarred with a brush	24	To be influenced in a negative way by something that should not have a "spoiling" effect
25	To be tarred with a brush	25	Be touched/affected by sth
26	To be tarred with a brush	26	To treat someone as if he is of a lesser importance; to ignore sb to be treated badly because of being of lesser importance)
27	To be tarred with brush	27	Treated the same way
28	To be tarred in the brush	28	Not to be interested in sb else's mess
29	To be tarred with a brush	29	Być traktowanym protekcjonalnie
30	To be tarred with a brush	30	To be influenced by something on a great scale
31	To be tarred with a brush	31	---
32	Be tarred with the brush	32	Be put in trouble; odczuć coś boleśnie
33	To be tarred with a brush	33	Wchodzić w ciemne konszachty
34	To be tarred with a brush	34	Być pod czyjąś kontrolą
35	To tar sth/sb with a brush	35	To treat sb/sth as inferior
36	To be tarred with the colonial brush	36	Być czymś zagrożonym
37	To be tarred with the colonial brush	37	Dać się, aby ktoś ingerował w czyjeś sprawy
38	To be tarred with a brush	38	Mieć chorą ambicję
39	Tar sb with sb's brush	39	Insult or offend sb
40	To be tarred with a brush	40	To be blamed for sth (unjustly)
41	Tar sth with a brush	41	Traktować coś/kogoś w jakiś sposób
42	Be tarred with a brush	42	---
43	They should not be tarred with a colonial brush	43	nie traktować/drażnić kogoś/czegoś przez wspominanie czasów kolonializmu
44	To be tarred with a brush	44	To run into problems
45	To be tarred with a brush	45	---
46	To tar sb with a brush	46	---
47	To be tarred with the colonial brush	47	To be .... by the British (or by any other colonialistic country)
48	To be tarred with the colonial brush	48	To be involved in colonial arguments
49	Tarred with the colonial brush	49	Influenced by
50	To be tarred with colonial brush	50	Mieszać się w czyjeś sprawy
51	To be tarred with a brush	51	---
52	Be tarred with a (colonial) brush	52	To be affected by (influenced/in a negative way) by sth // the (colonial) brush affects/spoils sth
53	Be tarred with colonial brush	53	Być zbrukanym/mieć naruszoną reputację sprawami kolonialnymi
54	To be tarred with a colonial brush	54	Być zbrukanym przez...
55	To tar sb with ... brush	55	To tarnish sb's reputation/opinion
56	To tarr sb with .... brush	56	To blacken sb
57	To be tarred with a brush	57	To be influenced by
58	To tar sth with a brush	58	To adulterate sth or sb's good conduct with a taint of sth rather inglorious

	Form		Definition
59	To be tarred with a colonial brush	59	?--
60	To be tarred with a colonial brush	60	To be given the right to do sth
61	To be tarred with a brush	61	(?) napotykać na coś trudnego
62	To be tarred with a colonial brush	62	Być przestraszonym
63	To be tarred with a brush	63	One should not meddle in the inappropriate matters
64	To be tarred with the brush	64	Zeszmacić kogoś, oczernić, winić za coś
65	To be tarred with a brush	65	To be dependant to & compliant to sb?
66	Be tarred with a brush	66	Być uległym, podporządkowanym komuś
67	Be tarred with a brush	67	--
68	To be tarred with the brush	68	Skorzystać, otrzeć się o coś
69	To tar sth with brush	69	--
70	To be tarred with the colonial brush	70	--
71	To be tarred with the colonial brush	71	Nie mieszać się w czyjeś sprawy
72	To be tarred with the brush	72	--
73	To be tarred with colonial brush	73	--
74	To be tarred with a brush	74	Szargać swoją opinię
75	Be tarred with sb's brush	75	Być pod wpływem kogoś

Idiom 3 A

	Form		Definition
1	To throw legal books at sb	1	Znaleźć powód do oskarżenia
2	To throw a book at	2	To ask sb lots of questions
3	Throw legal books at sb	3	Find evidence in the codes that sb's actions are illegal
4	To throw every legal book at sbd	4	Użyć całej dostępnej wiedzy przeciw komuś
5	To throw a book at sb	5	Używać wiedzy w celu pokazania komuś, że jest w błędzie
6	To throw a legal book at sb	6	Zastosować przepis prawny przeciwko komuś
7	To throw a legal book at sb	7	Zastosować przepis prawny przeciw komuś
8	To throw legal books at somebody	8	Odwoływać się do przepisów prawnych
9	To throw every legal book at sb/sth	9	Użyć każdego możliwego argumentu ???
10	Throw every legal book at sb	10	No idea!
11	To throw a legal book at smb	11	Użyć wszelkich środków aby nie dopuścić do czegoś
12	To throw a legal book at sb	12	To sacrifice all the things you have to get sth else
13	To throw books at sbd	13	To try proving sth to sb showing him or her rules that support out cause
14	To throw one's legal books (at one's considerable library) at sb	14	To criticise sb
15	To throw a book at sb	15	Zademonstrować coś, pokazać ?
16	Throw every legal book at sb	16	--
17	To throw every book at somebody	17	To be mad, go crazy

	Form		Definition
18	To throw a book at sb	18	To prove sb to be wrong and support it with some knowledge
19	To throw a book at sb	19	To prove sb to be wrong & support it with some knowledge
20	To throw legal books at sth	20	Udowadniać komuś, że nie ma prawa czegoś robić
21	To throw every legal book from one's library	21	Wykorzystywać kruczki prawne znane sobie
22	To throw a book in one's library	22	To use all the possible means against
23	To throw every legal book at	23	To take to court
24	To throw every book in a library at sb	24	To go mad at somebody about something
25	To throw a book at sb	25	To present an argument against
26	--	26	--
27	To throw a legal book at sb	27	To find reason to sue sb
28	To throw a book at sb	28	To prove sb to be wrong and support it with some book knowledge
29	To throw a book in a library	29	Chcieć udowodnić swoją rację poprzez zarzucanie argumentami
30	To throw a book in a library	30	To want to proove one's own rights
31	To throw one's books at sb	31	Krzyczeć na kogoś, denerwować się na kogoś
32	Throw one's book at sb	32	Protest fiercely; nie zgadzać się na
33	To throw every legal book at somebody	33	Wykorzystywać kruczki prawne jed- nocześnie uniemożliwiając wykonanie czegoś
34	To throw legal books	34	Udowadniać przy pomocy litery prawa
35	To throw books at sb	35	Get furious and throw abuses
36	To throw every legal book from sb's library at sb.	36	Cytować fragmenty z książek/dzieł
37	To throw a book in considerably big library at sb	37	Rzucać oskarżenia pod czyimś adresem
38	To throw legal books at somebody	38	Wściekać się na kogoś
39	Throw a (legal) book at sb	39	Use legal ways of assessing your rights
40	To throw a book at sb	40	To get nervous at sb
41	Throw a legal book at	41	Wykorzystać środki prawne/znajomość przeciwko
42	Throw the book at sb	42	To criticise sb, scold heavily
43	He threw at her every legal book he had in his astonishing library.	43	Skrytykować kogoś
44	To throw one's every possible book in one's rich library at sbd	44	To use one's own arguments against sbd
45	To throw a book at someone	45	Wyzywać kogoś
46	--	46	--
47	To throw every (legal) book in the li- brary at smb	47	To persuad smb into/out of something in an aggressive way
48	To throw every legal book at sb	48	To provide sb with lawful interpretations
49	Throw all the legal books in one's con- siderable large library at sb	49	To use one's theoretical knowledge to explain to people that what they are after is not achievable

	Form		Definition
50	To throw all the legal books in one's considerably library	50	Wykorzystać każdą możliwość (prawną) przeciw komuś
51	To throw every legal book at sb	51	To use every legal way to stop sb from doing sth
52	To throw legal books	52	(?) to use law, rules
53	Throw a legal book at sb	53	Doszukiwać się haczyka prawnego
54	To throw (every) legal book at sb	54	Wstąpić na drogę sądową z kimś
55	To throw a book at sb	55	To use rules/regulations to fight sb
56	To throw a book at sb	56	To make sb account for his/her actions
57	To throw every legal book in his library	57	To "hide" behind the law
58	To throw books at sb	58	To pelt sb with definitions, very bookish knowledge
59	To throw book at sb	59	To accuse sb of sth, to attack sb
60	To throw every legal book from one's considerable library at	60	To use every possible method to solve a problem
61	To throw a legal book at sb	61	Pozywać do sądu
62	To throw every legal book at sb	62	Być złym
63	To throw the book at	63	To criticize sb or punish sb severely
64	To throw books at somebody	64	Robić awanturę
65	To throw legal books	65	Quote law (rules & laws)
66	Throw a book at sb	66	Przywołać prawa, opinie, argumenty na poparcie/odparcie czegoś
67	To throw a book	67	Użyć każdego możliwego argumentu
68	To throw every legal book in sb's considerable library	68	Użyć każdy znany sobie prawny kruczek z bogatego zasobu
69	To throw every considerable book at sb	69	Użyć wszelkich argumentów
70	To throw every legal book in one's considerable library	70	---
71	To throw every legal book in his considerable library at him	71	Zdenerwować się do tego stopnia, że nie panować nad sobą i zrobić wszystko by się odegrać – tonący brzytwy się chwyta
72	To throw a book in one's library	72	---
73	To throw a legal book at sb	73	---
74	To throw a book at smb	74	Wykorzystać swoją wiedzę przeciw komuś
75	Throw a book at sb	75	Oskarżać o coś

Idiom 5 A

	Form		Definition
1	To have an axe to grind	1	Mieć własne problemy do przejścia
2	To grind with an axe	2	?--
3	Have one's own axe to grind	3	Be in need for a financial or technological jump forwards
4	To have one's own axe to grind	4	Mieć swoje zadanie do wypełnienia
5	To have an axe to grind	5	Mieć swoje cele
6	To have an axe to grind	6	Mieć orzech do zgryzienia
7	To have one's axe to grind	7	Każdy ma swój orzech do zgryzienia

	Form		Definition
8	To have one's axe to grind	8	Mieć problem z którym trzeba się uporać
9	To have one's own technological axe to grind	9	Posiadać swoje metody
10	To have one's own technological axe to grind	10	Mieć swój własny sposób, metody
11	To have an axe to grind	11	Mieć swój punkt widzenia
12	To have an axe to grind	12	To have interests in different field
13	To have one's own axe to grind	13	To have one's own interest in sth
14	To have one's own axe to grind	14	To have one's own perception, attitude to sth
15	To have an axe to grind	15	---
16	To have one's own axe to grind	16	To have one's own profits in mind, not being willing to compromise
17	To have one's own axe to grind	17	To have one's own interest, solution, idea
18	Axe to grind	18	To have one's own business, take care of one's own business
19	Axe to grind	19	To take care of one's business
20	Each vendor has its own axe to grind	20	---
21	Each vendor has its own axe to grind	21	Nie wiem
22	One needs to grind one's axe	22	One needs to prepare and develop
23	To have an axe to grind	23	To have not an easy task to do in order to gain sth
24	Every vendor has its own axe to grind	24	Everything before becoming a success needs to go through a series of problems
25	To have own axe to grind	25	To have own business in sth
26	To have an axe to grind	26	Mieć własne interesy którymi się zajmujemy
27	To have an axe to grind	27	To have some problems to overcome
28	To have some axe to grind	28	To tackle some difficult problem
29	To have sb's own axe to grind	29	Mieć swoje własne problemy z czymś
30	To have one's own axe to grind	30	No idea
31	To have an axe to grind	31	Mieć trudny orzech do zgryzienia
32	Have an axe to grind	32	Cope with sth; zmierzyć się z czymś, znosić coś
33	To have an axe to grind	33	Mieć swoje zalety do wykorzystania
34	To have one's own axe to grind	34	Mieć własne wymagania
35	To have an axe to grind	35	Mieć jakiś własny interes w czymś i dlatego nie być obiektywnym
36	Every vendor has its technological axe in the grind	36	Każdy działa według swoich własnych zasad
37	Have sb's own axe to grind	37	Wtrącać swoje pięć groszy
38	To have one's axe to grind	38	Mieć swój sposób działania
39	Everyone has their own axe to grind	39	Everyone has their own way of doing things/dealing with problems
40	To have an axe to grind	40	To have a problem to solve
41	Have an axe to grind	41	Używać odpowiednich środków do wybranego celu
42	To have axe to grind about sth	42	To have sth against sth, to be critical about sth

	Form		Definition
43	Everyone had an axe to grind	43	Każdy miał swój pomysł, który chciał zrealizować
44	To have one's own axe to grind	44	Wtrącić swoje pięć groszy
45	To be an axe in a grind	45	---
46	To have an axe to grind	46	To have own problem to overcome
47	To have one's own axe to grind	47	To use one's own methods/ways to achieve the goal
48	To have one's own axe to grind	48	To have one's own reasons/point of view
49	Have one's own axe to grind	49	"Własny orzech do zgryzienia"
50	To have an axe to grind	50	Mieć własny problem (mieć twardy orzech do zgryzienia)
51	To have an axe to grind	51	---
52	Have an axe to grind	52	To have your own task (duty) to fulfill
53	Have its own axe to grind	53	Mieć twardy orzech do zgryzienia
54	To have one's own axe to grind	54	?---
55	To have an axe to grind	55	Something needs to be improved, to have to hone on sth
56	To have one's own axe to grind	56	To deal with problems individually, in one's specific way
57	To have sb's own axe to grind	57	To have sb's own interest
58	To have one's own axe to grind	58	To have one's own way in dealing with things
59	To have one's own axe to grind	59	To have different aims
60	To have an axe to the grind	60	---
61	To have an axe to grind	61	(?) próbować przeprowadzić rzeczy na swój własny sposób
62	To axe the grind	62	Spełniać wymogi
63	Every vendor has its own axe to grind	63	---
64	To have one's own axe to grind	64	Mieć swój własny pomysł, rozwiązanie
65	To have an axe to grind	65	To have one's own idea & try to persuade it by all means
66	Have an axe on one's own grind	66	Mieć własne zdanie
67	An axe to grind	67	---
68	To have an axe to grind	68	Dostosować coś na swój użytek
69	To have your own axe to grind	69	---
70	To have one's own axe to grind	70	To convince others to one's ideas
71	Everyone has its own technological axe to a grind	71	Mieć swój własny złoty środek (sposób) na jedną rzecz
72	To have your own axe to grind	72	Dbać o własny interes
73	With axe & grind	73	---
74	To have an axe to grind	74	Mieć swoje własne problemy
75	Have many axes to grind	75	Dużo problemów do rozwiązania

Idiom 1 B

	Form		Definition
1	--	1	--
2	Be one feather in a crowded cap	2	Być zapowiedzią tego, co nastąpi w przyszłości
3	One feather in a crowded cap	3	One thing among many others
4	A feather in a cap	4	Sth done that we should be proud of
5	To be a feather in a cap	5	--
6	To be only one feather out of many (in the cap)	6	Być tylko jednym z wielu, z których mozna być dumnym
7	A feather in one's cap	7	Sth to be proud of
8	One feather in your cap	8	Just one of many things you have done and can be proud of
9	A feather in your cap	9	A one of numerous successes
10	One more feather in one's cap	10	One more thing to be proud of
11	To be a feather in a cap	11	To be merely one of the many (and not significant) in a lot
12	A feather in a cap	12	Something one is very proud of
13	One feather in the crowded cap	13	Powód do dumy
14	A feather in one's cap	14	A success, sth to be proud of
15	A feather in an increasingly crowded cap	15	Coś z czego można byc dumnym
16	Feather in a cap	16	Sth that we should be proud of
17	To be a cap in a feather	17	To be one of the many things of the same kind (positively)
18	To be a feather in a cap	18	To be sth one should be proud of
19	Be a feather in a cap	19	To be successful
20	A feather in a crowded cap	20	One of the things you've done that you should be proud of
21	A feather in your cap	21	Powód do dumy
22	One feather in a cap	22	A pleasant thing that you've done or experienced
23	Have a feather in a cap	23	Have sth to be proud of
24	One feather in a cap	24	One element/point among many others (success)
25	To be one feather in a cap	25	Sth that one can be proud of
26	One feather in your cap	26	Something you should/can be very proud of
27	A feather in one's cap	27	Something one is proud of
28	One feather in a crowded cap	28	Kropla w oceanie
29	A feather in a cap	29	One in many
30	A feather in sb's cap	30	An achievement
31	A feather in a cap	31	Success
32	To be one feather in the cap	32	To be one of the many
33	To be one feather in a cap	33	To be just one part of sth bigger, more important
34	Another feather in one's cap	34	Kolejny sukces
35	A feather in the cap	35	One of the things you can be proud of
36	A feather i n sb's cap	36	To have sth to be proud of
37	A feather in a cap	37	A thing to be proud of
38	To be a feather in one's cap	38	To be the reason for sb to be proud of

	Form		Definition
39	A feather in one's cap	39	Something one has done that one should be proud of
40	A feather in a cap	40	Quite a success
41	A feather in your cap	41	Another successful achievement
42	A feather in a cap	42	Małą część czegoś, nieistotna
43	A feather in a cap	43	Jeden z wielu sukcesów
44	A feather in sb's cap	44	Osiągnięcie
45	A feather in one's cap	45	A thing you achieved and may be proud of
46	Another feather in a cap	46	Another reason to be proud of
47	Feather in a cap	47	Być z czegoś dumnym
48	To be a feather in a cap	48	O osiągnięciu, z którego jest się dumnym
49	To be a feather in a cap	49	To be a thing to be proud of
50	A feather in a cap	50	A progress, a step in
51	Be merely a feather in an increasingly crowded cap	51	Być wierzchołkiem góry lodowej (I didn't check it)
52	One feather in a cap	52	To be very successful
53	A/ one feather in your cap	53	Something you can be proud of
54	To be a feather in a cap	54	Sth that one may be proud of
55	A feather in a cap	55	One thing out of many somebody has done to be proud of
56	A feather in a cap	56	---
57	To be/have a/one feather in a cap	57	Mieć coś w dorobku, z czego można być dumnym
58	Feather in a cap	58	Sth you should be proud of
59	One feather of the crowded cup	59	---
60	To be a feather in a cap	60	Być powodem dumy
61	To have a feather in one's cap	61	To do sth that's you're proud of
62	To be a feather in one's cap	62	To be one of one's achievements, sth to be proud of
63	A feather in a cap	63	Jedno z wielu osiągnięć
64	To be a feather in one's cap	64	To be proud of sth
65	To have feathers in the crowded cap	65	Mieć ważniejsze sprawy, nie tylko jedną
66	A feather in one's cap	66	Coś z czego można być dumnym (jedna z wielu rzeczy)
67	A feather in one's cap	67	Osiągnięcie, z którego jest się dumnm
68	To have a feather in one's cap	68	Zrobić, mieć coś z czego jesteśmy dumni

Idiom 2 B

	Form		Definition
1	To be tarred with the same brush	1	To be blamed for sth
2	Be tarred with the same brush	2	Be blamed for somebody else's faults
3	Tarred with a brush	3	Affected by sth
4	Be tarred with the brush	4	Be blamed for sth
5	To be tarred with sb's brush	5	Być obwinianym za czyjeś błędy

	Form		Definition
6	To be tarred with the same brush	6	Być obwinianym za prze-winienia/przestępstwa innych
7	To be tarred with the brush	7	To be blamed for someone's faults
8	To be tarred by someone else's brush	8	To be blamed for sb else's faults
9	To be tarred with a brush	9	To be blamed for sth
10	To tar sb with a brush	10	To pin blame on sb, to charge sb with false accusations
11	To be tarred by the brush	11	To be influenced negatively by a kind of conflict
12	To be tarred with someone's brush	12	To be blamed for someone else's faults
13	Be tarred with brush	13	Być obwinianym za
14	To be tarred with the same brush	14	To be blamed for somebody else's faults
15	Be tarred with a brush	15	Be punished for sth one did not do him/herself
16	To be tarred with a brush	16	To be treated in the same way as sb else
17	To tar sb with the same brush	17	To punish sb severely for sb else's crime or offence
18	Be tarred with the same brush	18	To be blamed for sth and burdened with the responsibility for a crime committed by somebody else
19	To tar sb with the same brush	19	To blame sb for sth
20	To be tarred with the brush	20	To be blamed for sth you did in the past
21	Be tarred with the same brush	21	Być obarczanym za winy innych
22	To tar with the same brush	22	To have an opinion/attitude to something that is influenced by something else that we have the same opinion about
23	Be tarred with a brush	23	Be blamed for sth that sb else has done
24	To be tarred with sb's brush	24	To be blamed for
25	To be tarred in/with a brush	25	---
26	Be tarred with the same brush	26	Be blamed for the faults of others
27	Be tarred with the same brush	27	To be made responsible for somebody else's mistakes
28	To be tarred with a brush	28	Obwiniać kogoś za swoje przewinienia
29	To be tarred by the same brush	29	To be blaimed for sb else's deed
30	To be tarred with the same brush	30	To be blamed for sb else's actions
31	To be tarred with the same brush	31	To be blamed with sb else's faults
32	To be tarred with the brush	32	To suffer as a result of sb's mistakes, faults
33	To be tarred with a brush	33	To be (accused) punished for all faults, mistakes, crimes
34	To be tarred with a brush	34	To be blamed for sb else's faults
35	To tar with the same brush	35	To blame for/accuse of sb else's crimes
36	To be tarred with sb's brush	36	Be responsible for sb's faults
37	To be tarred with the same brush	37	To be blamed for what someone else did
38	To be tarred with a brush	38	To be blamed for someone else's faults
39	Be tarred with sb else's brush	39	Be blamed for sb else's faults
40	To be tarred by a brush	40	To be blamed for sth one did not do
41	Be tarred with the same brush	41	Be blamed with sb else's mistakes
42	To tar sth	42	---
43	To be/get tarred with the same brush	43	Być winionym za czyjeś błędy

	Form		Definition
44	To be tarred with (the same) brush	44	To be blamed for sb else's crimes
45	To be tarred with the same brush	45	To be treated in the same way, to be equal
46	Be tarred with a brush	46	Be blamed for sth
47	Be tarred with a brush	47	Winić się za coś
48	To be tarred with the same brush	48	Być obwinianym, sądzonym lub karanym za cudze winy
49	To tarr sb with a brush	49	Blame for
50	To be tarred with a brush	50	To blame somebody for doing something
51	Be tarred with the same brush	51	Być obwinianym o coś
52	To tar with a brush	52	Repeatedly stalk
53	To be tarred with a brush	53	To be held responsible for somebody else's crimes or faults
54	To be tarred with brush	54	To be blamed for
55	Be tarred with a brush	55	Be blamed for somebody else's blames or faults
56	Be tarred with a brush	56	Be blamed for someone else's faults
57	To be tarred by the brush	57	Być ocenianym na podstawie czegoś
58	Be tarred with brush	58	Be punished
59	Tarred with the same brash	59	To blame for sb else's crimes, faults
60	To be tarred with a brush	60	Mieszać się w coś/niepokoić kogoś
61	To be tarred with the brush	61	To be blamed by other's faults
62	To tar sb with the same brush	62	To blame sb for the faults of others
63	To be tarred with a brush	63	Być karanym za coś, czego się nie popełniło/zrobiło = za czyjeś czyny/błędy
64	Be tarred with a brush	64	To be influenced by sth
65	To tarred with the brush	65	Nie zgodzić się z czymś
66	To be tarred with a brush	66	Być obwinionym za coś, czemu winny jest ktoś inny
67	To be tarred with the same brush	67	To be blamed for sb's faults
68	To be tarred with the same brush	68	Być winionym za czyjeś niedociągnięcia

Idiom 3 B

	Form		Definition
1	To throw a legal book at sb	1	-------(gdzieś już wcześniej słyszałem, ale nie znam znaczenia)
2	Throw the book at	2	Charge sb with all possible accusations
3	Throw books at	3	React angrily, violently
4	Throw the book at	4	Punish, criticize sb
5	To throw the book at sb	5	Robić komuś zarzut
6	To throw a legal book at	6	Zarzucić kogoś aktami prawnymi, podać komuś akty prawne w momencie oskarżenia
7	To throw the book at	7	To punish someone for sth, charge someone with sth (znany jednak przypomniałam sobie ten idiom po 1 zadaniu)
8	Throw the books at sb	8	To accuse sb of sth and punish him severely

	Form		Definition
9	Throw the book at sb	9	To charge sb with as many offences as possible
10	To throw book at sb	10	To prove that sb is wrong by giving evidence
11	To throw the book at	11	To accuse someone of every possible crime etc. to punish sb severely
12	To throw a book at somebody	12	To act offensively
13	To throw books at	13	To blame
14	To throw the book at	14	To punish somebody severely or charge him for sth
15	Throw a legal book at	15	Karać za coś, oskarżać
16	To throw a book at sb	16	To accuse sb of every possible thing
17	To throw a book at sb	17	To accuse sb of every possible offence
18	To throw a book at	18	To punish as severely as possible or charge sb with all possible offences
19	To throw the book at	19	To do whatever possible
20	To throw a book at	20	To find every possible argument (a legal one) to punish sb
21	Throw the books at (sb)	21	Rzucać oskarżenia pod czyimś adresem
22	To throw a book at sb	22	To use all things possible against sb
23	Throw the book at	23	Punish sb or charge sb with
24	To throw a (legal) book at	24	To punish
25	Throw a book at sb	25	To charge sb with some offences
26	Throw the book at sb	26	Charge sb with as many accusations as possible
27	To throw a book	27	To put blame on somebody for everything possible
28	To throw a book at sb	28	Karać kogoś surowo
29	To throw the book at	29	To accuse sb of every possible offence
30	Throw books at sb	30	Use arguments from a book
31	To throw book at sb	31	Hm
32	To throw a book at sb	32	To accuse sb of sth
33	To throw a book at sb	33	To punish sb, very severely
34	To throw books at sb	34	?
35	To throw the book at	35	Punish hardly or charge with many accusations
36	Throw a book at	36	To get angry with sb
37	To throw a book at sb	37	To accuse, blame sb, cast accusation
38	To throw a book at someone	38	To punish severely
39	Throw the book at	39	Accuse sb of every possible misdeed
40	To throw a book at	40	To shout at sb/be furious about sb
41	To throw a book at sb	41	To make all possible accusations
42	To throw a book at sb	42	---
43	To throw a legal book at sb	43	Użyć wszelkich środków
44	To throw (every legal) book at sb	44	To use (legal) expertise to stop sb
45	To throw books at sb	45	To punish sb severely
46	Throw any legal book at....	46	---
47	Throw a legal book at sb	47	Być zdenerwowanym na kogoś
48	To throw a book at sb	48	Nie potrafię wytłumaczyć
49	Throw a book at sb	49	Accuse of sth

	Form		Definition
50	To throw a book at	50	To punish somebody (sprawdzane w słowniku)
51	Throw books at sb	51	Krytykować kogoś
52	To throw a book at	52	To overwhelm with repetition
53	To throw every book at sb ?	53	---
54	To throw books at	54	To punish sb
55	To throw a book at somebody	55	To punish somebody severely
56	Throw a book at sb	56	To punish sb severely
57	To throw a book at sby	57	Próbować znaleźć sposób by kogoś za coś ukarać/ukarać kogoś
58	Throw a book at sb	58	Point at sb's faults
59	To throw any legal book at	59	---
60	To throw the book at	60	Ukarać kogoś/zbesztać kogoś
61	To throw the book at sb	61	To offend them
62	To throw a book at sbd	62	To punish him severely
63	To throw a book at sm	63	To punish sm severely or to charge sm as many offences as possible
64	To throw a book from ones library	64	To give vent of anger
65	To throw books into one's library	65	Nie zgodzić się z opinią, odrzucić argumenty
66	To throw legal books at	66	No idea :-)
67	To throw legal books at sb ... (?)	67	Wytaczać wszelkie argumenty przeciwko ... (?)
68	---	68	---

Idiom 5 B

	Form		Definition
1	To have an axe to grind	1	Use a lot of ideas and talk all the time in order to persuade sb
2	Have an axe to grind	2	Talk about sth over and over again in order to persuade someone
3	To have one's own axe to grind	3	To speak about sth again and again
4	Have an axe to grind	4	Repeat sth in order to persuade
5	To have an axe to grind	5	Mieć sposób na przekonanie
6	To have one's own axe to grind	6	Bardzo dużo mówić w celu przekonania innych do swoich poglądów
7	To have an axe to grind	7	To have a problem to deal with
8	To have an axe to grind	8	To say sth repeatedly so that to persuade other people to accept your beliefs
9	To have an axe to grind	9	To do sth again and again because you want sth very much
10	To have one's own axe to grind	10	To repeat over and over again one's own opinion, idea disregarding other people's
11	To have an axe to grind	11	To try to persuade s.o. that one's own proposal should be the base for consensus
12	To have an axe to grind	12	To talk a lot about one's actions

	Form		Definition
13	To have one's own axe to grind	13	To do a lot of things (e.g. to speak, repeat) so as to put one's idea across
14	An axe to grind	14	To talk about sthg again and again in order to persuade them into it
15	Axe to grind	15	Broń dzięki której we'll persuade sb to do as we want them to do
16	To have an axe to grind	16	To have a very difficult task to solve
17	To have an axe to grind	17	To talk about sth over and over again in order to persuade sb about it
18	To have one's own axe to grind	18	To have sth to say to persuade sb else's beliefs
19	To grind an axe at	19	To persuade smb to follow one's ideas
20	To have an axe to grind	20	To add more and more/to talk more and more trying to persuade people about that you are right
21	Have an axe to grind	21	Forsować (jakąś/jakieś) ideę/idee
22	To have an axe to grind	22	To talk about sth constantly so that others would accept it
23	To grind an axe	23	Talk over and over again about sth to persuade others to it
24	To have one's own axe to grind	24	To persuade sb again and again
25	Grind one's axe	25	To try to present one's own view and position on a given topic and make one believe that it's the best one
26	Have an axe to grind	26	Persuade sb continuously about sth
27	Have an axe to grind	27	To have an issue about which one has to convince others, persuade, defend it
28	To have an axe to grind	28	Powtarzać coś do upadłego aby komuś coś wyperswadować
29	To have an axe to grind	29	To repeat sth over and over again until convincing others to it
30	Grind your axe	30	Repetitively talk about sth to persuade the others
31	To have an axe to grind	31	To persuade others to one's beliefs
32	To have your own axe to grind	32	To be preoccupied with your own affairs, to do sth on your own, regardless of others
33	To have an axe to grind	33	To say sth many times in order to persuade sb to do sth
34	To have one's own axe to grind	34	To persuade others to accept one's own ideas
35	To have an axe to grind	35	To try again and again and persuade others to your way of thinking
36	To have an axe to grind	36	To have one's own beliefs and try to persuade others to accept them
37	To have an axe to grind	37	To have a voice to persuade others as to one's ideas
38	To have an axe to grind	38	To persuade sb into buying sth by repeating one's arguments
39	Have one's own axe to grind	39	Try to convince sb to one's views by repeating sth over and over again

	Form		Definition
40	To have an axe to grind	40	To support/promote persistently one's own idea
41	Have an axe to grind	41	Deliberately try to persuade people to believe in your ideas
42	To grind an axe	42	Mierzyć się z problemem
43	To have an axe to grind	43	W kółko powtarzać aby kogoś przekonać o czymś
44	To have an axe to grind	44	To have business with sb
45	To judge one's own axe to grind	45	To judge according to one's own criteria
46	Another technological axe to grind	46	Przekonać kogoś do czegoś
47	Have an axe to grind	47	Podeprzeć się swoim zdaniem w danej kwestii
48	To have an axe to grind	48	Nie potrafię wytłumaczyć
49	To have an axe to grind	49	To try to persuade sb
50	To have an axe to grind	50	To have one's own opinion
51	To have an axe to grind	51	Postulować coś, nakłaniać do czegoś
52	To make an axe with a grind	52	Thoroughly examine
53	To have an axe to grind	53	To repeat sth over and over again
54	To have an axe to grind	54	To popularize what one believes in
55	Have an axe to grind	55	Have one's own method to persuade sb
56	Have an axe to grind	56	To give some reasons for sth
57	Have one's axe to grind	57	Repeat sth over and over so that sby would finally believe in what you are saying
58	Have an axe to grind	58	Way of thinking or doing sth so that others may be encouraged or persuaded
59	To axe the grind	59	To say sth again and again in order to persuade others to your own beliefs/ideas
60	To have an axe to grind	60	Mieć dar przekonywania
61	To axe its own grind	61	To say sth again and again in order to persuade the others to accept your point of view/idea
62	To have an axe to grind	62	To repeat sth all over again in order to persuade them
63	To have one's axe to grind	63	Popierać coś
64	---	64	---
65	---	65	---
66	To have an axe to grind	66	Mówić o czymś "w koło Macieju" żeby przekonać innych do swojego punktu widzenia
67	To have an axe to grind	67	Używać swoich argumentów w kółko, w celu przekonania innych do swoich racji
68	To have an axe to grind	68	Mówić wciąż te same rzeczy, powtarzać